Accounting Handbook for
MEDICAL PRACTICES

Accounting Handbook for MEDICAL PRACTICES

Rhonda W. Sides, CPA   Michael A. Roberts, CPA

John Wiley & Sons, Inc.
New York • Chichester • Weinheim • Brisbane • Singapore • Toronto

ISBN 0-471-37009-6

Printed in the United States of America.

10 9 8 7 6 5 4 3 2 1

Contents

About the Authors

Rhonda W. Sides, CPA, has become associated with Horne CPA Group as Director, Nashville Physician Services in Nashville, Tennessee. She specializes in practice valuations, cost accounting, operational assessments, and financial feasibility issues related to group and integrated delivery system development. She lectures nationally for various health care and financial organizations, including Southern Medical Association, and is actively sought for her ability to combine the practicality of accounting with the needs of health care practice management. Rhonda is a licensed CPA in Georgia and Tennessee, and is a member of the Georgia and Tennessee Societies of CPAs, the American Institute of CPAs, and the Healthcare Financial Management Association. Rhonda is also a candidate member of the American Society of Appraisers. She co-authored another John Wiley & Sons book, *Valuation of a Medical Practice*, 1999. Rhonda also is an adjunct professor at Belmont University, Nashville, Tennessee.

Michael A. Roberts, CPA, is the Shareholder in Charge of the Franchise Services Division of Home CPA Group in Nashville, Tennessee. His expertise is in compliance, tax planning, financial reporting, and mergers/acquisitions for various national corporations. He is the editor of *Focus on Franchising,* a quarterly newsletter that is distributed throughout the franchisee groups of Domino's Pizza, Inc., Quizno's Classic Subs, Inc., and other national companies. He lectures nationally on financial reporting, tax planning, and management advisory services for franchisees. Mike is a licensed Certified Public Accountant in Tennessee, Mississippi, Louisiana, Alabama, and North Carolina. His professional memberships include the American Institute of CPAs and the Mississippi and Tennessee Societies of CPAs.

Preface

In today's ever-changing world of healthcare, most physicians, medical practice administrators, and their professional advisors are bombarded with a myriad of complex issues on a daily basis. Information that is learned today can easily be obsolete tomorrow. One exception in this fast-paced world is the practice of accounting. This book provides you with a survival guide that addresses the issues and challenges of accounting and financial decision-making for medical practices. It is a "must-keep" handbook that provides you with the tools for building a foundation of knowledge that will give you stability while you are challenged to keep up with all the other regulatory and governmental complexities of healthcare. *Accounting Handbook for Medical Practices* will serve you for years to come.

This handbook teaches financial accounting and analysis as should be applied particularly to *your* business—the medical practice. In this handbook, you will find specific examples, and discussions for accounting methods and standards, financial analysis formulas, chart of accounts, cost analysis, tax issues, and internal controls for cash flow and practice assets. We have cited many examples based on our real-life experiences in working with physician practices as accountants and consultants. We hope that these examples will give you insights and helpful information with which to run your own medical practice.

In writing this handbook, we have tried to make it uncomplicated and easy to understand as opposed to the ongoing challenges of healthcare. We hope that this information, along with our personal in-

sights, will give you some valuable tools and help you develop knowledge in this area.

Please feel free to contact us with any comments or questions on
this handbook at the addresses and numbers below.

Rhonda W. Sides, CPA
Mike A. Roberts, CPA
HORNE CPA GROUP
216 Centerview Drive, Suite 121
Brentwood, TN   37027
615-377-9946
fax 615-377-9983
rhonda.sides@hcpag.com
mike.roberts@hcpag.com

Financial Statement Overview

LANGUAGE OF FINANCIAL DECISIONS

Accounting is the system that measures business activities by processing information into reports, and communicating the findings to decision makers. It is not bookkeeping! Here's a tidbit for you: Did you know that bookkeeping is the only word in the English language that has three double letters? Bookkeeping is a procedural element of accounting, just as arithmetic is a procedural element of mathematics. Bookkeeping is the record keeping part of accounting. Beware of over-sophisticated accounting procedures. Keep to the basics.

All businesses must retain/maintain accounting records. These form the source document, and are not necessarily financial statements.

Why It Matters

- Industry experts estimate that the cost of inefficiencies is currently at least 20 to 30 percent of revenues. Most health care entities are suffering from lack of profits, not lack of revenues.

- Market share is being captured by low-cost/high-quality providers.

- Increasing revenue may lead to lower margins.

- It is necessary to establish fees, insurance agreements, financial policies and billing procedures.

Know Where You're Going

A favorite phrase is "You have to know where you're going before you can know when you've arrived." This fundamental idea has guided us through a lot of messes over the years. What should we see, what result is reasonable, what is supposed to be the answer? In other words, if theory were applied to the situation at hand, what would the outcome be?

Here we are, in a very complex, changing environment with competition intruding and the government intervening from every angle, and "health care" becoming the buzz word in political campaigns. Service providers are asking, "How do we fight back?" The answer is simple: Become more sophisticated. We didn't say that the financial statement process must become more sophisticated, but that the decision makers must. The first step is to form a clear vision of where you are going or want to go. What obstacles have to be overcome? What contributions do you feel are warranted by you and the team around you? Your vision of the elements of effective practice management may differ somewhat from the following, but ours may influence you:

- Service-oriented personnel (teamwork and cross training)
- Financial planning and budget analysis
- Well-designed physical facility
- Written policies/procedures and appropriate job descriptions
- Efficient collections and accounts receivable follow-up
- Good information systems/practice management software
- Appropriate coding and medical records management

In addition to "you have to know where you're going," you have to have some perspective of what happens in a typical physician practice if you intend to affect the results in a way that will eventually be reflected in the financial statements. In actuality, the financial statements are the report card of the business—the conscience of the business. Exhibit 1.1 outlines a typical service delivery routine in a physician practice.

Know When You've Arrived

The financial statement process, as noted earlier, is not bookkeeping—although bookkeeping is a requisite element of the financial statement process.

Know Where You're Going, Revisited

Now that we understand the work flow in a medical practice, we need to apply the same thought process to understanding the financial statement process. It is difficult to identify when and where the financial statement process actually begins, so we will not elaborate on that point here. Let it suffice to say that at some point the process begins, and it is your task to summarize the individual processes in a meaningful output, that being the financial statement.

The *financial statement* is a culmination of many tasks, gathering information from many sources, analysis of perceived variances, and confirmation of balances with third-party information. The *chart of accounts*, discussed in chapter 2, is the basis for presenting the financial statement information in a format that is acceptable to the user. In many instances, the user is not informed of alternatives to this presentation style and, more often than not, does not know what to ask for. The traditional process for financial statement review is that the user gets a financial statement prepared internally or by an outside accountant, opens the statements to review the cash balance or some other account that he/she generally believes to be the representation of where the company is financially, and then quickly stuffs the statement in a cabinet, never to be bothered again. This is where, in our opinion, opportunity abounds. Expectation is often low to nonexistent although the information is available. All that is needed from the preparer and the user are creativity and a thorough understanding of the financial statement process.

Exhibit 1.1
Typical routine of physician service delivery

Patient check-in:
- ✓ Demographic information is obtained
- ✓ Past medical history is obtained
- ✓ Insurance information (referral and authorization numbers) is obtained and verified
- ✓ Superbill/encounter form is prepared and attached to chart
- ✓ Demographics are entered into computer system
- ✓ Patient name is recorded on daily summary (paper system)
- ✓ Patient name is checked off on schedule and sign-in sheet
- ✓ Patient waits

Patient service delivery
- ✓ Back office performs procedures
- ✓ Physician or nurse codes superbill (denotes services performed)
- ✓ CPT codes and ICD-9 codes are checked
- ✓ Additional tests, outgoing appointment are scheduled by back office
- ✓ Follow-up appointment is made

Charges:
- ✓ Encounter forms are picked up at check-out area
- ✓ Encounter forms are examined for clarity, then properly coded and prepared for charge entry (includes verification of financial information, if not already completed)
- ✓ Charges are keyed into computer system
- ✓ Charges are recorded on daily summary
- ✓ Encounter forms are compared with patient sign-in sheet

Payments:
- ✓ Co-pays are collected
- ✓ Fees are collected
- ✓ Payments are keyed into computer system
- ✓ Payments are recorded on daily summary
- ✓ Money is deposited

Insurance claims and statements:
- ✓ Insurance claims are generated the same or following day and are QA'd by a claims control system
- ✓ Claims are electronically transmitted
- ✓ Statements are generated daily
- ✓ Information is entered into daily production report, permitting monitoring of the daily balance necessary for EOM purposes

Exhibit 1.1 (Continued)

End-of-day procedures:
- ✓ Daily summary is balanced
- ✓ Daily reconciliation is completed
- ✓ Encounter forms, daily summary, and system report are reconciled
- ✓ Deposit slip is gathered
- ✓ Insurance claims and statements are generated

Reimbursement:
- ✓ Payment, including daily pickup of lock box deposit from bank, is entered
- ✓ Electronic remittance is input to system
- ✓ Payments in computer system are confirmed against pertinent account

Follow-up:
- ✓ Private pay and insurance accounts are reviewed daily
- ✓ Edit reports and unacceptable electronic transmits are worked and corrected
- ✓ Insurance companies are contacted
- ✓ "Largest, oldest, first"—The biggest and oldest balances handled first

Collections:
- ✓ All EOB's are examined for low payments, denials, and unacceptable UCR
- ✓ Insurance companies are contacted
- ✓ All accounts aged 90 days or more are examined for possible turnover to collection agency
- ✓ Collection letters are sent out
- ✓ Accounts are sent to collection agency
- ✓ Bad debt recovery is monitored closely

UNDERSTANDING THE FINANCIAL STATEMENT PROCESS

Normal Balances of Accounts

The sum of the increases recorded in an account is usually equal to or greater than the sum of the decreases recorded in the account. For this reason, the normal balances of all accounts are positive rather than negative. For example, the total debits (increases) in an asset account will ordinarily be greater than the total credits (decreases). Thus, asset accounts normally have debit balances.

The rules of debits and credits and the normal balances of the various types of accounts are summarized in Exhibit 1.2. Note that the

Exhibit 1.2
Rules of debits, credits, and normal balances

Balance Sheet Accounts	Increase	Decrease	Normal Balance
Assets	Debit	Credit	Debit
Liabilities	Credit	Debit	Credit
Owner's Equity—Capital and			
Retained Earnings	Credit	Debit	Credit
Drawing and Dividends	Debit	Credit	Debit
Income Statement Accounts			
Revenue	Credit	Debit	Credit
Expenses	Debit	Credit	Debit

drawing, dividend, and expense accounts are considered in the positive sense. Increases in these accounts, which represent decreases in the owner's equity, are recorded as debits. When an account that normally has a debit balance actually has a credit balance, or vice versa, it indicates either an accounting error or some unusual situation that should be investigated. For example, a credit balance in the office equipment account could result from an accounting error; a debit balance in an accounts payable account could result from an overpayment.

A handy acronym tossed around from time to time is DEACLR, meaning that the normal debit (D) accounts are expenses (E) and assets (A), and the normal credit (C) accounts are liabilities (L) and revenue (R). Stated another way, debits are expenses and assets, credits are liabilities and revenue. If you know what you should see, then you can deal with information that differs from what you expect.

Cash versus Accrual Method of Accounting

In situations in which the presentation blurs the distinction between the cash and accrual methods of accounting, the accrual method should be presented as the overriding one (see chapter 3 for a more in-depth discussion of these two types of accounting). In our opinion, the accrual method presents a more thorough summary of operations and financial position at a given point in time. The cash method or modified cash method is a means of determining cash flow; it is used to minimize exposure to income tax on revenue to be collected in the future, that is, accounts receivable. It is also the easier method to manipulate. For example, let's assume that on November 30 the practice has a year-to-date profit of $125,000 after all traditional modified cash basis accruals are deducted. Let's further assume that the practice normally generates a profit in December of $25,000. So it is anticipated that the practice will have taxable income for the year of $150,000. The practice's patients want to make sure they use their respective cafeteria plan balances before year end. Herein lies a classic example of competing goals—those of the practice versus those of the patient.

Under the cash method of accounting, the practice would generally encourage patients to postpone payment until after being notified by the insurance company of their co-payment obligations. Understanding the rules regarding their patient's cafeteria plans is bonus: The practice knows that the definition of benefits is dependent on the date of service and not the date of payment. Therefore the staff can explain to the patients that they are making a holiday gesture and can encourage them to postpone payment until the following year. The practice would also postpone invoicing the insurance carrier and at the same time would purchase additional supplies and pay any obligations that would not ordinarily be accrued. This could easily result in a significant change in taxable income.

On the other hand, the accrual method of accounting would require that the practice identify accounts receivable that may need to be written off as uncollectable as well as expenses that should be accrued; purchase supplies that would normally be consumed over the next thirty days; and pay taxes on the balance. The objective is the same, the outcome probably quite different, and the direction for the most part different as well.

As mentioned before, the accrual method of accounting more accurately presents the results of operations and financial position at a specific point in time. Accrual method accounting is less susceptible to manipulation due to short-term timing differences. Further, it is not the favored method of accounting for medical practices, which generally have significant accounts receivable balances. No one wants to pay income tax on phantom income—and receivables, uncollected, are phantom income. It is doubtful that anything presented here will alter that perspective. Therefore, the accounting system should accommodate both theories of presentation. For management of the practice, use the accrual basis financial statement presentation style; for income tax reporting, use the modified cash method.

The accrual method of accounting records revenues as earned and expenses as incurred. In other words, revenue is recorded when services are rendered regardless of when they are billed to third-party payers; and expenses are recorded when the obligation to pay becomes fixed, following the same logical process you would use for your personal expenses. When you buy something you owe for it. Using a credit card doesn't change the fact that you just purchased something. You just repositioned whom and when you will pay.

If the intent is to share information with banks or other lending institutions, it would be in the best interest of the borrower to present accrual basis financial statements. Without sharing information about receivables relative to a medical practice and due to income tax planning that generally takes place relative to reportable income, the chances of securing a loan would be minimal at best if you presented cash basis financial statements.

The cash method is, as it implies, the reporting of transactions as they are paid or when cash is received. Generally, most practices use what is referred to as "modified cash basis" reporting, in which they record some liabilities before cash is actually paid but rarely record revenue before cash is received—a little like getting your cake and eating it too.

Unless a medical practice maintains an inventory of goods for resale to patients, it can use the modified cash basis of accounting for income tax reporting. If it does maintain such an inventory, it must use the accrual basis for tax reporting. An example of a medical practice that would be required to use the accrual basis is an optometry practice that sells eyeglasses and contact lenses.

A textbook example of a typical medical expense, the reporting for which differs significantly under these methods, is professional liability (or malpractice) insurance. Generally, the premium is paid annually or semiannually and is paid prior to the coverage period. Therefore, it is a prepaid expense because the benefit (i.e., coverage) has not commenced. To illustrate the recording of this transaction please review the journal entries in Exhibit 1.3.

To record January's expense for malpractice insurance for Doctor Domino, the same second entry would be made at the end of every month through June. At the end of the six-month period the account

Exhibit 1.3
Journal entry—transaction

Cash Method

Dr	Professional Liability Insurance	$6,000
Cr	Cash in Bank	$6,000

To record Doctor Domino's malpractice insurance for the period January 1, 2000, through June 30, 2000.

Accrual Method

Dr	Prepaid Expense—Professional Liability Insurance	$6,000
Cr	Cash in Bank	$6,000

To record payment of Doctor Domino's malpractice insurance for the period January 1, 2000, through June 30, 2000

To Record/Post Expense for Current Month

Dr	Professional Liability Insurance	$1,000
Cr	Prepaid Expense—Professional Liability Insurance	$1,000

---

balances will be exactly the same as reported under the cash method. However, during the course of the six-month period, under the accrual basis, management has the opportunity to evaluate the practice on a monthly basis with the advantage of a more accurate recurring cost structure; whereas under the cash method, only the June 30 statement would be of similar usefulness. This is a significant improvement in opportunity through a minor change in presentation.

Another significant deviation between the methods of presentation is that under the cash method, practices tend not to monitor as closely the bad debt experience of their operations as compared to those of their peer group. Out of sight, out of mind, as the adage goes, and so goes the profit!

Ratio/Percentage Analysis

In most instances, presentation follows method, as prescribed in accounting literature. The ideal is to present data in the manner that best informs the reader. All too often data are presented in the controllable/noncontrollable format with percentages based on total revenue. Review Exhibit 1.4 and the alternative presentation in Exhibit 1.5

Exhibit 1.4

Dr. Quizno Clinics statement of revenue and expense—modified cash basis
August 31, 1998 and 1997

	Actual			Percentages	
	1998	**1997**	**Variance**	**1998**	**1997**
Service fee revenue	1,328	896	432	0.10%	0.07%
Income—professional services	1,014,128	965,979	48,149	76.34%	80.62%
Lab fee revenue	257,334	209,814	47,520	19.37%	17.51%
Radiology/imaging revenue	55,630	21,554	34,076	4.19%	1.80%
Total net revenue	1,328,420	1,198,243	130,177	100.00%	100.00%
Non-physician expenses					
Non-physician salaries	348,431	367,798	19,367	26.23%	30.69%
Non-physician benefits	53,176	73,849	20,673	4.00%	6.16%
Information services	22,478	24,550	2,072	1.69%	2.05%
Laboratory expenses	43,904	41,368	(2,536)	3.30%	3.45%
Radiology/imaging expenses	38,941	10,777	(28,164)	2.93%	0.90%
Medical/surgical supplies	89,992	121,956	31,964	6.77%	10.18%
Building/occupancy costs	139,186	141,669	2,483	10.48%	11.82%
Equipment lease expenses	23,914	2,194	(21,720)	1.80%	0.18%
Admin. supplies/service expenses	11,580	19,282	7,702	0.87%	1.61%
Outside services	99,779	59,632	(40,147)	7.51%	4.98%
Promotion/marketing	4,685	14,448	9,763	0.35%	1.21%
Recruiting expenses	8,048	6,413	(1,635)	0.61%	0.54%
Other operating expenses	31,068	3,155	(27,913)	2.34%	0.26%
Interest expenses	54,386	90,614	36,228	4.09%	7.56%
Total non-physician costs	969,568	977,705	8,137	72.99%	81.59%
Net revenue before distribution	358,852	220,538	138,314	27.01%	18.41%
Physician salaries/ advances	327,365	275,425	(51,940)	24.64%	22.98%

for an example of using data, through accounting analysis, to supply the reader with critical information.

Based on the income statement in Exhibit 1.4, one might conclude that the practice is doing quite well as compared to the prior year. Net revenue before distribution is up 63% over the prior year, while net revenue is up only 11%. The clinic has made significant improvements in controlling costs while at the same time increasing revenue.

Exhibit 1.5
Dr. Quizno Clinics statement of revenue and expense—modified cash basis
August 31, 1998 and 1997

	Actual			Percentages	
	1998	**1997**	**Variance**	**1998**	**1997**
Service fee revenue	1,328	896	432	0.10%	0.07%
Services—physician	760,596	821,082	(60,486)	56.97%	68.53%
—non-provider	253,532	144,897	108,635	19.09%	12.09%
Lab fee revenue	257,334	209,814	47,520	19.37%	17.51%
Radiology/imaging revenue	55,630	21,554	34,076	4.19%	1.80%
Total net revenue	1,328,420	1,198,243	130,177	100.00%	100.00%
Non-physician expenses					
Physician's asst./nurses	106,300	89,760	16,540	41.93%	61.95%
RN/LPN	85,095	105,437	20,342	33.56%	72.77%
Total direct patient wages	191,395	195,197	3,802	75.49%	134.71%
Lab research / technician	63,008	84,209	21,201	24.48%	40.14%
Administrative services	46,028	45,392	(636)	3.46%	3.79%
Business managers	48,000	43,000	(5,000)	3.61%	3.59%
Total non-physician wages	348,431	367,798	19,367	26.23%	30.69%
Non-physician benefits	53,176	73,849	20,673	4.00%	6.16%
Information services	22,478	24,550	2,072	1.69%	2.05%
Laboratory expenses	43,904	41,368	(2,536)	3.30%	3.45%
Radiology/imaging expenses	38,941	10,777	(28,164)	2.93%	0.90%
Medical/surgical supplies	89,992	121,956	31,964	6.77%	10.18%
Building/occupancy costs	139,186	141,669	2,483	10.48%	11.82%
Other operating expenses	31,068	3,155	(27,913)	2.34%	4.44%
Interest expenses	54,386	90,614	36,228	4.09%	7.56%
Grouping for presentation	148,006	101,969	(46,037)	11.14%	8.51%
Total non-physician costs	969,568	977,705	8,137	72.99%	81.59%
Net revenue before					
distribution	358,852	220,538	138,314	27.01%	18.41%
Physician salaries/advances	327,365	275,425	(51,940)	24.64%	22.98%

Now take this same data, modify the format, adjust the presentation (as in Exhibit 1.5), and see if your conclusions remain the same.

The only thing to change in the presentation in Exhibit 1.5 is the wage section. Note how Lab Research/Technician wages decreased by 25%, but as a percentage of Lab Fee Revenue, the costs dropped by 39%—a significant improvement in costs associated with a respectable increase in revenue. This presentation uses available information to inform the user of changes in patterns that impact the bottom line. Please remember that you must educate the user whenever you make presentation changes such as this and when subsequent modifications occur. The following paragraphs explain the presentation modifications that are presented in Exhibit 1.5.

The Total Direct Patient Wages as a percentage of revenue is based on Services—Non-Provider and not Total Net Revenue. Why? It is perceived that the wages associated with this category are directly involved in the delivery of professional services to the patient and not in the other categories of revenue.

The Lab/Research Technician wages are calculated as a percentage of Lab Fee Revenue. Why should we consider anything else? Why shouldn't we monitor the wage costs classification to revenue from the same specialization? No, we are not ignoring the value of retaining specialists on staff who contribute to the goodwill and overall efficiency of the practice; but ignoring that there is a *definable* value in relation to this *perceived* value is not prudent business management.

The wages for Administrative Services and Business Managers are calculated as a percentage of Total Net Revenue as the allocation of costs exceeds the benefits to be derived from any greater specificity (for purposes of reviewing and monitoring interim financial statements).

Please note that the calculation of Total Non-Physician Wages as a percentage of Total Net Revenue is no different than that in the previous example. Yes, the columns no longer foot/total and do not follow traditional accounting literature, but the benefits to be derived outweigh the negatives of footings.

Total Direct Patient Wages as a percentage of Services—Non-Provider is 75.49% as compared to 134.71%. Provided the practice implemented some monitoring strategy for improving efficiency, its members should be pleased to see the results in a readable and meaningful format. The Physician's Assistant/Nurses wage as compared to the RN/LPN wage implies that the change from non-direct assistants to direct is more efficient.

Let's take this example one step further for the analysis of other categories that also impact the bottom line. Please note the change in costs for Radiology/Imaging Expenses, now presented as a percentage of Radiology/Imaging Revenue. The analysis doesn't stop here; there are a significant number of other opportunities.

Many other presentation opportunities are available, such as monitoring bad debt expense as a percentage of specific receivable categories. Here also is a significant issue; most current practices' accounts receivable programs are not integrated with their accounting software, requiring significant manual reconciliation between the accounts. Often due to the burdens of reconciliation, many practices put their receivables monitoring on so-called "autopilot." Managing receivables creates a significant amount of revenue. You see, if you really evaluate receivables, they represent 100% revenue! All costs of the clinic have already been incurred. It would be wise for a practice to present an interest charge on receivables (see Exhibit 1.6) as part of the revenue section of the income statement.

Current Assets/Liabilities

Classification as "current" implies that the asset will be consumed or the liability paid within the next 12 months. These balances are usually verified on an annual basis. When preparing interim financial statements, maintain the perspective of "current" as being the next 12 months. For example, the balance in the current maturity–L/T debt account is not reduced on a monthly basis by the principal portion of the debt and then replenished on the accounting anniversary. A rolling 12-month balance is maintained. It is also questionable to move the net change in current maturities on a monthly basis. The accuracy of the financial statements is not significantly improved. We suggest that, as in the example, the current portion be reflected on an annual basis with the monthly adjustment for payments of principal being posted to the long-term portion of the liability.

Various Journals

In most businesses, the use of various accounting journals to make journal entries is commonplace. These journals are the Cash Receipts Journal, Cash Disbursements Journal, Sales Journal, Purchases Journal, and the General Journal. Most medical practices do not make use of the Sales and Purchases Journals, as they are primarily used for recording sales on

Exhibit 1.6
Dr. Quizno Clinics statement of revenue and expense modified cash basis
August 31, 1998 and 1997

	Actual			Percentages	
	1998	1997	Variance	1998	1997
Service fee revenue	1,328	896	432	0.10%	0.07%
Services—physician	760,596	821,082	(60,486)	56.97%	68.53%
—non-provider	253,532	144,897	108,635	19.09%	12.09%
Lab fee revenue	257,334	209,814	47,520	19.37%	17.51%
Radiology/imaging revenue	55,630	21,554	34,076	4.19%	1.80%
Total net revenue	1,328,420	1,198,243	130,177	100.00%	100.00%
Non-physician expenses					
Physician's asst./nurses	106,300	89,760	16,540	41.93%	61.95%
RN/LPN	85,095	105,437	20,342	33.56%	72.77%
Total direct patient wages	191,395	195,197	3,802	75.49%	134.71%
Lab research / technician	63,008	84,209	21,201	24.48%	40.14%
Administrative services	46,028	45,392	(636)	3.46%	3.79%
Business managers	48,000	43,000	(5,000)	3.61%	3.59%
Total non-physician wages	348,431	367,798	19,367	26.23%	30.69%
Non-physician benefits	53,176	73,849	20,673	4.00%	6.16%
Information services	22,478	24,550	2,072	1.69%	2.05%
Laboratory expenses	43,904	41,368	(2,536)	3.30%	3.45%
Radiology/imaging expenses	38,941	10,777	(28,164)	70.00%	50.00%
Medical/surgical supplies	89,992	121,956	31,964	6.77%	10.18%
Building/occupancy costs	139,186	141,669	2,483	10.48%	11.82%
Other operating expenses	31,068	3,155	(27,913)	2.34%	4.44%
Interest expenses	54,386	90,614	36,228	4.09%	7.56%
Grouping for presentation	148,006	101,969	(46,037)	11.14%	8.51%
Total non-physician costs	969,568	977,705	8,137	72.99%	81.59%
Net revenue before					
distribution	358,852	220,538	138,314	27.01%	18.41%
Physician salaries/advances	327,365	275,425	(51,940)	24.64%	22.98%

account and purchases on account. Medical practices typically do not use their accounting system for recording accounts receivable. It is very common for a medical practice to use a completely separate and non-integrated system for accounts receivable management. This is due primarily to the requirements of healthcare in general and to the manner in which accounting and billing are performed for medical practices.

Physician Compensation

Most medical practices, throughout the year, account for monies distributed to the owner/physician as salary. In some cases, this salary is treated just like any other wage compensation paid to other employees; in other cases, it is classified simply as an advance, with no withholding or matching of traditional employer taxes. In the latter case, at the end of the year, an adjusting entry is required to reclassify the advance as a distribution in which the monies are not treated as compensation for income tax reporting purposes. This is based on the level of ownership and the style of reporting for income tax purposes, and is further discussed in chapter 7.

Balance Sheet

The balance sheet is a report card stating the financial health of the organization. It can only make representations based on the facts available to it. It is both a spokesperson sharing available information and a historical picture, explaining to the public what assets the organization has available to meet the demands of rendering services to the public; how it has acquired those assets (through the use of invested or borrowed money); how quickly its obligations can be paid; how well the business has been operated in the past; and whether the owners themselves have enough confidence in the business to invest their own capital. A significant amount of information may be gained through a review of the balance sheet. Therein lies the rationalization for preparing accrual basis financial statements. A stable, profitable business should have a representative balance sheet. It is often difficult to make a similar representation with typical cash basis presentations.

Income Statement

Why is an income statement so important to business owners? Because it indicates to a large degree whether the business has achieved or failed its primary objective: earning a "profit" or net income.

Shifts in Practice's Payer Mix

Many areas of the country have experienced or are experiencing a shift from commercial insurance to managed care. Some areas of the country have experienced a shift from 20 percent managed care to 70 percent in as little as twelve months. Shifts in payer mix will have a significant impact on practice revenue. Failure to recognize this shift and make appropriate adjustments have a detrimental impact on physician compensation.

For example, when a practice has ballooning gross revenues and still is losing money, a thorough evaluation of the payer mix generally will identify the problem. In one organization in which we were involved, the PPO and capitation patients were contributing a first year $100,000 gross. The physician couldn't understand why accrual basis profits were declining. We found that his costs to treat those patients amounted to nearly $130,000. Although the shift in payer mix had contributed to the negative impact on profits, in reality, the larger problem was a lack of understanding of the internal cost structure of the practice. The shift in payer mix did result in lower earnings for the practice, but the problem was rooted in not understanding the costs of delivering services to the PPO and capitation patients or in underestimating those costs.

This makes understanding a fee structure and an overhead analysis crucial when considering a proposal that requires a reduction in fees covering a large group. Even the most naïve practitioner immediately understands the concept that it's unwise to work highly skilled fingers clear through their latex gloves to produce a loss. Of course, if you don't know you are handing the equivalent of a five-dollar bill to every patient who gets a blood test, how can there be a problem?

Exhibit 1.7 is a sample chart that can be used to monitor payer mix as it currently exists, and to review quarterly (or at minimum, annu-

Exhibit 1.7
Sample chart—monitoring payer mix

Percent of patients in each insurance class:	
Medicare	_____ %
Medicaid	_____ %
Champus	_____ %
Workers' Comp.	_____ %
HMO FFS	_____ %
PPO FFS	_____ %
Capitation	_____ %
Blue Cross/Blue Shield	_____ %
Commercial Pay	_____ %
Self Pay	_____ %

ally) the shift that is taking place. The figures should be based on production generated, not production collected.

Standard Journal Entries

A significant number of journal entries to the general ledger on a monthly basis are recurring in nature. In the previous example of malpractice insurance, the recurring entry from prepaids to insurance will occur for at least six months. If set to be a monthly recurring entry, should the balance in prepaids goes to zero along with the next month's entry occurring without another payment for the prepaid covering the next six months, a credit would be reflected on the balance sheet. This would alert the bookkeeper that something may be wrong. It could be that the prepaid was posted to expense, or that the insurance premium may not have been paid. Either way, a situation exists that needs investigation. This is, in our opinion, the way it is supposed to work. The system should alert you to issues and allow you to deal with those issues and then move on.

Most software packages also allow you to set an entry for automatic reversal in the following month. This is of significant value in cases in which you make journal entries for accounts that should be adjusted on a monthly basis. Examples of items that fall into this category would be accruals for payroll taxes, inventory balances taken on a monthly basis, and accrued wages, to name a few.

CLINICS WITHOUT WALLS

An arrangement that is not as rare today as it was twenty years ago is one in which physicians join together to leverage administrative functions, an arrangement generally referred to as a "clinic without walls." Here each doctor maintains his or her separate office but shares the administrative functions, including billing and collections, with several other doctors. For bookkeeping, each office is considered a profit center, with a separate financial statement report.

Collections present specific problems when each practice individually invoices its patients through the centralized billing office. Even though the invoices are sent from a single location, payments are often received at the respective physicians' offices, as are collections for current services. All deposits go into a central bank account maintained for the group, not individual ones for each physician. You can imagine the trust necessary to make such an arrangement work. It is imperative that the accounting function support the needs of each individual practice unit. Detailed general ledger reports must be presented in layman's terms, ledgers must agree with receivable and collection reports, and administration of the separate practices must be better than would have been achieved in individual practices. It would be naïve to expect that the arrangement would continue should the collections of one particular practice go from an average receivable balance of, say, 65 days to 85 days. This represents capital that must come from somewhere, and it is doubtful that the other physicians would be pleased.

KEEPING THE BOOKS

Everyone thinks there is nothing to it—any person with a basic level of intelligence can easily manage, everyone is trustworthy, and bookkeeping is nothing more than reconciling the bank account, writing a few checks, and processing payroll checks with a computer that does all the calculations. So why do so many businesses find themselves with no cash, a significant amount of unpaid bills to vendors, and their accounting records in such a mess that it will cost a small fortune for someone else to come in and make sense of the whole thing? The problem is rooted in the perspective of the decision maker as to the level of knowledge required by the bookkeeper. Maintaining and presenting data in the most useful manner is akin to piecing together jigsaw puzzles. We have encountered many individuals who had the requisite technical training but lacked the common sense to bring it all together.

All too often the accounting staff attempt to record transactions based on the way things happened rather than on the obligations of the parties. See, for example, the journal entries for malpractice insurance given earlier. Other examples are personal use of company vehicles, collections in advance of services such as in many ob/gyn practices, and the physician compensation issue, already noted. Exercise caution when non-business accounting activity finds its way into the accounting for the business, as in the personal use of company vehicles. The Internal Revenue Service imposes on employers reporting obligations that have no bearing on the earnings of the company. These reporting modifications may affect the employee's Form W-2, yet have no impact on the financial operations of the business. The adjustments affect the employee's personal income tax situation only. All too often, accounting staff attempt to make some journal entry for the adjustments to the employee Form W-2 when no adjustment is necessary.

Overhead creates another perplexing dilemma. Consider a business that is 100% leveraged as compared to one that is 50% leveraged. Also consider that the 100% leveraged business has an owner who is accustomed to a 100% higher recurring salary than is the owner of the other business. Do the facts require that the 100% example must have an overhead higher than that of the 50% example? Yes, to arrive at true cash flow breakeven. But is that a reasonable burden to place on the respective businesses in evaluating their respective performance? Not likely.

So, what exactly is overhead? *Overhead* should represent costs that are not directly identifiable to a particular process or product output; costs that are essential to the overall business; costs for which the direct allocation to a particular process or unit is not cost-justified. Overhead cannot be a basket to accumulate expenditures that are later charged back/allocated as a percentage of revenue or other costs. Overhead should and must be controlled.

Is it reasonable to consider or anticipate that a minimum level of overhead exist relative to a given business? In other words, is there a fixed element to overhead? Yes.

What level of overhead is reasonable? Overhead should be identified at the beginning of the particular year or process: what is categorized as overhead; reason it isn't charged based on the necessity of the expenditure; what is an acceptable amount of cost to be non-identified—all should be documented. It would be futile to argue that not every business or process has an associated level of overhead. An evaluation of the business is necessary to determine what level is reasonable. Good luck!

Sample Chart of Accounts for a Medical Practice

OVERVIEW

Many small businesses operate with limited management information—typically, a budget, a monthly profit and loss statement, a monthly balance sheet, and a monthly cash flow statement. Situations such as this are ripe for the ambitious consultant who is engaged to evaluate the current reporting and to demonstrate the impact of alternative reporting. A successful project to install a management reporting system that addresses users' needs beyond traditional general ledger financial statement reporting will draw appropriate visibility. Successful reporting will take into consideration the company's critical success factors with styling of the reporting to present those factors. Before modifying existing reporting, the consultant must be sufficiently knowledgeable about the company's operations to access whether the correct critical success factors have been identified.

All projects should begin with a thorough evaluation of existing management reporting, the current accounting process, user needs, and of course existing software availability. Assuming that some users seek information that is currently not available, a determination of how to collect this information is necessary, as well as at what incremental cost.

Part of any thorough evaluation should incorporate an evaluation of the existing chart of accounts for the general ledger system. The structure of the chart of accounts must be flexible, allowing groups of

Exhibit 2.1
CRAHCA chart of accounts—broad identification of segments

Account Number	Category
1000	Assets
2000	Liabilities and owners' equity
3000	Revenues
4000	Adjustments and allowances
5000	Human resource expenses
6000	Physical resource expenses
7000	Purchased services and general and administrative expenses
8000	Non-operating revenues and expenses

differing sizes and complexity to meet their respective financial information objectives. If a group expands in size or complexity, the chart of accounts should be sufficiently flexible to allow the needs to be met by expanding the existing system rather than rebuilding the entire system.

In developing the chart of accounts, significant and thorough evaluation of the specific needs of the company must be considered above all else. Generally, the opportunity to follow industry-specific formats will not interfere with the needs of the practice. We have, however, seen many instances in which the chart of accounts failed to address the needs of the practice. We suggest as a general rule that you first investigate industry literature, specific trade associations, and other peer groups within your specific practice before launching your own chart of accounts development. It is unlikely that you will succeed without considerable experience. The Center for Research in Ambulatory Health Care Administration (CRAHCA) has developed a chart of accounts for medical groups that you may consider adopting, provided your accounting system will accommodate the account codes.

For illustration purposes, we will start with the CRAHCA chart of accounts for a discussion of how complex a system can be or should be, and why. The CRAHCA starts out with a broad identification of segments of the chart of accounts and then further details the accounts (see Exhibit 2.1) to gather information for comparison (see Exhibit 2.2). When reviewing these exhibits, please take note of the complexity, versatility, and detail contained in them. The CRAHCA chart of accounts should accommodate the majority of businesses within the medical community. In many instances, the detail goes beyond necessity unless

Exhibit 2.2
CRAHCA chart of accounts—detailed

Account Number	Category
1110–1140	Unrestricted cash at banks
1150–1160	Unrestricted cash on hand
1160	Petty cash
1170	Marketable securities and short-term investments
1210	**Accounts Receivable—Fee for Service**
1211	Accounts receivable—Private pay
1212	Accounts receivable—Blue Cross/Blue Shield
1213	Accounts receivable—Commercial insurance
1214	Accounts receivable—Medicare
1215	Accounts receivable—Medicaid
1216	Accounts receivable—Workers' compensation
1217	Accounts receivable—Other state agencies
1218	Accounts receivable—Collection agencies
1219	Accounts receivable—Other pay types
1220	**Accounts Receivable—Prepaid Contracts**
1221	Accounts receivable—Capitation—HMO (Plan A)
1222	Accounts receivable—Capitation—HMO (Plan B)
1223	Accounts receivable—Capitation—Medicare
1224	Accounts receivable—Capitation—Medicaid
1225	Accounts receivable—Capitation—State, County, City
1226	Accounts receivable—Capitation—Individual (non-group)
1227	Accounts receivable—Reinsurance claims
1228	Accounts receivable—Co-payments and coordination of benefits
1229	Accounts receivable—Other prepaid contracts
1230	**Allowance for Uncollected Receivables**
1231	**Allowance for Estimated Uncollectible Receivables— Private Pay**
1240	**Allowance for Contractual Adjustments**

you use the information to compare your practice to industry data. If you don't need the peer group information, you should eliminate many of the detailed line items, such as accounts 1210–1229. These items, unless needed to manage the practice, are of little value on their own merits. Comparing this data to peer group information can assist the practice in determining if the practice is under-performing or out-performing the peer group. The comparison is not possible unless you gather the information in the same manner as does the rest of the peer group.

As you can see, the detail necessary to gather information from a diverse industry can seem overwhelming. You should also realize that although many of the account categories may not have application to your practice, you should follow the chart of accounts to facilitate peer group analysis. In some instances, you may not gather information in the detail as outlined, which will lead you to erroneous results as compared to your peer group. In our opinion, once you begin to make exceptions, the process is of little use. For example, many small business owners quickly rationalize why their business, which fails to generate a profit, is worth a small fortune when they want to sell it. They somehow conjure up exceptions as to why the business really made money yet due to the accounting, or perhaps the lack thereof, the company really made a profit. Our approach is to eliminate the exceptions. A puzzle with missing pieces gives an incomplete picture. Your accounting system may have marginal room for exceptions; but when you do begin making exceptions, you'll soon have no means to manage your business except for increasing revenue. You should also realize that in some instances, this increased revenue may in fact result in less contribution margin than lower levels of revenue, but you may be in such a quandary that you have no perceived alternative. The old adage, "Sales cure all evils," is in most cases true; but the level of sales necessary to cure the evils of poor accounting may be more than the market can support or the business can manage.

For a more complete listing of the CRAHCA chart of accounts, we suggest that you contact your trade association for that information. This chart of accounts should be adequate to accommodate the needs of your organization.

MARKET CHANGES TO CONSIDER

"Change is as inevitable as death." "You are either moving forward or backward." "Embrace change or suffer the consequences." All are familiar phrases that you have probably heard over the last ten years, or have actually used to express yourself in dealing with clients, family, and friends. Change occurs even in financial statement presentation, due perhaps to new rules imposed by regulatory bodies, or to change in the way the practice is operated, or in the way taxes are calculated, or in the information available for evaluation.

An example of a change that modified the traditional financial statement presentation is a case in which the tax laws were changed to allow businesses to amortize intangible assets, such as goodwill. Traditionally, goodwill was amortized for book reporting but not tax reporting. Other intangibles were amortized for both book and tax reporting. Generally, the presentation on the balance sheet was net of amortization, with the amortization expense being reflected on the income statement. When and if the other intangibles were sold, the gain or loss would be calculated based on the remaining basis of the asset. Depreciation/amortization recapture was not required as it is for equipment. The net presentation was sufficient for the rules. Now the rules have changed and amortization is subject to recapture. Recapture means that if amortization was taken for income tax purposes and that asset was subsequently sold, resulting in a gain as compared to the remaining basis of the asset, amortization up to the amount of the gain is recaptured as ordinary income in the year of sale. The traditional presentation—"net of amortization"—will not inform the reader of the potential obligation for ordinary income recapture; therefore, a change in presentation is in order. Accumulated amortization for assets that have a reasonable likelihood of being sold in the future will require a separate amortization account for each category. For example, organization costs are amortized. The likelihood of organization costs' being sold in a typical business situation is not high. Therefore, a change in presentation is not appropriate, nor is it necessary.

You must challenge yourself to look for changes in presentation such as the ones noted above when they arise. Many changes occur due to improvements in information gathering, or to changes in the way the business is operated. We have seen situations in which the benchmark percentages remain valid although the foundation on which they are based have changed. Many management information systems have been developed in prior years with the mistaken belief that the management reporting responsibilities consist solely of generating a monthly balance sheet and income statement. These objectives certainly are important, because management validates business performance from historical numbers, and, in some cases, derives a measure of job security from such numbers. Measuring performance solely on financial results, however, has its limitations. Exhibit 2.3 reflects a sample chart of accounts for your consideration. This chart of accounts is non-specific to the particular practice, and caution should be exer-

Exhibit 2.3

Sample medical practice—chart of accounts

Balance Sheet

ASSETS

Current Assets
  Petty Cash
  Cash—Checking
  Cash—Savings
  Cash—Payroll
  Cash—Money Market
  Cash—Refunds
  Accounts Receivable
  Accounts Receivable—Employee
  Accounts Receivable—Owners
  Prepaid Expenses
    Total Current Assets

Property, Plant & Equipment
  Automobile
  Equipment
  Furniture & Fixtures
  Building
  Leasehold Improvements
  Land
  Accumulated Depreciation
    Net Property, Plant & Equipment

Other Assets
  Investments
  Deposits
  Goodwill
  Accumulated Amortization—Goodwill
  Covenant Not to Complete
  Accumulated Amortization—Covenant
  Patient Files
  Accumulated Amortization—Patient Files
    Total Other Assets

Total Assets

Liabilities and Stockholders' Equity

Current Liabilities
  Checking Account Overdraft
  Line of Credit
  FICA Withholding

Exhibit 2.3   (Continued)

Federal Income Tax Withholding
State Income Tax Withholding
Accounts Payable
Note Payable #1—Current
Note Payable #2—Current
Note Payable #3—Current
Retirement Plan Contribution
Charge Cards Payable
  Total Current Liabilities

Long-Term Liabilities
Note Payable #1—Long-Term
Note Payable #2—Long-Term
Note Payable #3—Long-Term
  Total Long-Term Liabilities

Stockholders' Equity
Common Stock
Paid-In Capital
Retained Earnings
Individual—Capital
Individual—Drawing
Current Year to Date Profit (Loss)
  Total Stockholders' Equity

Total Liabilities and Stockholders' Equity

Income Statement

Revenues
Product Sales
Physician Production
Non-Provider Production
Professional Discounts
  Contractual Discounts
  Bad Debt Write -Offs
  Patient Refunds
  Cash Adjustment
    Total

Total Revenues

Expenses
Labor Expenses
  Labor—Clerical
    Clerical Wages

continued

Exhibit 2.3   (Continued)

Payroll Taxes—Clerical
Clerical Casual Labor
Clerical Retirement Plan
Clerical Medical Insurance
    Total

Labor—Non-Provider
  Wages
  Payroll Taxes—Non-Provider
  Non-Provider Casual Labor
  Non-Provider Retirement Plan
  Non-Provider Medical Insurance
    Total

General Employee Expense and Benefits
  Unallocated Retirement Expense
  Unallocated Medical Insurance
  Workers' Compensation Insurance
  Want Ads/Staff Recruitment
  Staff Outings/Meetings/Snack
  Staff Continuing Education/Travel
  Staff Meals
  Staff Uniform Expenses/Allowance
  Staff Laundry for Uniforms
  Gifts/Awards
  Other General Employee Expenses
    Total

Total Labor

Direct Production Costs
  Product Purchases
    Product Purchases
      Total

  Supplies
    Small Instruments
    Clinical Supplies
    Drugs for Patient Distribution
    Other supplies
      Total

  Inside Lab
    Lab Casual Labor
    Lab Tech Wages
    Payroll Taxes—Lab Tech
    Medical Insurance—Lab Tech

Exhibit 2.3 (Continued)

Lab Continuing Education/Travel
Lab Meals
Inoculations
Retirement Plan Expense
  Total

Total Direct Production Costs

Capital and Facility
  Facility
    Facility Maintenance
    Building Rent
    Parking—Staff and Patient
    Utilities
    Trash/Waste Removal Expense
    OSHA Disposal
    Real Estate Taxes
    General Liability and Casualty Insurance
    Burglar Alarm Expense
    Building Interest
    Building Depreciation
    Building Repairs/Maintenance
    Office Flowers and Decorations
      Total
  Equipment
    Equipment Lease
    Expendable Equipment Purchases
    Equipment Interest
    Equipment Depreciation
    Personal Property Taxes
    Other Insurance
    Equipment Repair/Maintenance
    Computer Support/Maintenance
    Gain/Loss on Sale of Equipment
      Total

Total Capital and Facility
  Administration Expense
    Office Supplies and Expense
      Reception Area Magazines
      Forms and Stationary
      Postage
      Fees
      Visa/MC Bank Charges

continued

Exhibit 2.3   (Continued)

Bank Draft Charges
Dues and Subscriptions
Office Supplies and Expenses
   Total
Professional Fees
   Legal Fees
   Accounting and Tax Return Expenses
   Payroll Service Fees
   Practice Consultant's Fees
   Cafeteria Plan Administration
   Retirement Plan Administration
   Other Professional Fees
      Total
Insurance
   Malpractice Insurance
   Business Overhead Insurance
      Total
Telephone
   Basic Telephone Expense
   Cellular Telephone Expense
   Long Distance Telephone
   Telephone Pager
   Telephone Answering Service
      Total
Taxes and License Fees
   License Fee
   Privilege License
   City License
   Franchise Tax
   Federal Income Taxes
   State Income Taxes
   Penalties
      Total
Marketing
   General Advertising
   Yellow Page Advertising
   Practice Promotion/Other
   Patient Gifts/Awards
   Flowers for Office/Patients
   Patient Newsletter
   Referral Expense
      Total

Exhibit 2.3 (Continued)

Total Administrative Expense

Net Income (Loss) Before Compensation and Benefits
  Physician Compensation and Benefits
    Associate
      Salary/Independent Contractor
      Payroll Taxes
      Workers' Compensation
      Fringe Benefits
      Professional Expenses
      Dues/Publications (Non-Club)
      Continuing Education
      Travel and Lodging
      Meals and Entertainment
      Medical Insurance
      Disability Insurance
      Retirement Plan Expense
        Total

  Auto
    Lease
    Insurance
    Gasoline and Oil
    Depreciation
    Interest
    Repairs and Maintenance
      Total

  Physician Compensation and Fringe Benefits
    Salary
    Payroll Taxes
    Retirement Plan Contribution
    Medical Insurance
    Disability Insurance
    Medical Reimbursement Plan
    Partnership Insurance
    Buy-Sell Life Insurance
    Buy-Sell Disability Insurance
      Total

  Practice Acquisition Expense
    Practice Acquisition
    Amortization Expense
    Seller Post-Close Consultant Fees
    Intangible Practice Debt Interest
      Total

continued

Exhibit 2.3   (Continued)

Other Income (Expenses)
  Other Income
  Interest Income
  Interest Expense

Total Other Income (Expenses)

Net Income (Loss)

---

cised before implementing this account scheme without modification.
To do so would not incorporate company-specific critical success factors, would not have taken into consideration the need of the users of
the respective business unit, and may not result in an improvement
over the current system of reporting.

ANALYZING THE CURRENT SITUATION

To enhance decision-making, management needs information about
business processes—information that goes beyond traditional general
ledger reporting. Besides being accurate and timely, such information
must be relevant to the actions that drive the business. The nature of
management information directly influences how the business is managed because managers frequently take actions based on the information reported.

Management that approaches its future from a strictly historical
perspective could be assuming unnecessary risks. This statement is
true for several reasons:

- Historical data become stale very quickly and may not accurately predict future events and occurrences.

- Accounting methods heavily incorporate estimation techniques; consequently, the general ledger balances tend to be ar-
  bitrary, not absolute. Realistically, the tax consequences to the
  owners often dictate how aggressively or conservatively (within
  reasonable boundaries) the company presents the numbers.

- Financial statements may suggest emerging problems, but
  rarely reveal solutions. Management must look behind the fi-

nancial statements to discover why business problems have occurred.

The controller, as chief information officer of the small to midsized company, plays a critical role in guiding the management information process. Ordinarily, the controller must take the initiative in revamping or installing the company's management reporting system. Reporting needs are very fluid and should change as the company changes; so any reporting system over two to three years old should be reevaluated. The opportunity to implement a meaningful management reporting system is a chance for the controller to prove or enhance his or her worth to the company, while favorably influencing the company's decision-making ability and overall competitiveness.

Overhauling a company's management information reporting system is a major project. Because of the associated risk, you should thoroughly prepare for the task and anticipate the outcome. At minimum, the new management reports should provide executives with dynamic, highly focused information that enhances decision-making. A reporting scheme that attracts the reader's attention also helps in devising management reports that help managers make better decisions.

Being aware of certain background factors before embarking on a management reporting project will greatly assist in completing the project successfully. Gathering information and evaluating existing management reporting with the use of the following topics should facilitate the project:

- Controlling Information Overload

- Identifying Critical Success Factors

- Reporting Multiple Performance Measures

- Presenting Information in Multiple Formats

- Knowing the Cost of Information

Controlling Information Overload

One consequence of computer automation is the creation of more and more information. Today's computers (regardless of their size) can generate incredible quantities of data at a faster and faster pace. The magnitude of paper being generated poses obvious storage problems and complicates management's ability to focus on what's really important. Typically, executive management would prefer less, but better, information. Your responsibility is to identify pertinent data and highlight it for management. Executive management typically demands information that is more summarized, more oriented to exceptions, and perhaps less frequent.

In the past we've overheard comments that you will soon need a computer to inform you of which reports to review. This is a reality in today's business world, and an issue that must be addressed for businesses to succeed in today's competitive marketplace.

Identifying Critical Success Factors

The reality that executive managers want concise, relevant information is further evidenced by the notion of critical success factors. Essentially, the theory of *critical success factors* states that for any business to prosper, there exist a limited number of areas in which the business must succeed. Critical success factors vary widely from business to business. Normally, a business should focus on three to six critical success factors. Emphasizing more than six could cause unnecessary distractions in the business. Our experience is that identifying and limiting critical success factors to three produces the most effective results. Critical success factors typically use hard, statistical data, but might also involve more subjective data. These factors generally change as the business changes; therefore, an annual review is necessary to verify their continued relevance.

The proper selection of critical success factors is greatly simplified if management has already defined the company's essential processes and future goals. In many businesses, critical success factors are known industry benchmarks; but note that these benchmarks do vary from organization to organization due to cost factors such as differing vendors for supplies, payer mix, and so forth.

Although originally designed for top management, the critical success factors can be equally applicable at other organizational levels throughout the business. The concept can be pushed down throughout a business, much like strategic planning. Each division or department might develop its own critical success factors, the most important of which should be corporate-level factors.

Reporting Multiple Performance Measures

Management should not be content with a reporting system that fails to address the underlying factors influencing the company's profitability. The preceding discussion of critical success factors may suggest that a monthly, single-page report is all that executive management needs to oversee a company; however, although this possibility exists, management will more likely prefer to focus on the company's critical success factors, while also having access to additional supporting information—a series of reports.

Often the reporting of critical success factors falls outside the traditional information gathering for the general ledger system and are tied to performance measures rather than financial measures. Although numerous financial measures exist for gauging a business's health, a well-rounded reporting package should address a company's productivity and quality measures as well. In reality, productivity and quality measures are so closely linked to profitability that it is difficult to determine which comes first—somewhat akin to the chicken-or-the-egg analogy.

Productivity is a relatively simple concept that focuses on the use of resources to produce certain results or outputs. Most simply, it is the ratio of output to input. A company can increase productivity by raising output, while holding input constant; by lowering input while holding output constant; by raising output faster than input; and so on.

The concept of productivity has typically been associated with manufacturing, where the investment of direct labor dollars could be expected to produce certain quantifiable results. Because productivity is primarily concerned with resource usage, productivity measurement is possible in many environments. A correlation must exist between some unit of input (hours, dollars, etc.) and some unit of output (pieces, billable hours, patients, etc.). If the population is too small, however, measurements could fluctuate widely, rendering them meaningless.

Examples of productivity measurements applicable to service industries include:

- In a physician practice, the number of patients seen relative to the number of hours worked

- In an auto dealership, the number of sales closed relative to the number of prospects contacted or possibly the number of days or hours on duty

- In an accounting firm, the number of chargeable hours to the number of hours paid

The potential for producing undesirable results with improperly designed productivity standards often results from a failure to understand the process comprehensively. For example, where costs of sales are measured against revenue before discounts or collection write-offs, the lack of controls in the billing and collection department may offset any profitability due to subsequent account charge-offs. Management may have perceived that the business was operating at optimum levels only to find out later that there is no cash available, due to the fact that the practice has been seeing patients who either lacked the ability to pay or simply had not paid—an alarming revelation to the doctor who thought a new car was in order.

The company's accounting system generally provides information that addresses many of management's financial concerns, yet does little to satisfy the productivity and quality considerations that are also vital in a well-rounded reporting package. Generally, if productivity and quality statistics are being captured, the process is likely happening independently of the company's accounting system.

Presenting Information in Multiple Formats

Most traditional accounting reporting has the classical rows-and-columns appearance associated with balance sheets, income statements, and statements of cash flow. Trained accountants are very comfortable with the classical presentation of numbers in rows and columns; others, however, may be intimidated by such presentations.

Successful management reporting contemplates how users will read and understand the information. Reports that fail to communicate do not achieve their intended purpose. Controllers should be sensitive to the needs of the audience when designing reports. Research has suggested that some people think best in numbers, some in words, and some in pictures; a controller should accommodate all parties by supplementing the numerical presentation with a narrative and graphs.

In developing this supplementary information, be keen to the notion of readability and appearance. Draw the reader into the information with report styling, but exercise caution in what your message is. For instance, where all information is capitalized, ask yourself, "What is the message?" Presenting everything in the same context implies that each thing presented is of similar value. If the reader is not guided through your presentation by the style used, the presentation is in need of revision. Get the reader to the point, allow the reader to make informed decisions, then stop. Don't feel compelled to restate the details; management, properly informed, can take the lead empowered with the outcomes of their prior decisions.

Normally, computer-generated reports will fall short of being meaningful to executive management yet may effectively provide control information to lower levels in the business. Remember to improve readability and application; reports must have visual effect and present relevant information. Reports with good information but no visual appeal will not be widely used.

Knowing the Cost of Information

When striving to generate management information, one frequently overlooked issue is the high cost associated with information gathering. This statement applies primarily to operating statistics that must be collected outside the traditional general ledger system, such as the number of full-time equivalent employees, the percentage of on-time deliveries, and virtually anything that concerns marketing analysis. The absence of cost-effective monitoring systems is a primary reason that progress has been stymied in the productivity analysis area.

The controller serves as the gatekeeper for company information, often deciding whether it should be collected. Controllers should not refuse to dig out tough information, but should confer with the other parties involved to determine the associated costs and benefits of the task. This cost/benefit analysis is particularly essential with ad hoc requests, when the data-gathering tasks are nonrecurring.

Information is power, but power must be in the right hands to achieve results that impact the profitability of the company.

Often overlooked is the cost of reporting inaccurate or misleading information. Since a management reporting system is intended to influence decision-makers, it should be expected that report information will occasionally trigger modifications of current business activities. If managers take action based on erroneous information, much energy will be expended correcting the misdirection. The price of reporting management information is high; the price of reporting poor management information is unaffordable.

SUMMARY

Data relative to internal operations is almost always obtainable. Data external to the company can prove much more difficult to capture; however, some information about the competition is ordinarily public. Information about competitors can be ethically collected from common customers, trade journals, and so forth.

Assuming that the data is available from a source inside or outside the company, an estimation of the cost of acquiring the information should be prepared. Data can be extremely hard to access, resulting in a costly acquisition or an unreliable measurement. Additionally, some data-gathering processes may be so burdensome that they disrupt the factor being measured. Any number of factors, like adding staff to facilitate data gathering, can increase the cost of the undertaking.

Productivity should be a critical success factor for most businesses. A fiercely competitive marketplace has complicated management's general solution to offset worker inefficiencies by simply passing higher costs through to the customer. Few businesses anymore have the luxury of ignoring productivity and hope to survive indefinitely.

Accountants are most comfortable reporting historical information, which is most useful in making mid-course correction. Historical information represents where you've been, but where you're going is more important. The greatest dangers and opportunities lie ahead. If you must know where you've been, look at the retained earnings section of the balance sheet. This will quickly show you what has historically happened. It is doubtful that you can develop a quick answer as to where you are going from a review of the financial statements.

Management's desire for timely, relevant information most certainly influenced the explosive growth in microcomputers. Besides productivity gains for certain tasks, microcomputers also enabled decentralized processing. If managers could not get the information they required through normal channels, they could simply build their own information systems.

The ultimate information reporting system might be one that produced few, if any, paper reports. Instead, the system could build report formats stored on a local area network. As information changed the reports would be updated and the files refreshed. Management at all organizational levels could extract and reformat information as it is evolving. We are currently working on a web-based solution to management reporting; our system will interact with independent client information, gathering it on a daily to hourly basis across the Internet. Reports will be updated at least daily. We use an intranet scheme to share information about the company with various levels of management on a real-time basis. There should be little doubt that the information system arena offers very promising alternatives.

Compilation, Review, and Audit Standards, Prospective Financial Statements, and Ethics

OVERVIEW

Rules and Standards

Following the rules, knowing which rules to follow, and properly completing the work are becoming more difficult as the "product" (client financial statements, with our report) is being viewed more and more as a commodity by the public. It is usually a good idea to have someone other than internal staff involved with the financial statement process. The extent of involvement is sometimes dictated by others. Generally the requirement for an audit is imposed by a third party. The customer/client does not really want the audit but must have one completed to satisfy some sort of compliance requirement imposed by a regulatory body, lending institution, investor, or as we have seen in some cases, imposed on itself as a precaution. This leads to a point—*you should understand why the report is being sought.* One of the fundamentals that have aided us in properly completing our work is clearly defining the user of the report. If the client is really not interested in the report, then why is someone being engaged to prepare it? The "who and why" really make a difference in your perspective. For example, when it is the lender who requires a specific report, you need to evaluate the lender's needs. The reason the lender wants the report is sometimes significantly different from the reason the client wants the report.

What guidelines should we consider or are we required to follow in issuing financial statements? Are those requirements/guidelines different for internally-generated financial statements as compared to those prepared by outside accountants? Are the requirements different for the different reports? Which report is necessary? These are all valid questions when evaluating or interpreting the report you have or need; see the overview of the levels of reporting and some of the reasons for obtaining specific reports (Exhibit 3.1).

The following discussion intentionally does not cover audited financial statement processes in detail. Audited financial statements represent the highest level of assurance to the public that the financial statements, taken as a whole, fairly present the financial position and results of business activities. Generally speaking, medical practices do not have audited financial statements, and rarely has an audited financial statement been a requirement for the practice to obtain funding. In the normal course of business, a compiled or reviewed financial statement is usually sufficient for a medical practice's third-party users. There are, however, instances in which an audited financial statement may be required, as when a medical practice is negotiating with a publicly traded company for the sale of the practice.

We encourage you to consider that the typical audit will and does impose significant additional responsibilities on the accountant, and that the specifics of an audit are beyond the scope of this chapter.

In January 1988 the American Institute of Certified Public Accountants (AICPA) membership adopted a new *Code of Professional Conduct*. Rule 202 states:

A member who performs auditing, review, compilation, management consulting, tax, or other professional services shall comply with standards promulgated by bodies designated by Council.

In connection with the adoption of the new *Code*, the AICPA Council has resolved:

... that the AICPA accounting and review services committee (ARSC) is hereby designated to promulgate standards under rules 201 and 202 with respect to unaudited financial statements or other unaudited financial information of an entity that is not required to file financial statements with a regulatory agency in connection with the sale or trading of its securities in a public market.

Exhibit 3.1
Comparison of compilation, review, and audit engagements

	Compilation Engagement	Review Engagement	Audit Engagement
1. Level of assurance	No assurance as to GAAP	Limited assurance as to GAAP	Statements are fairly presented in accordance with GAAP
2. Entities covered	Nonpublic only	Nonpublic only	Public or nonpublic
3. Required knowledge of client's	Knowledge of the accounting principles and practices of the industry and general understanding of the the client's business	Same degree of knowledge same as with compilation *plus* an increased understanding of the client's business	Extensive knowledge economy, the relevant industry, and the client's business (SAS No. 22)
4. Required inquiry procedures	Inquiry not required unless the information supplied by the client is questionable	Inquiry and analytical procedures required *plus* additional if the information appears questionable	Inquiry and analytical procedures (SAS No. 56) and other audit procedures required
5. GAAP disclosures omitted	Substantially all disclosures required by GAAP may be omitted without restriction on use (exception, see SSARS No. 3)	All disclosures required by GAAP must be included or report must be modified to include the disclosures	Inadequate disclosure requires qualified or adverse opinion
6. Known departures from GAAP	Disclosure required in modified compilation report (exception, see SSARS No. 3)	Disclosure required in modified review report	Departure from GAAP requires qualified or adverse opinion
7. Accountant's independence	Accountant does not have to be independent	Lack of independence precludes issuing review report	Nonpublic entity—provide compilation report (SSARS No. 1 if not independent) Public entity—provide non independence disclaimer (SAS No. 26) if not independent
8. Need to understand the control structure and assess control risk	Not required	Not required	Required by SAS No. 55
9. Engagement letter	Recommended	Recommended	Not discussed in SAS
10. Representation letter	No mention	Required	Required by SAS No. 19

As a result of the above rulings, the pronouncements of the ARSC represent the authoritative body for CPAs when they provide accounting and review services to nonpublic entities.

An audit, review, or compilation of financial statements is an attestation engagement (as compared to the types of engagements in Exhibit 3.1). Other attestation engagements include any other engagement the purpose of which is to express an opinion or any other form of assurance regarding certain written assertions made by a responsible party, such as the entity's management. Examples of other attestation engagements include, but are not limited to, the following:

- An engagement to compile or review a client's historical financial statement

- An engagement to compile or examine a prospective financial presentation intended for general or limited use

- An engagement to express an opinion or any other form of assurance on the design and/or the operating effectiveness of a client's internal control structure

- An engagement to express an opinion or any other form of assurance on an account, item, or component of financial statements

- An engagement to render a report on the application of agreed-upon procedures

- An engagement to render a general purpose report expressing an opinion regarding the fair value of a business or a financial interest

Statements of Standards on Accounting and Review Services (SSARS) No. 1 summarizes the accountant's reporting obligation for compilation and review engagements. In summary, SSARS No. 1 states:

a. A compilation is the minimum level of service that an accountant can provide before submitting unaudited financial statements of a nonpublic entity to a client or others.

b. The accountant should not consent to the use of his name in association with unaudited financial statements unless he has compiled or reviewed them and his report accompanies them, or the financial statements are accompanied by an indication that the accountant has not compiled or reviewed them and that he assumes no responsibility for them.

c. The accountant should issue a report prepared in accordance with SSARS No. 1 or SSARS No. 3 whenever he compiles or reviews financial statements of a nonpublic entity.

Whenever an accountant generates financial statements or materially modifies client-prepared financial statements, he has submitted financial statements. When this occurs, the accountant must at least perform SSARS No. 1 compilation procedures and attach a compilation report to the financial statements. The report should not refer to any other procedures that the accountant may have performed. To do so might lead the reader of the financial statements to conclude that the accountant is, in fact, offering some form of assurance.

So Tell Me More

SSARSs apply to all compiled and reviewed financial statements. They were written to provide reporting guidance for unaudited financial statements.

A *compilation* is defined as "presenting in the form of financial statements information that is the representation of management." Please reread this definition. It states, that we as accountants, present in the form of financial statements information that is the representation of management. The standards (discussed later) do not require that any work be performed. The standards require that based on authoritative guidance, we present information provided by the client in the form of financial statements. A general overview of what is or is not a financial statement is provided below. As additional clarification, no actual analysis of accounts, preparation of workpapers to support accounts, reconciliation of the bank statement and other bookkeeping services are not required by the standards.

A *review* is defined as "performing inquiry and analytical procedures that provide an accountant with a reasonable basis for expressing limited assurance that there are no material modifications that should be made to the statements in order for them to be in conformity with generally accepted accounting principles (GAAP) or, if applicable, an other comprehensive basis of accounting (OCBOA)." The standards for review services do require that we actually apply procedures to the information provided by the client in fulfilling our responsibilities.

The objective of a review differs substantially from the objective of a compilation. The inquiry and analytical procedures performed in the review should provide the accountant with a reasonable basis for expressing limited assurance that there are no material modifications that should be made to the financial statements. No such limited assurance is provided by a compilation.

Statements of Standards on Accounting and Review Services No. 1 defines a *financial statement* as follows:

> A presentation of financial data, including accompanying notes, derived from accounting records and intended to communicate an entity's economic resources or obligations at a point in time, or the changes therein for a period of time, in accordance with generally accepted accounting principles (GAAP), or a comprehensive basis of accounting other than generally accepted accounting principles.

This statement provides the guidance necessary to enable the accountant to comply with general standards of the profession set forth in Rule 201 of the AICPA *Code of Professional Conduct* in the context of a compilation or review engagement, and establishes additional standards deemed appropriate for such engagements.

The accountant should consider, among other matters, the following attributes when determining whether a financial presentation is a financial statement or a trial balance, and when modifying the presentation to eliminate any features in it that blur the distinction between a financial statement and a trial balance.

- Generally, a financial statement presents a combination of similar general ledger accounts with groupings of corresponding subtotals and totals. Some examples include "current assets," "current liabilities," and "revenues." In addition, contra accounts are generally netted against the primary account in financial statement presentations (i.e., "organization costs net of amortization"). In contrast, a trial balance consists of a listing of all of the general ledger accounts and their corresponding debits or credit balances.

- Financial statements generally contain titles that identify the presentation as one intended to present financial position, results of operations, or cash flows. Typical titles for financial statements include:

    (1) Balance Sheet

    (2) Statement of Income or Statement of Operations

    (3) Statement of Retained Earnings

    (4) Statement of Cash Flows

    (5) Statement of Changes in Owners' Equity

    (6) Statement of Assets and Liabilities (with or without owners' equity accounts)

    (7) Statement of Revenue and Expenses

    (8) Summary of Operations

    (9) Statement of Operations by Division

    (10) Statement of Cash Receipts and Disbursements

- Typical titles for trial balance presentations are:

    (1) Trial Balance

    (2) Working Trial Balance

    (3) Adjusted Trial Balance

    (4) Listing of General Ledger Accounts

- The balance sheet in a set of financial statements segregates assets, liabilities, and owners' equity accounts and presents these three elements based on the following equation:

**Assets = Liabilities + Owners' equity
(Balance Sheets Balance)**

The elements of the income statement and their relationship to net income are presented based on the following basic equation:

Revenues – Expenses + Gains – Losses = Net Income

- In a trial balance, no attempt is made to establish a mathematical relationship among the elements, except that the total debits equal total credits.

- The income statement in a set of financial statements generally contains a caption such as "Net Income" or "Net Revenues over Expenses" that identifies the net results of operations. Trial balance presentations generally do not contain similar captions.

- The balance sheet in a set of financial statements usually presents assets in the order of liquidity and liabilities in the order of maturity. In a trial balance, the accounts are generally listed in account-number order as they appear in the general ledger.

- In a set of financial statements, the income statement articulates with the balance sheet because the net results of operations are generally not closed out to retained earnings.

Principles versus Standards

When considering the guidance that is provided by the accounting profession to relative to financial statements accountants, it is important to remember the differences between principles and standards as they relate to accounting responsibilities and the public. Basically, *principles* are guidelines and definitions of certain alternative means of presenting financial data, and apply to anyone who is involved with the financial statement process. For example, the method used to compile a set of financial statements—such as generally accepted accounting principles (GAAP), income tax basis, cash basis, and so forth—all relate to accounting principles. These are the underlying foundation to the accounting profession regardless of who practices in the profession. These principals apply to CPAs, bookkeepers, accounting clerks, or anyone else involved in the financial statement process.

Standards, on the other hand, are quite different. Standards are regulatory guidelines that are promulgated by the oversight agencies that regulate Certified Public Accountants. These standards, such as Statements on Auditing Standards (SASs), Statements of Standards on Accounting and Review Services (SSARSs), and others, have been developed to assure the public that the services provided by CPAs, regardless of whether in public practice, will be held to a certain standard of ethics and competency.

CPAs must adhere to the standards promulgated by the profession. Bookkeepers, on the other hand, are not required to follow the standards; this is a specific aspect of accounting that sets the two groups apart. The standards, in addition to the items noted herein, require that the person or persons be adequately supervised and receive continuing professional education, among many other guidelines that will generally not be adhered to by bookkeepers performing services similar to those of CPAs. This distinction in services is not generally recognized by smaller business organizations due to their limited exposure. From their perspective, bookkeeping is bookkeeping whether done by a CPA or a public accountant. The standards require that the CPA bookkeeper have a more thorough understanding of the financial statement presentation process and of the standards considered in completing the process.

Generally Accepted Accounting Principles (GAAP)

While accountants agree on the existence of a body of knowledge called generally accepted accounting principles, or GAAP, determining that a particular accounting principle is generally accepted may be difficult because no single reference source exists for all such principles. In January 1992, the Auditing Standards Board issued SAS No. 69, *The Meaning of "Present Fairly in Conformity with Generally Accepted Accounting Principles" in the Independent Auditor's Report.* Statement on Auditing Standards No. 69 describes GAAP in general terms as

> . . . a technical accounting term that encompasses the conventions, rules, and procedures necessary to define accepted accounting practice at a particular time. It includes not only broad guidelines of general application, but also detailed practices and procedures. Those conventions, rules, and procedures provide a standard by which to measure financial presentations.

Statement on Auditing Standards No. 69 outlines the hierarchy of sources of GAAP as follows.

> a. Accounting principles promulgated by a body designated by the AICPA Council to establish such principles, pursuant to Rule 203 of the AICPA Code of Professional Conduct. This consists of FASB Statements and Interpretations, APB Opinions, and AICPA Accounting Research Bulletins.

b. Pronouncements of bodies, composed of expert accountants, that deliberate accounting issues in public forums for the purpose of establishing accounting principles or describing accounting principles that are generally accepted, provided those pronouncements have been exposed for public comment and have been cleared by a body referred to in category a. This consists of FASB Technical Bulletins and, if cleared by the FASB, AICPA Industry Audit and Accounting Guides and AICPA Statements of Position.

c. Pronouncements of bodies, organized by a body referred to in category a and composed of expert accountants, that deliberate accounting issues in public forums for the purpose of interpreting or establishing accounting principles or describing existing accounting principles that are generally accepted, or pronouncements referred to in category a but have not been exposed for public comment. This consists of AICPA Accounting Standards Executive Committee (AcSec) Practice Bulletins that have been cleared by the FASB and consensus positions of the FASB Emerging Issues Task Force.

d. Practices or pronouncements that are widely recognized as being generally accepted because they represent prevalent practice in a particular industry, or the knowledgeable application to specific pronouncements that are generally accepted. This includes AICPA accounting interpretations and implementation guides, "Qs and As" published by the FASB staff, and practices that are widely recognized and prevalent either generally or in the industry.

e. In the absence of a pronouncement covered by Rule 203 or another source of established accounting principles, other accounting literature may be considered, depending on its relevance to the circumstances. Other accounting literature includes, for example, FASB Statements of Financial Accounting Concepts; AICPA Issues Papers; International Accounting Standards Committee; Government Accounting Standards Board (GASB) Statement, Interpretations, and Technical Bulletins; Technical Information Service Inquiries and Replies included in the AICPA Technical Practice Aids; and accounting textbooks, handbooks, and articles.

Generally, the accounting principles in category a are undisputed as GAAP. If the accounting treatment of a transaction or event is not covered by category a but is covered by category b, c, or d, the accountant should be prepared to justify a conclusion that another treatment is generally accepted. If there is a conflict between sources within those categories, the accountant should follow the source specified in the higher category (for example, follow category b treatment over category c) or be prepared to justify a conclusion that a treatment specified by a source in the lower category better presents the substance of the transaction. Generally, the accountant should consider other accounting literature, (category e) only in the absence of relevant accounting principles in category a, b, c, and d.

Alternatives When Faced with a GAAP Departure.   Normally, a material GAAP departure is readily determinable. However, the continual proliferation of standards makes it more difficult to remember all the subtle GAAP requirements.

Although compiled financial statements may omit substantially all disclosures required by GAAP and not be considered a material GAAP departure, the omission of material *disclosures* from reviewed financial statements is a GAAP departure. In this situation, the accountant is required to include in the review report all of the omitted disclosures or, if the details to be disclosed have not been determined, the specific nature of the omitted disclosures. If, in the course of a compilation or review engagement, the accountant becomes aware of material *measurement* departures from GAAP, he or she has three possible courses of action:

- Persuade the client to revise the statements to conform with GAAP

- Refer to the departure in his report

- Withdraw from the engagement

Revision of the financial statements is, of course, the preferred course of action. If revision is not feasible, delineating the departure in the accountant's report is appropriate unless the accountant concludes that management's intention is to mislead the reader. If modification of the report to disclose the departure is not adequate and the client refuses to revise the statements, the accountant should withdraw from the engagement and consider consulting legal counsel.

If modification of the accountant's report is appropriate, the nature of the departure from GAAP should be disclosed in a separate paragraph, and the effects (dollar amount) of the departure should be disclosed, if known. If the effects are not known, the accountant is not required to determine the level of departure but must state in the report that no determination of the effect of the departure has been made.

Rule 203 of the AICPA *Code of Professional Conduct* addresses a rare situation in which accountants are associated with financial statements that contain a departure from GAAP because compliance with GAAP would actually result in misleading financial statements. Rule 203 states that

> If, however, the statements or data contain such a departure and the member can demonstrate that due to unusual circumstances the financial statements or data would otherwise have been misleading, the member can comply with the rule by describing the departure, its approximate effects, if practicable, and the reasons why compliance with the principle would result in a misleading statement.

Statement on Auditing Standards No. 58, *Reports on Audited Financial Statements,* contains guidance for auditors in these circumstances. Similar guidance did not exist for accountants who are performing a review engagement; therefore, ARSC issued Interpretation No. 19 of SSARS No. 1. The interpretation states that, when the circumstances contemplated by Rule 203 are present in a review engagement, the accountant should include a separate paragraph in the review report that contains the information required by the rule. However, Rule 203 does not apply to a compilation engagement. Interpretation No. 19 states that when confronted with this situation in a compilation engagement, the accountant should treat the item as a departure for GAAP and report accordingly.

Defining a Material GAAP Departure.   Determining whether GAAP departures are material to individual financial statements, to specific line items or subtotals within financial statements, or to the financial statements taken as a whole remains one of the most difficult decisions for the professional. *Materiality* is defined by the Financial Accounting

Exhibit 3.2
Benchmark samples of GAAP departures

Effect of Departure on Income before Tax	Materiality to Financial Statements
1–5%	Not material
6–9%	Danger area—could be material
10% or greater	Probably is material

If income before tax approaches zero, the percentages may be applied to what would be considered normalized income before tax for similar entities in similar industries.

Standards Board (FASB) in its Statement of Financial Accounting Concepts No. 2, "Qualitative Characteristics of Accounting Information," as

The magnitude of an omission or misstatement of accounting information that, in light of surrounding circumstances, makes it probable that the judgement of a reasonable person relying upon the information would have been changed or influenced by the omission or misstatement.

Some might argue that the FASB definition is nebulous, but a more definite statement is probably impossible since materiality is a matter of judgment based on the circumstances. While no quantitative guidelines exist, accountants often use benchmarks to assist in assessing the materiality of GAAP departures. A benchmark used by some firms is given in Exhibit 3.2.

Other Comprehensive Basis of Accounting (OCBOA)

Unaudited financial statements of nonpublic companies prepared in accordance with an "other comprehensive basis of accounting" (OCBOA) are clearly governed by SSARS No. 1. *Other comprehensive basis of accounting* is defined in SAS No. 62, *Special Reports*, Paragraph 4, as follows:

For purposes of this statement, a comprehensive basis of accounting other than generally accepted accounting principles is one of the following:

a. A basis of accounting that the reporting entity uses to comply with the requirements or financial reporting provisions of a governmental regulatory agency to whose jurisdiction the entity is subject (An example is a basis of accounting insurance companies use pursuant to the rules of a state insurance commission).

b. A basis of accounting that the reporting entity uses or expects to use to file its income tax return for the period covered by the financial statements.

c. The cash receipts and disbursements basis of accounting, and modifications of the cash basis having substantial support, such as recording depreciation on fixed assets or accruing income taxes.

d. A definite set of criteria having substantial support that is applied to all material items appearing in financial statements, such as the price-level basis of accounting.

Other Definitions

Sometimes it may be difficult to distinguish between the income tax basis, cash basis, and accrual basis of accounting, especially when terms like GAAP, OCBOA, and so on are thrown in. These terms, most of which may not be well defined in authoritative literature, are often used interchangeably. Adding to the confusion is the frequent use of the term "modified cash basis." The following discussion is intended to present simple rules of thumb for identifying the basis of accounting used.

Accrual Basis

Generally, accrual basis financial statements present financial position and results of operations in accordance with GAAP. *Accrual accounting* is defined as the method of recording transactions, by which revenues and expenses are reflected in the accounts in the period in which they are considered to have been earned and incurred, respectively, regardless of whether such transactions have been finally settled by the receipt or payment of cash or its equivalent.

A common tendency is to assume that a financial statement that excludes accounts receivable or accounts payable is not presented on the accrual basis. However, *if the omission of accrual entries does not have a material effect on financial position and results of operations, the statements should be referred to as accrual basis statements.*

Cash or Modified Cash Basis

The *cash basis of accounting,* in its pure form, recognizes revenues and expenses based on the receipt and disbursement of cash. The pure cash basis treats all disbursements of cash as expenses; thus, the purchase of fixed assets or inventory is recognized as an expense rather than as an asset. Stated another way, under a pure cash basis of accounting, the conventional balance sheet contains only cash and equity, and the conventional income statement reflects all cash receipts as revenues and all cash disbursements as expenses.

In practice, the pure cash basis of accounting is seldom used. Instead, the cash basis of accounting has generally become recognized as a hybrid or modification of the cash-accrual basis. In fact, SAS No. 62 states that one option in preparing OCBOA statements is the cash basis or modifications that have substantial support.

Modification of the cash basis must have substantial support. The AICPA's *Technical Practice Aids* offers the following clarification of the term *substantial support* (though written for an audit engagement, it also applies conceptually to an SSARS engagement):

> Modifications have evolved through common usage in practice. Examples of modifications recognized as having substantial support in practice are recording:
>
> a. Property, plant, and equipment purchased as assets.
>
> b. Accumulated depreciation.
>
> c. Material amounts of inventory purchased for cash as assets.
>
> d. Liabilities arising from the receipt of borrowed cash.
>
> e. Employee FICA and withholding taxes not deposited with the IRS.
>
> f. Federal income taxes accrued on current year's cash income.

If the cash basis statement has so many modifications that it is, in reality, an accrual basis statement, it should be reported on as such. This is also supported by *Technical Practice Aids,* which states (again, though written for an audit engagement, it also applies conceptually to an SSARS engagement):

If the modifications are so extensive that the modified "cash-basis" statements are, in the auditor's judgment, equivalent to financial statements prepared on the accrual basis, the statement should be considered GAAP basis. The auditor should use the standard form of report modified as appropriate.

If the cash basis statements have a modification that does not have "substantial support," the AICPA *Technical Practice Aids* recommend that the ". . . auditor should include an explanatory paragraph in his or her report (preceding the opinion paragraph) and should include in the opinion paragraph the appropriate modifying language and a reference to the explanatory paragraph."

Some accountants prefer identifying hybrid cash/accrual basis financial statements as "modified cash basis" financial statements. Others prefer the term "cash basis." Whichever term is used, the financial statements should be appropriately titled and the accountant's compilation or review report should refer to the titles used.

The cash basis of accounting can offer certain tax advantages and can simplify accounting requirements. However, the cash basis may not be appropriate for certain entities. For example, for merchandising or manufacturing companies that have significant inventory and sales on account, satisfactory net income measurements call for the adoption of the accrual basis. On the other hand, failure to recognize accruals and prepayments for many professional organizations and companies selling services can result in relatively minor deviations that are largely counterbalanced in periodic reporting.

The cash basis or modified cash basis, while widely used in the profession, is not viewed by many as the OCBOA that offers the best solution to the standards overload problems of GAAP. One reason is the difficulty of identifying which modifications of the cash basis are appropriate in the circumstances and which are departures from the cash basis. A frequently mentioned alternative to GAAP that presently has more appeal is the income tax basis of accounting.

Income Tax Basis

Many entities maintain their accounting records on a basis identical to, or substantially identical to, that required to file their income tax returns. When financial statements are prepared from such records, determining the proper description of the basis of accounting used can become a confusing issue. For example, the basis of accounting allowed by tax law could range from the accrual to the cash basis. Between these two options, tax law may allow special accounting treatments that conform neither to accrual nor cash basis principles. Sometimes, of course, all that is needed will be copies of the client's tax return, not tax basis financial statements. In these situations, practitioners are not required to report on the tax return. The general guidelines discussed in the following paragraphs are useful in deciding how to describe and report on such financial statements.

If the basis of accounting used to file the tax return is accrual, the additional cost of preparing GAAP financial statements normally will be minimal. Accordingly, it is usually preferable to describe and report on such financial statements as GAAP. However, this general advice is not appropriate if an agreement, such as a partnership agreement, specifically calls for use of the tax basis because (1) it is confusing to the users of the financial statements to refer to the statements as GAAP when they expect the tax basis (even if the two are the same); and (2) in future years, the entity may elect a tax accounting treatment that would be materially different from GAAP, resulting in a confusing accountant's report.

Practice varies when the tax return is filed using a cash basis of accounting. First, the client must decide whether the cost to convert to GAAP financial statements exceeds the benefits. Some firms, in deciding whether to present the financial statements on the basis used for filing the tax return, identify and report on the statements as cash basis or modified cash basis; other firms choose to identify and report on them as tax basis financial statements.

When the basis of accounting used to file the tax return contains an unusual tax election that is not appropriate for either GAAP or cash basis financial statements, and the cost of converting to GAAP exceeds the benefits, the financial statements are normally identified and reported on as tax basis. Examples of such tax elections include, but are not limited to:

- Depreciation computed in accordance with the accelerated cost recovery system, or the modified accelerated cost recovery system, resulting in material differences from depreciation computed on estimated useful lives

- Deduction of statutory depletion

- Deduction of intangible development costs on producing wells

- Use of installment sales accounting

- Use of property valuations allowed for tax purposes that differ materially from historical cost (stepped-up basis)

- Accounting for investments in other entities at costs that could require consolidation or equity basis accounting in GAAP financial statements

- Accounting for leases that meet the requirements of capital leases under SFAS No. 13 but are treated as operating leases for tax purposes

Internally-Generated Financial Statements

Should internally-generated financial statements or those prepared by the corporation's chief financial office contain the standard compilation report? *An outside accountant to report upon financial statements that are the representation of another party, (the CPA attests to an assertion made by someone other than the CPA) namely, the management of a nonpublic company, uses a compilation.* The compilation report describes the outside accountant's limited responsibility and inability to express an opinion or any other form of assurance based on the limited procedures performed. Attestation services require independence on the part of the accountant.

The CFO, on the other hand, is a part of management and is intimately involved in the preparation of the financial statements. A CFO has direct responsibility for the design and operation of the accounting system, the design and operation of most internal control procedures, and much of the control environment.

There are no standards on how a company's CFO should report on the company's financial statements when those statements are transmitted to third parties. However, it seems appropriate for a CFO to issue a report stating management's responsibility for the financial statements. Such a report might be modeled after the management responsibility letter typically contained in annual reports, and may be worded as follows:

The accompanying balance sheet of Company X as of December 31, 19XX and the related statements of income, retained earnings, and cash flows for the year then ended have been prepared by management, who is responsible for their integrity and objectivity. These statements have not been compiled, reviewed, or audited by outside accountants.

Company X maintains a system of internal accounting controls designed to provide reasonable assurance that assets are safeguarded and that transactions are properly executed, recorded, and summarized to produce reliable records and reports.

To the best of management's knowledge and belief, the statements and related information were prepared in conformity with generally accepted accounting principles, and are based on recorded transactions and management's best estimates and judgments.

Signature of chief financial officer

Reference to the Accountant's Report on the Financial Statements

Each page of compiled or reviewed financial statements should include an appropriate reference to the accountant's report, such as "See accountant's compilation report" or "See accountant's review report."

When comparative financial statements are presented and either the accountant or the level of service is different for one of the periods presented, the standard references discussed above are inappropriate.

Compilation Reports and the Small Business

When dealing with the accounting standards and principles you must follow the rules, but first you must know which rules apply. You must understand why a report is being produced and the purpose of that "product." Once the "who and why" are known, you must navigate through the standards to assure that you apply those necessary for the particular circumstances.

As noted, this process can be quite cumbersome; however, it is necessary and should be considered regardless of where you fall into the financial statement process.

There is growing interest within the accounting profession in finding the small business's alternatives to the measurement and reporting requirements of GAAP. One solution often mentioned is the more frequent use of OCBOA financial statements. In 1981, the AICPA's special committee on accounting standards overload was formed to consider alternative means of providing relief from accounting standards that are not cost-effective, particularly for small, closely-held businesses. In its final report published in 1983, the committee concluded:

> Small, nonpublic entities can gain some measure of relief from accounting standards overload by issuing compiled, reviewed, or audited financial statements prepared on a comprehensive basis of accounting other than GAAP in accordance with existing disclosure and measurement standards and with the existing reporting requirements for CPAs.

Although this is a helpful alternative, the reader of financial statements should be aware that statements prepared in accordance with GAAP, regardless of the level of assurance provided by the accountant's report, actually present the most fair presentation of the financial condition of the reporting entity. Stated again, financial statements prepared under the guidelines of GAAP represent the highest degree of reliability for the user. Any departure from GAAP should prompt the reader to discern what effect the departure may have on the financial statements taken as a whole.

Here are a few remaining comments relative to compilation reports. The AICPA's special committee report states the following:

> A compilation is limited to presenting information that is the representation of management in the form of financial statements. We have not audited or reviewed the accompanying financial statements and, accordingly do not express an opinion or any other form of assurance on them.

The compilation report states that the information is the representation of management. Nothing in the standards requires the accountant to do analytical or audit work on the information provided; he or she must simply present the information, provided by management, in the form of financial statements. The standards require the accountant to exercise professional judgment relative to the information, and stop there. More often than not, the accountant does more work on compilations than is required by the standards. Other accountants, however, believe that this additional work may alter their reporting responsibility, and that if they performed a higher level of work, they would be required by the standards to prepare a review or audit report as well. The standards state that the accountant may issue a lesser report, provided that the reason for doing so is not due to the discovery of information that actually calls for a qualified report; and provided that the lower level of reporting does not allow the presentation of items that, had they been presented according to the standards for the review or audit, would have been less favorable. Stated another way, if the accountant, when performing work for a review or audit, becomes aware of issues that are unfavorable, considering a compilation report as an alternative is inappropriate. The standards for a compilation still require the accountant to exercise professional judgment; awareness of an adverse finding without disclosure of that information is a violation of the standards—compilation or not, full disclosure or not. Whether to do more work than is required is generally at the discretion of the accountant, based on the accountant/client relationship.

Often the client expects the financial statement prepared by the accountant to be exact, correct in all aspects; the client is, of course, unaware of the standards' requirement that, in the case of a compilation only, the statements be presented in the form of financial statements, without further requirement except as noted, based on the accountant's professional judgment.

Remember: The principles guide everyone in the process of accounting. The standards and the requirements to adhere to those standards are what distinguish the accountant apart from the traditional bookkeeper. Clients are generally unaware of the differences and what those differences mean to them. The accountant generally performs more services than required to satisfy the client's expectations of the accuracy of the financial statements. If clients knew of the accountant's limited responsibilities under the standards, they would probably require more specific arrangement letters from accountants setting forth the terms of agreement. As we explain to staff in our organization, we go farther than the required minimum in order to insure that we are satisfying our responsibilities to the profession and to our reputation.

Proposed Amendment to SSARS No. 1

The Accounting and Review Services Committee of the AICPA has drafted a proposed amendment to SSARS No. 1 that would codify the Committee's thinking about independence and compilation services. The following is a draft of the proposed amendment:

> This statement recognizes that accountants may perform services for clients that are equivalent to those ordinarily performed by management. Such services entail making management decisions for clients or having the authority to do so. If an accountant performs services for a client that entails making management decisions for a client or having the authority to do so, the accountant would be deemed to be acting as a member of client's management and would be precluded from compiling that client's financial statements covering the period during which the accountant performed these services or had the authority to do so.

The proposed draft distinguishes between the certified public accountant who must comply with SSARS when associated with financial statements, and the certified public accountant who may not issue a compilation report in accordance with SSARS. The amendment would preclude a CPA from compiling a financial statement under SSARS if he or she is considered a part of management.

The amendment, if adopted, would be the standard for CPAs not in public practice.

PROSPECTIVE FINANCIAL STATEMENTS

Prospective financial information presents financial position, results of operations, and cash flows. It takes the form of either financial forecasts or financial projections and should include the summaries of significant assumptions and accounting policies, disclosed as footnotes. Although prospective financial statements may cover a period that has partially expired, statements for periods that have completely expired are not considered to be prospective financial statements—nor are pro forma financial statements and partial presentations (defined later in this section).

A *financial forecast* is a prospective financial statement that presents, to the best of the responsible party's knowledge and belief, an entity's expected financial position, results of operations, and cash flows. A financial forecast is based on the responsible party's assumptions of expected conditions and course of action. It may be expressed in specific monetary amounts as either a single-point estimate of forecasted results; or as a range falling between two points that are based on key assumptions, and within which the responsible party may reasonably expect the item or items subject to those assumptions to actually fall. The range, if one is included, is not specified in a biased or misleading manner (for example, with one end that is significantly less-expected than the other). Minimum presentation guidelines for a financial forecast are set forth in the Presentation Guidelines discussed later.

A *financial projection* is a prospective financial statement that presents, to the best of the responsible party's knowledge and belief, an entity's expected financial position, results of operations, and cash flows, given one or more hypothetical assumptions. A financial projection is sometimes prepared to offer one or more hypothetical courses of action for evaluation, as in response to the question "What would happen if . . . ?" A financial projection is based on the responsible party's assumptions of expected conditions and course of action, given one or more hypothetical assumptions. A projection, like a forecast, may contain a range.

The *responsible party* is the person or persons responsible for the assumptions underlying the prospective financial information. The responsible party usually is management, but it can be persons outside the entity who currently do not have the authority to direct operations (for example, a party considering acquiring the entity).

Two other definitions should also be mentioned at this point: the compilation of prospective financial information, and the examination of that information. The *compilation* of prospective financial information is a professional service that involves the assembly, to the extent necessary, of prospective financial information; a consideration of whether the assumption or presentation is obviously inappropriate; and the issuance of a compilation report in which the accountant expresses no conclusion or any other assurance. (The *assembly* step involves the manual or computer processing of mathematical or other clerical functions related to the presentation of the prospective financial information. Assembly does not refer to the mere reproduction and collation of such statements, or to the responsible party's use of the accountant's computer processing hardware or software.)

The *examination* of prospective financial information, on the other hand, is a professional service that involves (1) evaluation of the preparation of the prospective financial information, the support underlying the assumptions, and the presentation of the information for conformity with AICPA guidelines; and (2) issuance of an examination report.

In summary, the major difference between the forecast and the projection is one of requirements and standards placed upon the accountant. The information presented as a forecast is held to a higher standard in the areas of independence, as it relates to objective basis, GAAP and consistency, evidentiary matters, and management's intent. In the majority of projects, a projection is the appropriate level of service to render. Minimum presentation guidelines for a financial projection are set forth in the Presentation Guidelines discussed later.

Pro-Forma Financial Statements

Financial statements that depict what the significant effects on historical financial information *might have been,* had a consummated or proposed transaction (or event) occurred at an earlier date, are called pro-forma financial statements. Although the transaction in question may be prospective, these presentations are essentially *historical* statements and *do not* purport to be prospective financial statements.

Partial Financial Statement Presentation

A presentation of prospective financial information that excludes one or more of the applicable items (see items 1–12 on page 67), as set forth in the Presentation Guidelines required for prospective financial statements, is called a partial financial statement presentation—that is, a partial presentation of a project or forecast.

Types of Prospective Financial Information and Its Uses

Entities prepare prospective financial information for a variety of reasons. For example, an entity may want to obtain external financing, consider a change in operations or accounting, or prepare a budget. The reason for which the prospective financial information is prepared determines its type.

Prospective financial information is for either "general use" or "limited use." This section discusses the differences between the two uses and the types of presentations that are appropriate for each.

General Use of Financial Statements

General use of prospective financial statements refers to the use of statements by persons with whom the responsible party is *not* negotiating directly, for example, use as an offering statement of an entity's debt or equity interest. Since recipients of prospective financial statements distributed for general use are unable to ask the responsible party directly about the presentation or to negotiate the terms or structure of a transaction with such party, the presentation most useful to them is one that portrays, to the best of the responsible party's knowledge and belief, the expected results. Thus, only a financial forecast is appropriate for general use.

A financial projection is not appropriate for general use, and should not be distributed to those who won't be negotiating directly with the responsible party (as in the previous example of a offering statement of an entity's debt of equity interests) unless the projection is used to supplement a financial forecast and is for the period covered by the forecast.

Limited Use of Financial Statements

Limited use of prospective financial information refers to use of the information by the responsible party and by third parties with whom the responsible party is negotiating directly. Examples include use in negotiations for a bank loan, use in submission to a regulatory agency, and use solely within the entity. Third-party recipients of prospective financial information intended for limited use can ask questions of the responsible party and negotiate the terms or structure of a transaction directly with such party. Any type of prospective financial information that would be useful in the circumstances would normally be appropriate for limited use. Thus, the presentation may be a financial forecast, a financial projection, or a partial presentation.

A partial presentation may also be appropriate in many limited-use situations. For example, a responsible party may prepare a partial presentation to analyze whether to lease or buy a piece of equipment, or to evaluate the income tax implications of a given election, since it may only be necessary to assess the impact on one aspect of financial results rather than on the financial statements taken as a whole. Therefore, a partial presentation is often appropriate for use by third parties who will be negotiating directly with the responsible party. A partial presentation, however, is not ordinarily appropriate for general use.

Presentation Guidelines

Title of the Presentation

Forecast.   The title used for a financial forecast should describe the nature of the presentation and should include the word "forecast" or "forecasted."

Projection.   Statement titles in financial projections should be descriptive of the presentation. Accordingly, they should not imply that the presentation is a forecast. In addition, titles should describe or refer to any significant hypothetical assumptions as such. For example, a break-even analysis might be titled "Projected Results of Operations and Cash Flows at Break-Even Sales Volume."

Format of the Presentation

Prospective information presented in the format of historical financial statements facilitates comparisons with financial position, results of operations, and cash flows of prior periods as well as those actually achieved for the prospective period. Accordingly, financial forecasts/projections should be in the format of historical financial statements that would be issued for the period(s) covered, unless there is an agreement between the responsible party and potential users specifying another format. Financial forecasts/projections may take the form of complete basic financial statements or may be limited to the following items (when such items would be presented for historical financial statements for the period).

1. Sales or gross revenues

2. Gross profit or cost of sales

3. Unusual or infrequently occurring items

4. Provision for income taxes

5. Income from continuing operations

6. Discontinued operation or extraordinary items

7. Net income

8. Primary and fully-diluted earnings per share

9. Significant changes in financial position

10. A description of what the responsible party intends the finan-
    cial forecast/projections to present, a statement that the as-
    sumptions are based on the responsible party's judgment at the
    time the prospective information was prepared, and a caveat
    that the forecasted/projected results may not be achieved

11. Summary of significant assumptions

12. Summary of significant accounting principles

Items 1 through 9 represent the minimum items that constitute a financial forecast/projection. *A presentation that omits one or more of Items
1–9 would be a partial presentation, and would not ordinarily be appropriate
for general use.* If the omitted applicable item is derivable from the information presented, the presentation is not be deemed to be a partial
presentation.

Items 10 through 12 are disclosures that should accompany the
forecast/projection, whether the presentation is limited to applicable
minimum items or presents more detail. The omission of item 10, 11, or
12 from a presentation that contains at least the applicable minimum
items would not create a partial presentation; it would create a *deficient*
presentation because of the lack of required disclosures.

Additional Guidelines for the Presentation

When evaluating the period to be covered by a financial forecast/pro-
jection, the responsible party should balance the information needs of

users with its ability to estimate prospective results; however, a reasonably objective basis should exist for each forecasted/projected period (month, quarter, year) presented.

Ordinarily, to be meaningful to users, the presentations of a financial forecast/projection should include at least one full year of normal operations. For example, an entity forecasting/projecting a major acquisition would present at least the first full year following the acquisition, and a newly formed entity would include at least the first full year of normal operations in addition to the start-up period.

Assumptions

The disclosure of *significant assumptions* is essential to the reader's understanding of the financial forecast/projection; accordingly, the responsible party should disclose those assumptions deemed to be significant to the statements. The basis or rationale for those assumptions should be disclosed to assist the user of the financial forecast/projection to understand the presentation and make an informed judgment about it.

Identifying those assumptions that, at the time of preparation, appear to be significant to the financial forecast/projection requires the careful exercise of judgment by the responsible party. By nature, financial forecast/projections embody a large number of assumptions, especially for a complex enterprise, and an attempt to communicate all assumptions is inherently not feasible. Furthermore, questions may arise after the fact, making significant certain assumptions that previously were considered unimportant. The assumptions disclosed should include:

- Assumptions of a reasonable possibility of the occurrence of a variation that may significantly affect the prospective results; that is, *sensitive assumptions*

- Assumptions of anticipated conditions that are expected to be significantly different from current conditions and that are not otherwise reasonably apparent

- Other matters deemed important to the prospective information or its interpretation

For financial projections, in addition to disclosing these three types of assumptions, the responsible party should also identify which of the assumptions are hypothetical. A hypothetical assumption is one used in a financial projection or partial presentation of projected information to present a condition or course of action that is not necessarily expected to occur, but is consistent with the purpose of the presentation. If the hypothetical assumptions are improbable, the disclosure should indicate that as well.

The presentation should further indicate which disclosed assumptions seemed particularly sensitive at the time of preparation. Of course, although the responsible party should try to identify those particularly sensitive assumptions, hindsight may later reveal sensitive assumptions that did not appear to be particularly sensitive earlier.

Particularly sensitive assumptions are those assumptions with a relatively high probability of sizable variation that would materially affect the financial forecast/projection. The impact on the financial forecast/projection might result from either (1) an assumption with a relatively high probability of sizable variation, or (2) an assumption for which the probability of a sizable variation is not as high but for which even a small variation would have a large impact.

Not all significant assumptions are particularly sensitive. For example, an assumption regarding the federal income tax rate may be significant but not particularly sensitive, whereas the assumption about the interest rate of a new debt issue may be both significant *and* particularly sensitive. The disclosure of a particularly sensitive assumption needs not include a quantification of the potential effects of variations in those assumptions. Furthermore, although all significant assumptions (sensitive or otherwise) should be disclosed, they need not be presented in such a manner or in such detail as would adversely affect the competitive position of the entity.

Introduction to the Summary of Assumptions

One assumption is so basic it is frequently considered to be implicit in the forecast/projection: the assumption that current conditions with enormous potential impact, such as the condition of peace and the absence of natural disasters, will continue to prevail. For this and other reasons, an introduction should precede the summary to make it clear that the assumptions disclosed are not an all-inclusive list of those used in the preparation of prospective information. The introduction should also describe what the responsible party intends the financial forecast/projection to present, and should include both a statement that the assumptions are based on the responsible party's judgment at the time the prospective information was prepared, and a caveat that the prospective results may not be attained.

The introduction to a financial forecast/projection that does not contain a range should be similar to the following.

> This financial forecast presents, to the best of management's knowledge and belief, the Company's expected financial position, results of operations, and cash flows for the forecast/projection period. Accordingly, the forecast/projection reflects its judgment as of (date), the date of this forecast/projection, of the expected conditions and its expected course of action. The assumptions disclosed herein are those that management believes are significant to the forecast/projection. There will usually be differences between the forecasted/projected and actual results, because events and circumstances frequently do not occur as expected, and those differences may be material.

For financial projections, the introduction preceding the summary of significant assumptions should also clearly explain any special purpose and limitation of the usefulness of the statements. For example, the introduction preceding the summary of assumptions for a presentation of results with sales at maximum productive capacity would be similar to the following example (which illustrates the introduction for a presentation with an improbable hypothetical assumption; the example should be modified as appropriate to the circumstances).

> This financial projection is based on sales volume at maximum productive capacity and presents, to the best of management's knowledge and belief, the Company's expected financial position, results of operations, and cash flows for the projection period if such sales volume were attained. Accordingly, the projection reflects its judgement as of (date), the date of this projection, of the expected conditions and its expected course of action if such sales volume were experienced. The presentation is designed to provide information to the Company's board of directors concerning the

maximum profitability that might be achieved if current production were expanded through the addition of a third production
shift, and should be considered to be a presentation of expected future results. Accordingly, this projection may not be useful for
other purposes. The assumptions disclosed herein are those that
management believes are significant to the projection. Management considers it highly unlikely that the stated sales volume will
be experienced during the projection period. Furthermore, even if
the stated sales volume were attained, there would usually be differences between projected and actual results, because events and
circumstances frequently do not occur as expected, and those differences may be material.

The following is an example of an introduction for a forecast/pro-
jection that does contain a range. In the situation illustrated, the
responsible party does not make a point estimate of occupancy of its
apartment building but expects, to the best of its knowledge and belief, that actual occupancy will be between 75 and 95 percent of available apartments.

This financial forecast/projection presents, to the best of management's knowledge and belief, the Company's expected financial
position, results of operations, and cash flows for the forecast/pro-
jection period at occupancy rates of 75 percent and 95 percent of
available apartments. Accordingly, the forecast/projection reflects
its judgements as of (date), the date of this forecast/projection, of
the expected conditions and its expected course of action at each
occupancy rate. The assumptions disclosed herein are those that
management believes are significant to the forecast/projection.
Management reasonably expects, to the best of its knowledge and
belief, that the actual occupancy rate achieved will be within the
range shown; however, there can be no assurance that it will. Further, even if the actual occupancy rate is within the range shown,
there will usually be differences between forecasted/projected
and actual results, because events and circumstances frequently
do not occur as expected, and those differences may be material,
and the actual results may be outside the range presented by the
forecast/projection.

Please see Exhibits 3.3 (sample engagement letter), 3.4 (sample
letter of representation), and 3.5 (sample independent accountant's re-

Exhibit 3.3
Sample engagement letter

Name of Firm
Address
City, State, ZIP Code

Date

Addressee
Name of Company
Street Address
City, State, ZIP Code

Dear Client:

This letter sets forth our understanding of the terms and objectives of our engagement and the nature and limitations of the services we will provide.

We will compile, in accordance with standards established by the American Institute of Certified Public Accountants, from information management provides, the projected balance sheet and the related projected statements of income, retained earnings, cash flows, and summaries of significant assumptions and accounting policies of CLIENT as of DATE and DATE, and for the years then ending. We will not express any form of assurance on the achievability of the projection or the reasonableness of the underlying assumptions.*

A compilation of a financial projection involves assembling the projection based on management's assumptions and performing certain other procedures with respect to the projection without evaluating the support for, or expressing an opinion or any other form of assurance on, the assumptions underlying it.

If for any reason we are unable to complete our compilation of your financial projection, we will not issue a report on it as a result of this engagement.

A financial projection presents, to the best of management's knowledge and belief, the Company's expected financial position, results of operations, and cash flows for the projection period. It is based on management's assumptions, reflecting conditions it expects to exist and the course of action it expects to take during the projection period.

Management is responsible for representations about its plans and expectations for disclosure of significant information that might affect the ultimate realization of the projected results.

There will usually be differences between the projected and actual results, because events and circumstances frequently do not occur as expected, and those differences may be material. Our report will contain a statement to that effect.

Exhibit 3.3 (Continued)

We have no responsibility to update our report for events and circumstances occurring after the date of such report.

At the conclusion of the engagement, management agrees to supply us with a representation letter that, among other things, will confirm management's responsibility for the underlying assumptions and the appropriateness of the financial projection and its presentation.

In order for us to complete this engagement, management must provide assumptions that are appropriate for the projection. If the assumptions provided are not appropriate and have been revised to our satisfaction, we will be unable to complete the engagement, and accordingly, we will not issue a report on the projection.

If management intends to reproduce and publish the projection and our report thereon, they must be reproduced in their entirety, and both the first and the subsequent, corrected drafts of the document containing the projection and any accompanying material must be submitted to us for approval.

The assistance to be supplied by your personnel in the preparation of schedules and analysis of accounts has been discussed with you. The timely completion of this work will assist us in achieving an efficient performance of our work.

Should you have any questions, we shall be pleased to discuss this letter with you at any time.

If this letter defines the engagement as you understand it, please sign and date the enclosed copy and return to us.

Sincerely,

Firm

Confirmed by:

_____

_____, 1999

*Due to the nature of the engagement, you may not know the exact titles and formats of the schedules. Consequently, you may use generic terms and define these specifically in the report and representation letter.

Exhibit 3.4
Sample letter of representation

Name of Firm
Street Address
City, State, ZIP Code

Date

Addressee
Name of Company
Address
City, State, ZIP Code

Dear Client:

In connection with your compilation of the forecasted statements of assets and liabilities as of DATE 2 and DATE 3 and the related schedules of cash flows and summaries of significant assumptions and accounting policies of CLIENT years ending DATE 2 and DATE 3, we make the following representations:

1. The financial projection presents our assumptions and, to the best of our knowledge and belief, the Company's expected financial position, results of operations, and cash flows for the projected period in conformity with the generally accepted accounting principles expected to be used by the Company during the projected period, which are consistent with the principles CLIENT uses in preparing its historical financial statements.

2. The financial projection is based on our judgment of the expected conditions and our expected course of action.

3. We have made available to you all significant information that we believe is relevant to the projection.

4. We believe that the assumptions underlying the projection are reasonable and appropriate.

5. To the best of our knowledge and belief, the documents and records supporting the assumptions are appropriate.

6. We believe the projected results are achievable; however, the projection may be favorably or unfavorably affected by many unforeseeable and uncontrollable factors.

7. There are no other significant matters that should be reflected or disclosed in the projected financial presentation in order to make it not misleading.

CLIENT, Title

Exhibit 3.5
Sample independent accountant's report

Name of Firm
Street Address
City, State, ZIP Code

Date

Addressee
Name of Company
Address
City, State, ZIP Code

Dear Client:

We have compiled the accompanying projected statements of assets and liabilities as of DATE 2 and DATE 3 and the related schedules of cash flow and summaries of significant assumptions and accounting policies of CLIENT for the years ending DATE 2 and DATE 3 in accordance with standards established by the American Institute of Certified Public Accountants. As discussed in Note 1 of the summary of significant accounting principles and assumptions, the accompanying statements are prepared on the income tax basis of accounting, and, accordingly, they are not intended to be presented in conformity with generally accepted accounting principles.

A compilation is limited to presenting in the form of a projection information that is the representation of management and does not include evaluation of the support for the assumptions underlying the projection. We have not examined the projection and, accordingly, do not express an opinion or any other form of assurance on the accompanying statements or assumptions. Furthermore, there will usually be differences between the projected and actual results, because events and circumstances frequently do not occur as expected, and those differences may be material. We have no responsibility to update this report for events and circumstances occurring after the date of this report.

Firm
City, State

Date

---

port) for generic examples of some of the necessary paperwork attendant to the reporting process.

ETHICS AND CODE OF PROFESSIONAL CONDUCT

Over the past several years, ethics, morals and principles have become hot topics in the media. This has created a dilemma for many practice administrators, especially when dealing with Medicare/Medicaid fraud and abuse, and has ultimately caused many physicians to reevaluate their Hippocratic oath as well as other ethical issues such as the right to die. In response to the media attention and to intense scrutiny by the Department of Health and Human Services, many healthcare institutions and organizations have formally adopted codes of ethics and ethical guidelines to help their employees deal with moral conflicts within the profession.

Like those in the healthcare industry, Certified Public Accountants must adhere to their own State Code of Ethics for licensure; however, adhering to the Code of Professional Conduct as established by the American Institute of Certified Public Accountants is voluntary. The mission of the AICPA is to provide its members with the resources, information, and leadership to enable certified public accountants to provide valuable services in the highest professional manner to benefit the public as well as employers and clients. In fulfilling this mission, the AICPA has created the following Preamble and Six Articles of the Principles of Professional Conduct.

> **Preamble: 01** Membership in the AICPA is voluntary; however, by accepting membership, the CPA assumes an obligation of self-discipline above and beyond the requirements of laws and regulations.
>
> **02** These Principles of the Code of Professional Conduct of the AICPA express the profession's acknowledgement of its responsibilities to the public, clients, and colleagues. The AIPCA guides its members in their performance of professional responsibilities and expresses the basic tenets of ethical and professional conduct.

Section 52 Article I: Responsibilities

In carrying out their responsibilities as professionals, members should exercise sensitive professional and moral judgments in all activities.

01 As professionals, certified public accountants perform an essential role in society. Consistent with that role, AICPA members have responsibilities to all those who use their professional services. Members also have a continuing responsibility to cooperate with each other to improve the art of accounting, maintain the public's confidence, and carry out the profession's special responsibilities for self-governance. The collective efforts of all members are required to maintain and enhance the traditions of the profession.

Section 53 Article II: The Public Interest

Members should accept the obligation to act in a way that will serve the public interest, honor the public trust, and demonstrate commitment to professionalism.

01 Members have a responsibility to the public in that others rely on their objectivity and integrity as CPAs to maintain the orderly functioning of commerce. Thus, responsibility to the public's interest (i.e., the collective well-being of the community of people and institutions that the profession serves), imposed upon CPAs.

02 In performing their professional responsibilities, AICPA members may experience conflicting pressures from those among the group. In resolving those conflicts, members should act with integrity, guided by the fact that their responsibility to the public is fulfilled when the clients' and employers' interests are best served.

03 Those who rely on the services of CPAs expect them to perform their duties with integrity, objectivity, due professional care, and a genuine interest in serving the public.

04 Members of the AICPA commit themselves to honor public trust and should seek continually to demonstrate their dedication to professional excellence.

Section 54 Article III: Integrity

To maintain and broaden public confidence, members should perform all professional responsibilities with the highest sense of integrity.

01 Integrity is the fundamental character to professional recognition and that in which the public obtains trust and ultimately the benchmark for which a member must test all decisions.

02 Integrity also requires a member to be honest and candid within the parameters of client confidentiality. Service and the public trust should not be sacrificed for personal gain and advantage.

03 Integrity is measured in terms of what is right and just. When a member is in a conflicting situation and there are no specific rules in reference to the issue, he should ask himself. "Am I doing what a person of integrity would do and have I retained my integrity?"

04 In order to maintain integrity, a member must adhere to the principles of objectivity, independence, and due care.

Section 55 Article IV: Objectivity and Independence

A member should maintain objectivity and be free of conflicts of interest in discharging professional responsibilities. A member in public practice should be independent in fact and appearance when providing auditing and other attestation services.

01 Objectivity is a state of mind that imposes the responsibility to be impartial, intellectually honest, and free of conflicts of interest. Independence prohibits relationships that might impair a member's objectivity in rendering attestation services.

02 Members often serve many interests in various capacities and must demonstrate their objectivity in different circumstances. Regardless of service or capacity, members should protect the integrity of their work, maintain objectivity, and avoid any inferior judgment.

03 An AICPA member in public practice must continually assess their client relationships and public responsibility in order to maintain objectivity and avoid conflicts of interest.

04 AICPA members that are not in public practice cannot maintain the appearance of independence, nevertheless, they have the responsibility to maintain objectivity in performing professional services. When employed by others to prepare financial statements, audits, tax or consulting services, they must be conscientious in their application of generally accepted accounting principles and honest in all their dealings with members in public practice.

Section 56 Article V: Due Care

A member should observe the profession's technical and ethical standards, strive continually to improve competence and the quality of services, and discharge professional responsibility to the best of the member's ability.

01 Due care requires a member to perform his professional duties with competence and diligence. It also obligates the member to perform his professional services to the best of his ability with concern for the best interest of those for whom the services are being performed.

02 Competence is a combination of education and experience. It begins with mastering the common body of knowledge required to become a certified public accountant and requires continuing education through a member's professional life to stay informed of new laws and regulations that are continually being imposed upon the profession.

03 Each member is responsible for determining his own level of competence and of evaluating whether his education, experience, and judgment are adequate to perform the client's requested task.

04 Diligence imposes upon its members to render services promptly and carefully and to observe applicable technical and ethical standards.

05 Due care requires a member to organize and adequately supervise any professional activity for which he is responsible.

Section 57 Article VI: Scope and Nature of Services

A member in public practice should observe the Principles of the Code of Professional Conduct in determining the scope and nature of services to be provided.

01 The public interest requires that CPAs have integrity, objectivity, and independence from conflicts of interest when performing their professional duties and as such, these duties should be performed with due care.

02 Each of these Principles should be considered by the members when determining whether or not to provide specific services which are dependent upon the varying circumstances. In some cases, they may represent a restraint on the nonaudit services that might be offered to a certain client. There are no specific rules that can be developed to help members reach these judgments; however, they must be satisfied that they are meeting the *spirit* of the Principles in this regard.

03 In order to achieve this, members should:

- Practice in firms that have internal controls which ensure that services are being performed competently and adequately supervised.

- Determine, in their own judgment, whether the nature and scope of performing a professional responsibility for an audit client would create a conflict of interest in the performance of the audit function for that client.

- Assess, in their own judgment, whether an activity is consistent with their role as a professional as compared to other members of the profession.

The moral dilemma of whether to formally adopt a Professional Code of Ethics will likely continue well into the future. One can only hope that the establishment of such a code will increase the quality of service and improve the professional standards of the practice. The foundation of any Professional Code of Ethics is the need to establish specific standards, assist those within the profession to continually improve their performance and expertise, and monitor such performance to enforce current standards and requirements.

Financial Statement Analysis for a Medical Practice

OVERVIEW

Financial statistics and ratio analyses are excellent tools for managers and physicians to use when analyzing a medical practice and comparing the practice to others. It is important for physicians and managers to have access to accurate data in order to make sound financial decisions for their practices. However, much caution should be used in judging a lone statistic at face value. In order to fully understand your practice's performance it is important to understand how the financial statistics and ratios behave together.

For example, it may appear at first glance that a medical practice has a problem with increasing overhead because the ratio analysis has determined that the overhead is high. However, the fact that this percentage is increasing does not mean expenses are also increasing. In the overhead expense ratio, the numerator in the expense equation represents overhead and the denominator represents professional revenue. While it may appear that overhead is increasing, in fact, the overhead may have remained the same while the revenue actually decreased. This is only one example illustrating the reason that ratios should be analyzed in their relationship to other variables within the practice. Remember that statistics and ratios can easily be manipulated. In order to get a true and accurate picture of the practice's financial state the statistics and ratios *must* be evaluated both as a whole and in relation to one another.

With a thorough financial statement analysis, medical practice management can determine the current financial health of the practice, make projections about future earnings, and detect potential problems. After gathering the kinds of information on the following list, which is taken from Statement on Auditing Standards No. 56, a medical practice will have the necessary information to make informed decisions concerning its financial status.

1. Financial information for comparable prior periods.
2. Anticipated results—for example, budgets or forecasts.
3. Relationships among elements of financial information within the period.
4. Information regarding the industry in which the entity operated.
5. Financial information with relevant nonfinancial data.

RATIOS

General Types

Liquidity—Short-Term Payments of Obligations

These ratios measure the practice's *liquidity,* or its ability to pay its short-term debt. *Short-term debt* is debt that has a maturity date of twelve months or less. A practice should strive to maintain a twelve-month liquidity, at minimum.

The main reason for liquidity analysis is to assure creditors that the practice has the ability to repay its debts in a timely manner.

Activity—Use of Assets to Produce Income

Investors are primarily interested in the consistency of the ability of the practice's management, which in most medical practices includes the physician, to generate a positive bottom line. The bottom line is what investors see as their opportunity—their return on investment. Once this ability is known, investors look at the revenue/sales of the physician, that is, the physician's ability to produce positive cash flow through providing medical care to the patients.

Exhibit 4.1
Pineway Family Practice balance sheet as of December 31, 1999

ASSETS		
Cash	$25,000	
Fixed Assets—Net Book Value	50,000	
Other Assets	200	
Total Assets		**$75,200**
CURRENT LIABILITIES		
Current Portion of Long Term Debt	6,500	
Payroll Taxes Payable	3,500	
Total Current Liabilities	10,000	
Long term debt	35,000	
Total Liabilities	$45,000	
STOCKHOLDER'S EQUITY		
Retained Earnings	$30,000	
Net Income/Loss	200	
Total Stockholders Equity	$30,200	
Total Liabilities & Stockholders Equity		$75,200

Profitability—Gain or Loss

Profitability minus Profit Margin equals Net Income/Cash Collections or Net Revenue (accrual). Profitability ratios measure just that—the "profitability" of a medical practice. This ratio not only reflects the level of profitability but also reflects the practice's decision-making capabilities.

Coverage—Debt/Investor

The coverage ratios measure the level of security that long-term creditors have in their investment. It indicates the practice's ability to cover debts due in the short-term.

To illustrate some of these financial performance indicators for a medical practice, we have included a general set of financial statements to use as a case study. See the sample balance sheet (Exhibit 4.1) and income statements (Exhibit 4.2) for Pineway Family Practice, P.C.

Exhibit 4.2
Pineway Family Practice income statement for 12 months ending
December 31, 1999

REVENUE		
Professional Receipts (Less patient refunds)	$900,000	
Other Income	20,000	
Total Income		**$920,000**
EXPENSES		
Depreciation Expense	7,000	
Staff Salaries	195,000	
Medical Supplies	35,000	
Administrative Supplies	20,000	
Telephone Expense	16,000	
Rent	68,000	
Equipment Lease	2,500	
Professional Services	4,000	
Computer Expense	1,500	
Professional Liability Insurance	12,000	
Insurance—General	3,500	
Staff Health Insurance	24,000	
Staff Retirement Plan	22,000	
Staff Payroll Taxes	15,000	
Answering Service	2,500	
Other Operating Expenses	1,800	
Physician Salary	450,000	
Physician Payroll Taxes	16,000	
Physician Health Insurance	6,000	
Physician Retirement Plan	18,000	
Total Expenses		**$919,800**
NET INCOME		**$200**

Ratios Illustrated

(For future reference we have also provided the following formulas at Appendix E for easy access.)

Current Ratio

The current ratio measures a company's immediate ability to play its current debt. To calculate the current ratio, divide the practice's total current assets by its current liabilities (as shown below). *Current liabil-*

ities are defined as the financial obligations of the practice that have a maturity date and are required to be paid within the next twelve months.

$$\text{Current Ratio} = \frac{\text{Current Assets}}{\text{Current Liabilities}}$$

The current ratio for Pineway Family Practice is shown below.

$$\text{Current Ratio} = \frac{\$25,000}{10,000} = 2.5$$

The result of this ratio, 2.5, indicates that Pineway Family Practice can cover its current liabilities upon immediate notice, if necessary. A good rule of thumb for this ratio is very simple: Always try to have a current ratio of at least 1.0. A consistent ratio of 1.0 means that the practice can rest easy that current (or short-term) liabilities can be met. This can be a concern for practices with large payrolls. Not only is payday a large drain on cash, so are payroll tax deposits, which are sometimes forgotten until they are due.

The median current ratio as published by the Medical Group Management Association (MGMA) is 1.37 for family practitioners. (These statistics are current as of the writing of this manual.) As a further point of reference, loan covenants generally require a 1.5 ratio.

Quick Ratio

The quick ratio, also referred to as the acid-test ratio, is similar to the current ratio because it measures a practice's ability to pay off its debts at any given point in time. It is called the quick ratio, however, because it measures the practice's ability to pay "quickly." Paying quickly resorts to the use of current assets that can be rapidly converted into cash if they are not already in cash form. Examples of these quickly liquidated assets are accounts receivable and marketable securities. Accounts receivable can be sold for a reasonable collectible amount if the practice needs immediate access to cash. Marketable securities can be sold at fair market value for immediate cash; however, most medical practices do not invest in marketable securities through the practice.

The quick ratio formula is as follows:

$$\text{Quick Ratio} = \frac{(\text{Cash} + \text{Accounts Receivable} + \text{Marketable Securities})}{\text{Current Liabilities}}$$

As a reminder when calculating this ratio, medical practices that use the modified cash basis of accounting do not reflect accounts receivable balances on the practice's balance sheet.

To illustrate the quick ratio using Pineway Family Practice's balance sheet as of December 31, 1999, see the calculation below. Assume that Pineway's accounts receivable balance is $160,000 as of December 31, 1999. As previously shown in the current ratio, Pineway's current assets are $25,000 and its current liabilities are $10,000.

$$\textbf{Quick Ratio} \; = \; \frac{\$25,000 \; + \; \$160,000 \; + \; 0}{\$10,000} \; = \; 18.5$$

This result, 18.5, indicates that the practice can easily cover its current liabilities of $10,000 by using both its cash and its other assets that can be quickly converted into cash. Likewise, the lower this ratio, the less likely the practice can effectively pay its short-term debt.

One point that should be made is that, in the medical industry, it must be understood and pointed out to unknowing creditors that the collection of accounts receivable of a medical practice has a longer cycle than many other types of businesses. Due to the amount of paperwork required to bill for medical services and the multiple parts after billing, it can be weeks or even months before an account has been fully collected through the normal course of billing.

Inventory Turnover Ratio

The inventory turnover ratio measures the number of times that a business's inventory is sold during a period, usually defined as a year. This ratio is not commonly used in the financial analysis of medical practices because medical practices typically do not have an inventory of goods or products to sell. A practice sells medical service—not a product that is purchased, put on a shelf, and then re-sold to the public. The medical practice's product is somewhat akin to time. The inventory turnover ratio is largely used by manufacturing and retail businesses, not service businesses. However, as with most things, there are exceptions, which brings us to why this ratio is applicable here.

One exception in the medical practice industry is that of an optometry or ophthalmology practice. These practices typically sell eyeglasses and contact lenses. In this case, the inventory turnover ratio would be an important ratio to monitor. A practice such as this, like any retail business, would want to sell through or "turn over" its retail inventory as quickly as possible and preferably before seasons change, styles change, clearance sales, discounts, and so forth.

The inventory turnover ratio is calculated as follows.

$$\text{Inventory Turnover Ratio} = \frac{\text{Cost of Goods Sold}}{\text{Average Inventory}}$$

The optimum result of this ratio would be high numbers, reflecting the fact that the practice is turning over its inventory quickly and thus enjoying strong sales.

Let's use a hypothetical example of C. U. Better's ophthalmology practice. For the year 2000, C. U. Better's cost of inventory that was sold (also referred to as cost of sales) was $300,000. If the practice has an average inventory balance (at cost) of $50,000, then the practice turned over its retail inventory of eyeglasses, contact lenses, and accessories 6 times during the year (see the calculation presented below). For purposes of this calculation, the average inventory can be calculated by dividing the sum of the beginning of year and end of year inventories by 2, or by averaging monthly balances throughout the year.

$$\text{Inventory Turnover Ratio} = \frac{\$300,000}{\$50,000} = 6$$

This ratio, when monitored routinely, helps identify slow moving inventory and potential problems due to above-market value pricing on certain inventory items.

Asset Turnover Ratio

The asset turnover ratio measures the efficiency of how the practice uses its assets to generate revenue. The higher this ratio, theoretically, the more efficient and effective the practice is at generating revenue.

This ratio is not commonly used in medical practices because there is an inconsistency in the way that medical practices purchase or lease assets. Many practices do not own the assets that are used in the practices to generate revenue. Therefore, these assets do not appear on their balance sheets. Also, many physicians personally own clinical and office equipment and other tangible assets used in their practices; again, the practices do not own the assets. Likewise, the assets do not appear on the practices' balance sheets because the physicians own the assets through separate entities. In these situations, the practices pay rent to the physicians for use of these assets.

Another reason that this ratio is not commonly used in medical practices is that typically, a medical practice's assets are not considered to be all that vital to the ability of the practice to generate revenue. The true ability of a medical practice to generate revenues lies in the ability of the physicians to treat patients. The assets in the practice—its computer system, exam tables, desks, and telephones—enhance the process of treating patients. One can, of course, argue that certain types of medical equipment are heavily relied upon by physicians in the treatment of their patients; however, by and large, the asset turnover ratio is not a statistic with great meaning in medical practice financial analysis.

The asset turnover ratio is produced by this formula:

$$\text{Asset Turnover Ratio} = \frac{\text{Net Revenue (or Cash Collections)}}{\text{Average Total Assets}}$$

The following calculation is based on the example financial statements of Pineway Family Practice for the year ending December 31, 1999. For the purpose of this calculation, assume that Pineway's average total assets are $45,000.

$$\text{Asset Turnover Ratio} = \frac{\$900,000}{\$45,000} = 20$$

A factor that skews this ratio, especially in medical practices, is the value of assets that is used in the ratio calculation. Medical practices can take advantage of large annual depreciation expense on newly purchased assets through an allowed tax deduction called Section 179 Expense Deduction. As of the writing of this book, the annual I.R.C. (Internal Revenue Code) Section 179, depreciation expense allowed is $19,000 for tax year 1999. Due to this deductibility, a medical practice's balance sheet typically reports a lower net book value on assets. This will, in effect, artificially inflate the results of the asset turnover ratio.

Working Capital Turnover Ratio

Working capital is defined as the amount of money that a medical practice has available at any given time to funnel back into the practice to support its daily operations. It is important for practice management to monitor working capital to anticipate appropriately short-term cash requirements.

To calculate working capital, subtract current liabilities from current assets (see Exhibit 4.1). In the example financial statements for Pineway Family Practice, the practice's working capital is $15,000. Its current assets are $25,000; its current liabilities are $10,000.

Working Capital = $25,000 (current assets)

minus $10,000 (current liabilities) = $15,000

This means that the practice has $15,000 available to meet its current operating expenses. Again, this is an important measurement for the practice to routinely monitor. There is an industry standard available for most specialties of medical practices for the median amount of working capital per FTE (full-time equivalent) physician. The current median amount of working capital per FTE physician for family practices according to the MGMA is $10,211. As illustrated in our example, Pineway is above average in working capital turnover.

A classic example of why this is so important is the following scenario: A medical practice has hired a new physician. Practically speaking, collections for services provided by the new physician will not flow back into the practice immediately. As is common with accounts receivable in medical practices, it takes time for collections to begin coming into the practice. Due to this, the practice must have funds from some other source in order to continue to run its operations.

When hiring a new physician, practice management must not fail to process the new physician's paperwork for credentials as soon as feasible. If this paperwork is not handled promptly, there will be a negative effect on working capital and cash flow, because managed care companies will not pay the practice for the patients the new physician is treating. Too often, this process is not completed in a timely manner. The end result is that not only will the practice experience a lag time in collections merely by the addition of a new doctor, but the lack of expedient credentialling can cause months of payment delay. An indirect result of this process is a domino effect, because staff must take time to follow up on the new physician's collections as well as on the credentialling process itself. Enough cannot be stated about the importance of medical practices' carrying out procedures accurately and in a timely manner on the first attempt.

Medical practices must also monitor this ratio because poor payment habits and poor financial conditions of payers have created cash flow problems for many medical practices nationwide. Practice management should anticipate problems such as these and be prepared to take action if the practice finds itself in a cash crunch. Practices may need to borrow cash from a lending institution on a short-term basis. This is only one example of why it is so important for a medical practice to monitor its financial condition from all angles on an ongoing basis. Things do change—practices must be prepared to handle the consequences.

When attempting to determine a practice's working capital, the practice revenue is divided by its average working capital as in the following formula. This ratio indicates the amount of working capital needed to maintain a certain level of revenue. If this ratio is declining, it may indicate a decreasing level of collections, a decreasing number of patients, or an increasing number of patients with low collectibility or no insurance.

$$\text{Working Capital Turnover Ratio} = \frac{\text{Revenue (Net Patient Fees)}}{\text{Average Working Capital}}$$

The denominator in this ratio should be the practice's average working capital, calculated by adding the beginning working capital of the period (for example, one year) and the ending working capital. Divide this sum by 2.

For example, let us say Pineway's beginning working capital at January 1, 1999, is $5,000. Per Pineway's December 31, 1999, financial statement, the practice's ending working capital is $15,000. Therefore, the average working capital is $10,000; the calculation to arrive at this number is ($5,000 + $15,000)/2 = $10,000.

The numerator in this ratio is $900,000, which is Pineway's professional revenue as reported on its income statement for the year ending December 31, 1999. Therefore, the practice's working capital turnover ratio is 90.

$$\text{Working Capital Turnover Ratio} = \frac{\$900,000}{\$10,000} = 90$$

This result means that the practice used its average working capital of $10,000 to bring in revenue of 90 times that amount. The more times a business turns over its working capital, the more revenue the business is generating.

Return on Assets

The rate of return on assets is a formula that, although used effectively in many industries, is not commonly used in analyzing the financial condition of medical practices. The reason is the same as that used earlier with regard to ratios that use fixed assets, such as the asset turnover ratio. Net income is also another item that cannot be compared equally from one medical practice to another. It is not a consistent indication of financial performance because most practices have zero net income—they do not typically retain earnings. However, they do typically distribute the additional net income to physicians. For this reason, the measurement of physician compensation is a much more reliable indicator of the financial performance of a medical practice (as is illustrated later in this chapter).

The following formula is used to calculate a medical practice's return on assets ratio.

$$\textbf{Return on Assets Ratio} = \frac{\textbf{Net Income}}{\textbf{Average Total Assets}}$$

To calculate the practice's return on assets ratio, let's use the Pineway Family Practice financial statements for the year ending December 31, 1999, as an example. The denominator in this ratio is the average total assets, which are typically calculated by adding the beginning and ending total asset balances and dividing the sum by 2. As calculated earlier in this chapter, Pineway's average total assets for 1999 is $45,000 (see Exhibit 4.1). Its net income for the year ending December 31, 1999, is $200 (see Exhibit 4.2). Therefore, its return on assets ratio is .44%, or less than 1% as follows:

$$\textbf{Return on Assets Ratio} = \frac{\$200}{\$45,000} = .44\%$$

As points of reference for medical practice, the current median percentages of return on total assets for several of the most common medical specialties are listed below. These are the current medians as published by MGMA; they further illustrate the fact that net income in medical practices ultimately becomes compensation in some form.

Family Practice	0.00%
General Surgery	2.72%

OB-GYN	1.88%
Pediatrics	0.00%
Internal Medicine	0.00%

Profit Margin on Revenue

The profit margin on revenue ratio is also a financial measurement that is widely used in many industries but is not commonly used in evaluating the financial performance of medical practices, for the same reason stated earlier regarding the return on assets ratio. Medical practices typically do not have a measurable or significant amount of net income.

The profit margin on revenue ratio is calculated as follows, using Pineway Family Practice's income statement for the year ending December 31, 1999, as an example.

$$\text{Profit Margin on Revenue} = \frac{\text{Net Income}}{\text{Net Revenue (or Cash Collections)}}$$

$$= \frac{\$200}{\$900,000} = .02\%$$

The result of this ratio for Pineway is less than 1%, or practically 0%. Again, this is not a meaningful result because net income can best be measured as physician compensation or that portion of physician compensation that is above average for a particular practice's specialty, number of years of physician experience, and so on.

Debt to Asset Ratio

The debt to asset ratio is used to monitor the practice's ability to service its debt—its short-term and long-term obligations. The lower the results of this ratio, the more favorable the ability of the practice to repay its debt and meet financial liabilities. The debt to asset ratio is calculated according to the following formula:

$$\text{Debt to Asset Ratio} = \frac{\text{Total Debt}}{\text{Total Assets}}$$

To illustrate, using Pineway's balance sheet as of December 31, 1999, we use the following formula and Exhibit 4.1:

$$\textbf{Debt to Asset Ratio } = \frac{\$45,000}{\$75,200} = 59.84\%$$

In the case of Pineway Family Practice, the practice's total debt to total asset ratio is 59.84%. This was calculated by dividing Pineway's total debt of $45,000 by its total assets of $75,200. This means that roughly 60% of the practice's total assets are tied up in amounts owed. As stated before, the lower this ratio, the better financial position the practice is in. If the ratio is low, then the practice has more available cash and assets with which to service additional debt, make purchases, or distribute as compensation.

In comparison to the current median standard as published by MGMA for the debt to asset ratio for family practitioners (86.42%), Pineway's debt to asset ratio is very favorable. Pineway has more cash and assets available for discretionary use than the majority of other family practices across the nation.

Using industry comparison data, available to physicians through MGMA, and other professional organizations and associations, the practice can safely draw the conclusion that most family practices have far more of their assets tied up in debt than does Pineway Family Practice. Therefore, this statistic would be a positive when trying to obtain a loan from a bank or other creditors. This does not of course, ensure that the practice would be able to obtain the loan, but it would give a more favorable impression to the bankers.

OTHER COMMON MEDICAL PRACTICE PERFORMANCE INDICATORS

There are various ratios and statistics that are commonly used by medical practices in addition to those noted previously. These financial performance indicators should be tracked consistently every month, quarter, or other routine reporting basis.

Practice management should be using this information to make financial and operational decisions. It is a relatively simple task to track this type of data, as is discussed in the following pages of this chapter. Tracking and monitoring performance data can be easily reported on spreadsheets; some accounting software packages report financial indicators with periodic financial statements; and some medical practices use outside accounting firms to perform the write-ups of the practices' financial statements. As part of this process, the accounting firms should provide the results of many of these financial statistics on an ongoing basis.

Again, this exercise is simple and easy to maintain. The benefit of having this information and using it to make managerial decisions far outweighs the cost of gathering the data. In essence, there is no excuse for a medical practice not to perform these financial tasks. A medical practice could have much more to lose if it does not use these indicators wisely.

Operating Expense Analyses

The following operating expenses are typically the largest line item expenses in a medical practice: malpractice insurance, office salaries, rent, and payroll taxes. These expenses should be monitored for increasing expenses and significant fluctuations. They should also be compared to industry averages, as has been highlighted in the following examples.

Overhead Expense Ratio

The overhead expense ratio is one of the most common gauges of a medical practice's spending habits. Overhead expense is made up of all the practice's operating expenses except provider compensation and benefits. The formula for calculating this ratio is:

Overhead Expense Ratio =

$$\frac{\text{Operating Expenses (excluding provider compensation \& benefits)}}{\text{Net Professional Revenue}}$$

To illustrate this ratio and other expense ratios, let's again refer to the income statement (Exhibit 4.2) for Pineway Family Practice for the year ending December 31, 1999. Provider compensation and benefits equal $490,000 ($450,000 + $16,000 + $6,000 + $18,000).

$$\text{Overhead Expense} = \frac{[\$919,800 - \$490,000]}{\$900,000}$$

$$= 47.76\%$$

Exhibit 4.3
Comparison of ratio to industry averages—Pineway Family Practice

Overhead Expense Analysis		
Practice	**MGMA**	**Variance**
47.67%	59.45%	(11.69%)

To compare Pineway's overhead ratio of 47.76% to the industry average, the current MGMA median for family practitioners' overhead expense is 59.45%, as shown in Exhibit 4.3. The results of this comparison indicate that the practice is using about 12% less of its revenue to operate than its peers use. This also means that there is more discretionary revenue left to be distributed as compensation to the owners, to be used for expanding the practice, to make contributions to retirement plans, of for other purposes. Because the practice has approximately 12% less operating expenses than the national average for its specialty, it is likely that the practice will have favorable comparisons in all of its major expense categories.

Staff Salaries Expense Ratio

Another operating expense ratio that a medical practice should evaluate is its staff salaries expense as a percentage of practice revenue. The formula for this ratio is indicated below.

$$\text{Staff Salaries Expense Ratio} = \frac{\text{Staff Salaries Expense}}{\text{Net Professional Revenue}}$$

Staff salaries include all personnel in the practice other than physicians and mid-level providers. Other than rent, staff salaries typically make up the largest line item expense on the practice's list of operating expenses.

See the following calculation for Pineway's Staff Salaries Expense Ratio.

$$\text{Staff Salaries Expense Ratio} = \frac{\$195,000}{\$900,000} = 21.67\%$$

As anticipated by the results of Pineway's overhead ratio, the practice's staff salaries expense ratio compares favorably to the current MGMA

Exhibit 4.4
Results of overhead ratio—Pineway Family Practice

Staff Salary Expense Analysis		
Practice	**MGMA**	**Variance**
21.67%	31.06%	(9.39%)

median of 31.06% for family practitioners, as seen in Exhibit 4.4. This result might indicate that the practice uses its human resources efficiently and effectively; or, it could mean that the practice pays low wages as compared to its peers. In that case, Pineway should evaluate its wage structure and salary review process. If the practice's pay scale is below average, there is a real possibility that the practice will lose some of its employees to competitors.

Supplies Expense Ratios

The supplies expense ratios measure the practice's spending for supplies and for some routine administrative services. These two expense categories have very high potential for waste and even petty theft—in fact, one of the biggest areas of petty theft and waste in businesses today is in the area of supplies, especially office supplies. It may not sound like a lot of money but it can add up to significant amounts.

As explained in Chapter 5, care should be taken to implement procedures in ordering, purchasing, and receiving supplies to control excessive use. Practice management should pay particular attention to rising costs inasmuch as they may be caused by a lack of internal control.

The formula for these two expenses is similar to the ratios presented before because they are calculated as a percentage of the practice's revenue.

To determine the *medical and surgical supplies expense ratio*, see the following calculation, using Pineway's income statement (see Exhibit 4.2) for the year ending December 31, 1999.

$$\text{Medical/Surgical Supplies Expense Ratio} = \frac{\textbf{Medical/Surgical Supplies}}{\textbf{Net Professional Revenue}}$$

$$\text{Medical/Surgical Supplies Expense Ratio} = \frac{\$35,000}{\$900,000} = 3.89\%$$

Exhibit 4.5
Medical/surgical supplies expense ratio—Pineway Family Practice

Practice	MGMA	Variance
3.89%	4.10%	(.21%)

Exhibit 4.6
Administrative expense analysis—Pineway Family Practice

Practice	MGMA	Variance
2.22%	1.98%	(.24%)

Pineway's medical/surgical supplies expense ratio is not significantly above or below the industry average for family practitioners when compared to the current MGMA median of 4.10%, as seen in Exhibit 4.5.

The following is the formula for determining Pineway's ratio for its expenditures related to *administrative supplies and services;* see Pineway's income statement to calculate this ratio.

$$\text{Administrative Supplies/Services Ratio} = \frac{\text{Administrative Supplies/Services}}{\text{Net Professional Revenue}}$$

$$\text{Administrative Supplies/Services Ratio} = \frac{\$20,000}{\$900,000} = 2.2\%$$

Pineway's result of 2.22% compares similarly to its expense ratio for medical and surgical supplies in that the deviation from industry averages is insignificant. When reviewing the supplies accounts, additional care should be taken to ensure that the expenses belong them. These accounts, especially administrative supplies and services, are often used as catch-all accounts. A good effective chart of accounts can assist with accurate record keeping.

As shown in Exhibit 4.6, the current MGMA median for family practitioners' administrative supplies/services expense is 1.98%.

FACILITY EXPENSE RATIOS

Another important expense item that should be monitored is a practice's expenditures for its facility or building and related expenses.

Exhibit 4.7

Building/occupancy analysis—Pineway Family Practice

Practice	MGMA	Variance
7.56%	7.58%	(.02%)

These expenses are usually a very significant portion of a practice's revenue. Practices should also anticipate increased rates in rent, utilities, and property taxes. If this ratio is increasing, the practice is not offsetting its rising costs with increases in revenue.

$$\text{Building/Occupancy Ratio} = \frac{\text{Building/Occupancy Expenses}}{\text{Net Professional Revenue}}$$

To calculate Pineway's *building and occupancy expense ratio,* see the following formula using Pineway's income statement (see Exhibit 4.2) for the year ending December 31, 1999.

$$\text{Building/Occupancy Ratio} = \frac{\$68,000}{\$900,000} = 7.56\%$$

Even though the calculation used only the rent expense from Pineway's income statement for illustration purposes, the practice may also have other building and occupancy expenses such as utilities, repairs, maintenance, and leasehold improvements that are listed separately on its financial statements.

Pineway's building and occupancy expense ratio of 7.56% is approximately at par (see Exhibit 4.7) with its peers nationally when compared to the current MGMA family practice median of 7.58%.

Other Profitability Measures

Other useful statistics in measuring the financial performance and profitability of medical practices are statistics that measure physician compensation and physician productivity.

As discussed elsewhere in this book, in the past physicians took home, as their pay, income that was left from the practice's revenue after operating expenses had been paid. No longer is this a dependable alternative for physicians. In analyzing and budgeting for the future of the practice, physician compensation and benefits should be treated as

Exhibit 4.8
Physician compensation/benefits analysis—Pineway Family Practice

Practice	MGMA	Variance
54.44%	38.84%	+15.60%

all other expenses. They should total to a fixed, expected expenditure that is included in the budget as a normal operating expense, even though in reality, if the practice were in a deficit situation, the deficit would come first from the allotted funds for physician compensation. So, for that reason, physician compensation is one of the most reliable measurements of a medical practice's profitability.

Physician Compensation and Benefits as a Percentage of Net Revenue

It is important for a practice to monitor its physician compensation and benefits, both relative to net revenue and to determine if the physicians are adequately compensated. To illustrate these calculations, let's continue with the example of Pineway Family Practice. Given Pineway's physicians' compensation and benefits, this ratio would be calculated as follows:

$$\text{Physician Compensation as a percentage of net revenue} =$$

$$\frac{\text{Physician Compensation/Benefits}}{\text{Revenue (or Cash Collections)}}$$

$$\text{Physician Compensation as a percentage of net revenue} = \frac{\$490,000}{\$900,000}$$

$$= 54.44\%$$

The current median statistic for this ratio nationally as published by MGMA is 38.84% for family practitioners. As seen in Exhibit 4.8, Pineway Family Practice compares favorably to this statistic. This means that the Pineway physicians, on average, are taking home a significantly larger piece of the pie than their peers are nationally.

Physician Compensation as a Percentage of Gross Charges

Another method of measuring the profitability of the practice is to measure physician compensation as a percentage of gross charges. Although gross charges are not the most reliable denominator to use in measuring physician practices because gross charges are not extremely consistent among practices, it is still a good indicator of the percentage of work that the physicians have performed versus the amount of benefit the physicians take home.

Given the physicians' productivity at Pineway, their compensation as a percentage of gross charges would be calculated as follows. We will assume for this calculation that Pineway's total gross charges for 1999 is $1,125,000.

Physician Compensation as a percentage of gross charges =

$$\frac{\textbf{Physician Compensation and Benefits}}{\textbf{Gross Charges}}$$

Physician Compensation as a percentage of gross charges = $\dfrac{\$450,000}{\$1,125.000}$ = 40%

Fee for Service Revenue Per FTE Physician

Like other available industry statistics, the amount of revenue collected as a result of services performed per FTE physician is also useful. Many outside creditors and banking institutions use this measure as an indicator of how handily a practice can pay its debt. This measure, which indicates the cash collected per FTE physician, is one that physicians and high level management applicants will want to review when considering employment opportunities with a medical practice. A new physician or administrator would want to be assured that he or she is choosing a solvent and stable operation.

Given the example of Pineway Family Practice, the revenue per FTE physician was $450,000 ($900,000 divided by 2 FTEs) as compared to the current median for family practitioners of $335,224 as published by MGMA. This comparison is shown in Exhibit 4.9; by this result, Pineway has obviously been a high-producing practice whose physicians have collected a far greater amount of revenue than the median

Exhibit 4.9
Fee for service revenue analysis per FTE physician—Pineway Family Practice

Practice	MGMA	Variance $	Variance %
$450,000	$335,224	$114,776	+ 34.24%

level of their peers in the same specialty. This is also a probable indicator that the practice has an effective billing and collection effort. This statistic is a direct reflection of the practice's ability to collect receivables, not just of high productivity.

MONITORING ACCOUNTS RECEIVABLE

As illustrated in the previous example, Pineway Family Practice likely has an effective billing function. Although most medical practices monitor their accounts receivable, they do not always perform this function effectively. Often, the physicians look at the practice's collections as compared to its charges and assume one thing—that managed care is not paying them enough; but before physicians and practice management can cite managed care as the reason for lower revenue, they must first take a look inward, at the practice's billing and collection efforts, to determine if improvements are warranted. The practice should evaluate each process with its billing department to determine what tasks, if any, can be performed more efficiently and effectively. The primary goal of the billing staff should be to collect revenue that it is due from both insurance companies and patients. Too often, the staff get bogged down in filling out forms and reviewing reports, rather than concentrating on the primary task at hand—"getting the money in the door." It is important that the practice have the proper procedures and protocols in place to monitor the effectiveness of collecting revenue.

Many medical practices try diligently to follow the proper procedures when collecting revenue; but too often, they do not know what the "proper procedures" are. For example, if a physician is asked about the protocols for following up on denied insurance claims, he or she will commonly either defer the question to the administrator or believe that the process is otherwise under control. When the billing staff who are responsible for denied claims are questioned, their response is often that the follow-up process is behind schedule—or that it is not being performed at all.

Often, the methods used in following up on these claims are not the most effective. For example, many times billing staff will do one of two things: They will either refile a claim blindly, or they will send a letter to several addresses hoping it will cover all the bases and eventually get to the right person. Neither one of these action plans works effectively. Usually, a practice should first call the insurance company directly to get resolution on a claim issue by finding out exactly what the practice should do—what information is required, where the information needs to be sent in order to expedite the claims processing, and so forth.

Of course, the first issues that should be addressed are the reason a claim was denied and how to fix the problem promptly. Rather than spending valuable time on handling denied and rejected claims, the staff should be addressing the issues causing the problems. Some of the most common denials of payment from insurance companies are due to errors made by the practice. Typical errors made by medical practices include: (1) not verifying a patient's eligibility for insurance coverage, (2) not filing claims on a timely basis, and (3) not obtaining the required authorization for services rendered. Other rejected claims are usually a result of missing or incorrect information required on the claim form, such as provider number, referring physician, diagnosis code, and so on.

Other financial items that medical practices should monitor regularly have to do with contractual adjustments, write-offs, and payments in the "unapplied credits" category.

Contractual adjustments and write-offs are areas of the practice's billing and collection system that can be manipulated by deliberately adjusting balances due from insurance companies and patients alike. There are several reasons for adjusting balances; the main one is that staff do not want to hassle with the follow-up process. Another reason is the deterrence of payment theft and its subsequent write-off, a problem discussed in more detail in chapter 5, "Internal Control Accounting Related to Medical Practices."

Another major issue with accounts receivable in medical practices is the process of entering payments into the computer system under a category called "Unapplied Credits." If a payment is received in error or in duplicate, for example, it should be input into the system under the patient's account; however, if the billing clerk cannot determine for which services the payment was received, the payment is labeled as "unapplied." Consequently, the payment just sits there until someone follows up to see where it should have been applied—but at this point, many practices abandon the process.

Sometimes payments are received in error that do not belong to the practice at all. It is very important for billing staff to be properly trained in handling payments that are received and do not belong to the practice; erroneous payments should not be deposited, but they aren't always caught in time. Once the billing staff have determined that a payment cannot be applied, they should determine their proper course of action. If the inquiry results in an erroneous payment or an overpayment by an insurance company, the practice should refund the payment immediately to the appropriate party with a letter of explanation. In such cases, the practice is encouraged to resolve the issue as soon as possible or risk an assessment of fraudulent and abusive billing practices.

To hold an erroneous payment or an overpayment issued by Medicare is illegal. Practice management and billing managers should continually monitor these issues. Documentation of how erroneous payments and overpayments are monitored should be kept in the practice's compliance plan. The documentation should include the procedures that are in place to handle these payments, if received. It should also include details of each specific review and what, if anything, was detected. Finally, the documentation should detail what the practice has done to correct the issue, such as phone calls, refunds, and so on. This documentation serves as proof to Medicare and other regulatory authorities that the practice has exercised diligence in complying with the law.

To effectively monitor accounts receivable, a medical practice should compute several financial statistics on a regular basis. In the following paragraphs are listed several accounts receivable indicators that practices should monitor, without fail, on a routine basis.

Accounts Receivable Turnover Ratio

This ratio is in the category of activity ratios of basic financial analysis. It depicts the number of times the practice has collected an amount equal to its average accounts receivable.

$$\text{Accounts Receivable Turnover Ratio} = \frac{\text{Net Revenue}}{\text{Average Accounts Receivable}}$$

To illustrate this calculation, let's assume that Pineway's average accounts receivable balance is $150,000. To calculate the average accounts receivable, average each month's balance *or* add the beginning and ending balances and divide by 2. To calculate Pineway's accounts receivable turnover ratio, see the formula below.

$$\text{Accounts Receivable Turnover Ratio} = \frac{\$900,000}{\$150,000} = 6$$

This means that Pineway collected its accounts receivable six times during the year. The higher this ratio, the more meaningful are the results of Pineway's liquidity ratios—the current and quick ratios—because of the practice's ability to collect cash quickly and effectively.

Accounts Receivable Collection Ratios

Two commonly used accounts receivable ratios in medical practices are the gross collection ratio and the adjusted collection ratio. These ratios measure the amount of money that the practice is collecting as a percentage of services rendered.

Gross Collection Ratio

The gross collection ratio is calculated as follows:

$$\textbf{Gross Collection Ratio} = \frac{\textbf{Net Professional Receipts}}{\textbf{Gross Charges}}$$

Pineway Family Practice had $900,000 of net professional cash receipts during 1999. As stated earlier, the practice had gross charges during the year 1999 of $1,125,000.

$$\textbf{Gross Collection Ratio} = \frac{\$900,000}{\$1,125,000} = 80\%$$

The current median gross collection ratio for family practitioners as published by MGMA is 75.88% for fee-for-service, 81.01% for fee-for-service and capitation revenues combined. By comparison, Pineway Family Practice is in the median range, but, if its revenue is primarily fee-for-service revenue, it appears to be collecting a higher percentage than its peers do by approximately 4%.

Adjusted Collection Ratio

To calculate the adjusted collection ratio, the formula is:

$$\textbf{Adjusted Collection Ratio} = \frac{\textbf{Net Professional Receipts}}{\textbf{Net Charges}}$$

In the case of Pineway, assume the practice's gross charges for the twelve months ended December 31, 1999, is $1,125,000, and that its contractual adjustments for the same time period is $210,000. First, Pineway must calculate its net charges by subtracting its contractual adjustments of $210,000 from its gross charges of $1,125,000, resulting in net charges of $915,000. Plugging the amount of net charges into the formula for adjusted collection ratio, we obtain the following:

$$\textbf{Adjusted Collection Ratio} = \frac{\$900,000}{\$915,000} = 98.36\%$$

The current median for net professional receipts (or collections) for family practitioners as published by MGMA is 98.65% from fee-for-service charges. By comparison, Pineway is in the median range of collections. This ratio is the more meaningful ratio of the two collection measurements discussed here, because it measures the amount of money that a practice can rightfully attempt to collect after agreed-upon contractual adjustments have been written off.

Months of Gross Charges

Months of Gross Charges in Accounts Receivable =

$$\frac{\textbf{Accounts Receivable Balance}}{\textbf{Average Monthly Gross Charges}}$$

This measurement reflects the amount of accounts receivable outstanding in terms of services rendered, illustrated by the following example: If Pineway's 1999 gross charges were $1,125,000, then the practice's average monthly gross charges are $93,750 ($1,125,000 / 12). Recall from a previous calculation that the practice's accounts receivable balance as of December 31, 1999, is $160,000. Thus, to calculate this ratio,

Exhibit 4.10
A/R months of gross charges analysis—Pineway Family Practice

Practice	MGMA	Variance
1.71 months	2.15 months	(.44) months

$$\text{Months of Gross Charges in Accounts Receivable} = \frac{\$160,000}{\$93,750} = 1.71$$

This means that the physicians have performed 1.71 months of work for which they have yet to be paid. By comparison, the current median number of months of gross charges for family practices as published by MGMA is 2.15, shown in Exhibit 4.10. Pineway's statistic compares very favorably to that of the physicians' peer practices across the country. Obviously, the lower this number, the better. When physicians and staff can relate this number to work performed with no pay, they understand the need to increase collection efforts where needed.

This statistic can also calculated by the number of days in the accounts receivable balance, as opposed to the number of months.

Aged Categories of Accounts Receivable

Medical practices should routinely monitor the amounts of uncollected balances in each aged category. These should be reviewed to find irregularities and to ensure that balances are being collected. As an example, let's assume that Pineway's accounts receivable is aged as shown in Exhibit 4.11 to compare the current median for aged categories of accounts receivable for the practice. It is good practice to compare against industry and specialty standards where available.

Total Accounts Receivable Per FTE Physician

The accounts receivable balance per FTE physician and per each individual physician are two helpful statistics for practices to monitor. When an accounts receivable balance increases gradually, its movement does not necessarily stand out as significant. However, when these two specific statistics are compared to industry averages, change

Exhibit 4.11
Aged Accounts Receivable—Pineway Family Practice

Number of Days	Practice	MGMA
0–30	45.50%	50.57%
31–60	15.76%	16.26%
61–90	10.82%	8.86%
91–120	6.11%	6.27%
>120	21.81%	25.35%

in the accounts receivable balance becomes more noticeable. In single-specialty practices, individual physician statistics are less meaningful because the billing staff typically does not differentiate among specific physicians when generating insurance claims and billing statements. This statistic is more useful in practices in which physicians, although in the same specialty, may perform different types of procedures from each other. For example, urologists perform a variety of complex procedures but not every urologist typically performs all of them. This difference may lead to different sets of billing and coding needs for particularly complex and costly procedures. It would not be unusual that these physicians may have large differences in their individual accounts receivable balances due to these variances. It is important that the billing staff have a good understanding of the proper billing procedures so as to expedite the claims processing by submitting a "clean claim."

Clean claim is a term used in the medical insurance industry to define a claim that includes all required information and that is reported in the required format. Clean claims should be a top priority for any practice because they can be immediately processed without coming back to the practice for more information. It should be a routine part of a billing manager's duties to ensure that the same set of problems does not cause one claim after another to be returned. If not monitored, claim returns can get out of control very quickly. Practices that have converted to new or upgraded computer systems should check to make sure that the claims are complete and accurate. Bottom line is, clean claims translate into faster cash received . . . period.

Additionally, all billing staff should be trained and encouraged to use the telephone to expedite the collection process. The longer the money sits on the table, the less chance a practice has of collecting it.

Exhibit 4.12
Accounts receivable per FTE physician—Pineway Family Practice

Practice	MGMA	Variance $	Variance %
$80,000	$84,343	(4,343)	(5.15%)

Pineway Family Practice has two full-time physicians. The average accounts receivable per FTE physician is $80,000 ($160,000 divided by 2 FTE physicians). This compares favorably (see Exhibit 4.12), although not significantly, with the average accounts receivable balance for family practices nationally on a per FTE physician basis, according to the current median of $84,343 as published by MGMA.

As an addition to the ratios that have been presented in this chapter, Exhibits 4.13 and 4.14 allow a medical practice to evaluate its accounts receivable and determine any potential problems that need to be addressed, and can be used as effective management tools. By completing the data in these charts, monthly or periodically, physicians and practice management can evaluate different aspects of accounts receivable at a glance.

Exhibit 4.14, "Aged Accounts Receivable Analysis," will, when used each month, assist management in evaluating trends in accounts receivable that should be investigated before a problem remains too long. For example, when account balances in older categories begin to increase, immediate action should be taken to determine the reason and all necessary steps should be taken to collect these receivables. This form reflects an "over 90 day" category. Some medical practice software programs will age accounts in 120-, 150-, and 180-day categories; but once an account becomes more than 90 to 120 days old it is difficult to collect, especially from patients. Practices should also consider the use of outside collection agencies to assist in the diligent collection of old accounts.

Exhibit 4.15, "Production and Collection Analysis," analyzes accounts receivable from several perspectives. The first chart is an excellent tool to calculate and monitor the practice's gross and adjusted collection ratios; these activities will aid the evaluation of production and contractual adjustments. This format is also useful in evaluating gross and net productivity for individual physicians and providers.

The second and third charts of this exhibit should be used rou-

Exhibit 4.13
Financial analysis worksheet—aged accounts receivable analysis

Month	Total A/R	Current	30 days	60 days	90 days	Over 90 days
Month 1						
Month 2						
Month 3						
Month 4						
Month 5						
Month 6						
Month 7						
Month 8						
Month 9						
Month 10						
Month 11						
Month 12						
Current %						
Survey Comparison						

tinely to highlight potential problems with payers. When payer variances are discovered, immediate action should be taken to review current EOBs (explanations of benefits) from the insurance companies to determine the cause of the variance. Also, the practice should waste no time in contacting the payers by telephone, if necessary, as soon as irregularities in payments have been discovered. It is important to be proactive in these instances to determine what action, if any, is required by the practice in order to be paid.

Income Statement Percentage Analyses

Percentage analyses allow financial managers to review financial activity at a glance when using percentages as an indicator. A variance, when methods such as these are used, is easy to spot.

Exhibit 4.14

Financial statement analysis

Production and Collection Analysis

Month	Production	Collection	Gross Coll. %	Adjustment	Adjustment %	Net Coll. %
Month 1						
Month 2						
Month 3						
Month 4						
Month 5						
Month 6						
Month 7						
Month 8						
Month 9						
Month 10						
Month 11						
Month 12						
Total						
Monthly Average						

Receivables Aging by Payer Class

Month	Total A/R	Current	30 days	60 days	90 days	Over 90 days
Medicare						
Medicaid						
Indemnity						
PPO plans						
HMO plans						
Workers compensation						
Self pay						
Other						

Receivables Aging by Specific Insurance Company

Month	Total A/R	Current	30 days	60 days	90 days	Over 90 days
Aetna US Healthcare						
Cigna						
Pacificare						
Kaiser						
Healthsource						
Beechstreet						
Blue Cross/Blue Shield						
Prudential						

Exhibit 4.15

Horizontal analysis—Pineway Family Practice income statement (expense portion)

	1999	2000	Variance	± % Change
Staff Salary Expense	$195,000	$198,000	$3,000	+1.5%
Medical Supplies	35,000	36,800	1,800	+5.1%
Administrative Supplies	20,000	21,500	1,500	+7.5%
Telephone Expense	16,000	17,000	1,000	+6.3%
Rent	68,000	69,900	1,900	+2.8%
Depreciation Expense	7,000	7,000	0	0.00%
Equipment Lease	2,500	2,900	400	+16.0%
Professional Services	4,000	4,500	500	+12.5%
Computer Expense	1,500	2,500	1,000	+66.7%
Professional Liability Insurance	12,000	12,850	850	+7.1%
Insurance—General	3,500	4,000	500	+14.3%
Staff Health Insurance	24,000	24,600	600	+2.5%
Staff Retirement Plan	22,000	22,250	250	+1.1%
Staff Payroll Taxes	15,000	16,000	1,000	+6.7%
Answering Service	2,500	3,500	1,000	+40.0%
Other Operating Expenses	1,800	2,900	1,100	+61.1%
Physician Salary	450,000	485,000	35,000	+7.8%
Physician Payroll Taxes	16,000	19,500	3,500	+21.9%
Physician Health Insurance	6,000	6,500	500	+8.3%
Physician Retirement Plan	18,000	22,000	4,000	+22.2%
Total Expenses	$919,800	$979,200	$59,400	+6.5%

Two common methods of percentage analysis employed by businesses are the horizontal analysis (Exhibit 4.15) and the vertical analysis (Exhibit 4.16). The *vertical analysis* measures the percentage of a line item's relative dollar amount to the total in its respective category in the financial statement. For example, in Exhibit 4.16, Pineway's staff salary expense is 21.2% of its total operating expenses, medical supplies are 3.8%, and so on. This type of analysis affords at a glance a picture of how the practice is spending its money; or in the case of different revenue sources, it provides the source of the most revenues. In medical practices, however, the percentage breakdown of revenue sources can usually be obtained from the practice's accounts receivable management software with little effort.

As its name implies, the *horizontal analysis* measures horizontally across comparative years, by line item, the percentage of increase or

Exhibit 4.16
Vertical analysis—Pineway Family Practice income statement, 1999
(expense portion)

Operating Expenses	Amount	% of Total Expenses
Staff Salaries	$195,000	21.20%
Medical Supplies	35,000	3.81%
Administrative Supplies	20,000	2.17%
Telephone Expense	16,000	1.74%
Rent	68,000	7.39%
Depreciation	7,000	.76%
Equipment Lease	2,500	.27%
Professional Services	4,000	.43%
Computer Expense	1,500	.16%
Professional Liability Insurance	12,000	1.30%
Insurance—General	3,500	.38%
Staff Health Insurance	24,000	2.61%
Staff Retirement Plan	22,000	2.30%
Staff Payroll Taxes	15,000	1.63%
Answering Services	2,500	0.27%
Other Operating Services	1,800	.20%
Physician Salary	450,000	48.93%
Physician Payroll Taxes	16,000	1.74%
Physician Health Insurance	6,000	.66%
Physician Retirement Plan	18,000	1.96%
Total Expenses	$919,800	100.00%

decrease in the variance of dollars. Users of the comparative information can easily scan the financial statement to look for trends. For example, if variances in expense amounts increase over several periods, the user should ask why. A positive finding would be that revenue had also increased, thus the practice would also experience an increase in variable expenses. The user should also inquire about any item that is significantly higher or lower than it was in previous periods. The rise may be due to a one-time expense, or it may be due to a misclassified item. Analysis like this is a quick, effective way for management to keep tabs on the business's spending.

Both the vertical and the horizontal analyses can provide useful information. In glancing at the vertical analysis, a manager may have in mind where the expenses should be or typically range; but when this information is used in conjunction with the horizontal analysis, a manager can identify trends that should be investigated. Creeping-up of expenses can happen over time but will not always be identified in a vertical analysis. On the flip side, although the expense amounts may not change, their percentage of the total expense may vary significantly. Therefore, it is a good idea for managers to analyze and review the financial picture from several perspectives. These two analyses are good tools to help managers keep their eyes open.

Internal Control Accounting Related to Medical Practices

OVERVIEW

The use of internal controls in medical practice is, unfortunately, a much overlooked process. However, it is one of the most important management tools available and should be put in place and monitored regularly. Implementing a solid internal control policy is imperative for a practice to protect its assets, especially its cash. A typical medical practice has an average annual cash flow of $500,000 to $2,000,000, a significant amount of which is in hard currency. This much money can be a temptation to many employees, and the medical practice must implement internal controls to protect itself from revenue loss and potential employee embezzlement.

An internal control policy should consist of specific procedures throughout a practice's cash cycle that will deter and hopefully eliminate all possibility of embezzlement and theft. Internal controls are not limited to cash controls, however, as is illustrated in the following real-life examples.

In the first example, the administrator of a certain large, multi-location primary care practice had check-signing authority. The mere fact that the administrator signed the checks was okay; however, this particular administrator also performed all bookkeeping functions for the practice—manually, no less. The practice did not use a computerized accounting package. Among the duties performed by the administrator were preparing the daily deposit slip, taking the deposit to the bank, and reconciling the practice's bank statements. The administrator had total control over the cash cycle. The physicians in this practice trusted their administrator completely. The problem with their total trust was demonstrated when the physicians found that the administrator's W-2 for the prior year showed $85,000. The physicians were alarmed because the administrator's annual salary was $40,000. The difference between these amounts was not attributable (as one might think) to additional compensation approved under a bonus incentive plan; the $45,000 difference was due, unfortunately, to blatant embezzlement that had been justified in the mind of the administrator. The only positive point was that the administrator had included this embezzlement as additional earnings, reporting the activity through the accounting records.

In the second example, immediately following the termination of another practice's administrator, it was discovered that most of the practice's current and most recent prior year records were missing—bank statements, deposit slips, accounts payable invoices, appointment schedule books, encounter forms, and payroll data. Also missing were complete personnel files of all active employees. Several major internal controls in this practice had not been in place; one serious failing, which caused the practice to forfeit so many records, was that the practice administrator had the only key to many of the file cabinets and desk drawers. It is never a good policy that only one person have access to vital records. Although it might sound like a good policy to limit accessibility to one person, this "one person" may be at the root of evil, which, unfortunately, turned out to be the case in this example. The managing physician frequently asked the administrator for various records and was refused or put off in a procrastinating manner; such behavior should be a warning to management that something is wrong.

SEGREGATION OF DUTIES

One of the first lines of defense is a proper "segregation of duties" (see checklist in Exhibit 5.1), on the principle that if it takes more than one person to commit a crime, then it is less likely that a crime will be committed. That is not to say that two employees will not collude in acts of theft, and care should be taken to assign duties to each employee in a manner that deters embezzlement as much as realistically feasible and

Exhibit 5.1
Segregation of duties checklist

DUTY	EMPLOYEE NAME
Opens mail	
Sorts mail	
Routes mail	
Endorses checks	
Copies checks	
Prepares deposit slip	
Takes deposit to bank	
Posts over-the-counter payments	
Posts payments received in mail	
Balances daily closing	
Performs month-end closing	
Approves purchases	
Writes checks	
Signs checks	
Approves refunds/write-offs	
Adjusts accounts for refunds/write-offs	
Maintains petty cash fund/change fund	
Has keys/combination to safe	
Has keys to petty cash/change fund	
Makes backup tapes	
Maintains backup tapes	
Has keys to narcotics	
Checks in merchandise	
Receives bank statement	

practical. Smaller practices are at a disadvantage with this control because they typically do not have enough staff to segregate duties.

A medical practice's main goal in instituting the proper segregation of duties is to ensure that no one employee has too much control over cash, a problem illustrated at the beginning of this chapter. Whether cash is incoming or outgoing, no single employee should have the authority to both accept and deposit cash, or to spend cash alone.

Incoming Cash and Payments

In a medical practice, the cash trail begins with cash and checks received over the counter by the receptionist as patients check in and out,

Exhibit 5.2
Daily deposit summary

DATE: _____ COMPLETED BY: _____

OFFICE LOCATION: _____

Revenue Deposit   _____
Other Deposits   _____

 • Credit Card Deposit   _____
 • Misc. Deposit   _____

Total Deposit   _____
Adjustments   _____

 • Credit Adjustments   _____
 • Debit Adjustments   _____
 • Voids   _____

---

or checks received through the mail. It is important from an internal control standpoint that the right elements are in place at the beginning of the cash cycle in order to prevent theft. One of the first safeguards that should be in place is the certainty that the employee who accepts monies over the counter is not the same employee who prepares the bank deposit slip. Such an overlap in duties would allow this person full opportunity to skim cash from the day's over-the-counter receipts. Cash co-payments are easily stolen without the proper deterrents in place.

Another function in the practice that must be safeguarded is the process of opening and routing the day's mail. The employee responsible for opening and routing the mail, which includes payments received, should not also be responsible for posting payments, which, again, allows the employee the opportunity to steal and the ability to cover up the theft. The employee who opens the mail should immediately endorse all checks received before routing them to the employee responsible for posting. The employee who opens the mail should also run two tape totals of amounts of all checks received. This employee may prepare the Daily Deposit Summary (Exhibit 5.2), but it is preferable, if the practice is large enough, to give this task to a different employee. One tape total should be passed to the employee who will take the deposit to the bank; the other should be forwarded to the employee who posts payments. This second tape should accompany the copies of checks and the EOBs received from insurance companies.

Exhibit 5.3
Daily cash reconciliation

DATE: _____

OFFICE LOCATION: _____

COMPLETED BY: _____

	Charges	**Payments**
Charges and Payments with Superbills	_____	_____
Charges and Payments without Superbills (Hospital Rounds, Nursing Home)	_____	_____
Received on Account		_____
Total Charges and Payments (per paper system)	_____	_____
Total Charges and Payments (per computer)	_____	_____
Total Deposit (per computer)		_____
Total Deposit deposited to bank		_____
Explanation of Any Differences in Totals:	_____	

The employee who posts the payments received in the mail should also run two tape totals on the amounts of these payments. One tape should be forwarded to the employee taking the deposit to the bank; the other should be kept with the daily batch of payment information and used to prepare a Daily Cash Reconciliation similar to the one in Exhibit 5.3. In computerized practices, these amounts should match the end-of-day closing reports that are run from the computer system. These reports should reflect the amount of daily deposits, and are tied back to the daily deposit slips and bank confirmations as controls for payments received.

Details of further segregation of duties in the cash cycle are given in the following section.

HANDLING PAYMENTS

Receipts for Cash Payments

Some practices do not use a paper receipt system for cash receipts such as copayments at the time of service. Patients are usually not alarmed by this lack and trust that the payment will be made to their account—but if an employee understands that he/she can steal the money and cover it up by creative patient accounting, then the practice does not have an effective internal control. The simple act of giving the patient a receipt reminds any employee who may be tempted that there is another variable in the game. It would be difficult for that employee to argue later with a patient who has a receipt from the practice proving that the payment was made. This fact alone may deter an employee from stealing money from the front desk operations.

Another control that should be implemented with regard to the incoming cash is the handling of petty cash and the change fund; the practice should also require staff to list each check separately on the deposit slip and to make deposits daily. Daily posting of payments as well as closing and balancing of each day's activity are imperative to effective internal control. Posting the current day's payments received may sometimes be prohibited because of late local mail delivery times; in this case, all of the previous day's payments should be posted the following day so that the payments are, at most, only one day behind. Don't discount the lost revenue from bad checks or closed accounts. Delays in making daily deposits increases exposure to the practice for theft, embezzlement, and insufficient funds.

Outgoing Payments

A rule of thumb for any business, not just medical practices, is that signature authority for company checks should be highly restricted. In medical practices, the physician-owners are usually the only people who are authorized to sign checks. In smaller practices, this may be only one physician. In larger practices, there may be several, allowing another internal control in place if check-signers rotate "check duty" or if practice staff are directed to go to whichever physician is around at the time. This control will prohibit a staff member's blindsiding one physician into signing checks he or she should not.

A strong word of caution to physicians: Know where your books and records are kept and make sure you have a key. Also, periodically go through your staff's file areas and drawers at night. Remember that if staff are aware that someone is watching and holding them accountable, it is less likely that they will commit theft or even be negligent in their duties.

Closing and Balancing the Day's Activity

Closing and balancing each day's activity in a medical practice is very important to maintain an appropriate level of control, as well as to keep a cycle of paperwork in process without letting it get behind. The daily closing process is the area in medical practices in which the most loopholes exist. Many practices make a good faith effort to perform this function diligently, but fail because the appropriate internal controls are not in place.

What should ultimately occur in the daily closing is:

1. All *payments* accepted over the counter during the day should be accounted for.

2. All *charges* incurred as a result of treating patients during the day should be accounted for.

3. All *patient encounters* during the day should be accounted for.

4. All *charge tickets* printed and/or used during the day should be accounted for.

In order to accomplish this, the practice *must* have mechanisms in place to tie all of these factors down.

Documenting the day's activity begins with the charge ticket, also referred to as an encounter form, router slip, or superbill. Whatever the name may be, this form should capture, at minimum, the data that will follow. In addition to the clinical information, such as CPT codes and ICD-9 codes, the charge ticket should allow for an itemized list of charges, the total charge for the encounter, receipts of over-the-counter payments such as copay and payments on account, and the date of service. These forms, when in carbon format, can also provide the patient with a hard copy receipt.

Patients that make a payment at the practice should *always* be given a receipt, although many practices offer various excuses for not doing so. One frequent excuse is that a CPT code may not have been properly captured on the ticket, and if the patient later is billed for more than was represented on the receipt, he or she may complain of fraudulent billing. Understandably, this is a valid concern for the practice; but it is not an excuse for not providing a receipt to the patient. The real issue is why the codes are being omitted from the forms.

In one example, a practice forwarded all charge tickets from the front reception counter to a business office employee in an upstairs office periodically throughout the day. One of the problems with this approach was that the charge tickets and payments received were not being counted or tracked at the front desk before they moved into the possession of the business office employee. This lack of control can easily result in the theft of cash, or at least provide an environment ripe for lost or misplaced charge tickets that may never find their way to billing. If anyone between the front desk and the business office wanted to steal the money, he or she could just take it and throw away the charge ticket, because at this point, the charges, the payments, even the patient visit, had not been entered into the practice's computer system.

The next step in this practice's system was that the business office employee pulled all chart documentation that corresponded with the charge tickets from the front desk. The business office did this to compare the chart documentation to the charge ticket to ensure that all charges and clinical codes had been captured. This may sound like a good internal control, but keep in mind that if the charge ticket is not passed along to the business office, it is not investigated; and at that point no information regarding these visits had been entered into the computer.

Another problem with this practice's system was the constant delay in the billing process. Because the business office was engaged in checking all the charge tickets against chart documentation, the filing of claims was at least one week behind—and so was the posting of payments (including cash). Although this practice was diligent in making a good faith effort to ensure that charges were not missed and that cash was protected, it was not addressing the issue effectively. Did the practice's system protect its cash? Did its system put controls in place that would deter an employee from theft? Did its system convince an employee that he or she would be caught if stealing from the practice? The answer to all of these questions is NO.

CHARGE TICKETS

A medical practice's charge tickets can work either for it or against it; they can help maintain internal controls or they can be a hindrance. The design and use of charge tickets is another main area in which practices often fail at maintaining internal control. With this problem in mind, it is recommended that charge tickets be pre-numbered to allow the practice a means of tracking patient encounters. At the end of each day, *prior to closing,* all tickets used should be accounted for, including tickets that were prepared for patients who rescheduled, cancelled, or did not show up for their scheduled appointments. It is important that each ticket is accounted for without being an added administrative burden on the staff. This can be accomplished by preparing a Daily Charge Ticket summary sheet like the one in Exhibit 5.4.

Charge tickets can be pre-numbered by the company that prints them. Also, many medical practice management computer systems can number the tickets sequentially, since the tickets are printed in-

Exhibit 5.4
Daily charge ticket summary sheet

DATE OF SERVICE: _____ COMPLETED BY: _____

BEGINNING SEQUENTIAL NUMBER: _____

ENDING SEQUENTIAL NUMBER: _____

Are all charge tickets accounted for?   Yes _____ No _____

MISSING CHARGE TICKETS:

Ticket Number	Reason	Attending Physician
_____	_____	_____
_____	_____	_____
_____	_____	_____

Total Daily Charges $_____
Total Daily Payments over the Counter $_____
   Cash $_____
   Checks $_____
   Credit Cards $_____

house. It does not matter which method is used as long as one of them is put into motion.

As a further step in checking and balancing each day's activity, the practice could use a simple form that documents all activity and monies for the day. An example of this form is included as Exhibit 5.5, Batch Control Sheet. It requires the receptionist or other staff member responsible for this activity to document the beginning and ending charge ticket numbers for the day, and to acknowledge by signature that all tickets are present. Additionally, the form requires documentation of the day's activities by patient, such as total charges, over-the-counter receipts, as well as total number of patient visits. It is also a good habit if the practice uses the daily patient sign-in sheet (see Exhibit 5.6, Sign In Sheet) to verify the number of patient visits, further ensuring that encounters have not been missed.

For a tighter element of control, clinical staff should always escort each patient to the check-out desk. In many practices, it has been experienced that some patients will walk out of the building without turning in the charge ticket, not realizing the impact of this act. Adding to this problem, physicians often hang onto the chart for future dictation, meaning that the only document left to accompany the patient to the check-out desk is the charge ticket. If a nurse would always escort the patient to the counter, the possibility of a patient's leaving the practice before payment has been addressed would be eliminated.

BANK ACCOUNTS

For the larger medical practice, it may be beneficial to maintain several bank accounts. Practices that make large daily deposits will benefit from having the daily receipts deposited into an interest-bearing account. Depending upon local bank relationships and interest rates offered, it is recommended that practices consider opening a Money Market Fund to take advantage of the best opportunity available.

It should be a priority for physicians and practice administrators to build and maintain relationships with local bankers. Banks and their officers can be a tremendous help to physicians in need, especially if the bankers are already familiar with a practice's physicians and financial status.

In addition to a Money Market Fund, many large practices also

Exhibit 5.5
Batch control sheet

DATE:
Total Cash & Checks: _____
Total Charges: _____
Total Cash, Checks, Charges: _____
Starting/Ending Superbill # ____ / ____

OFFICE: _____
COMPLETED BY _____

Number	Patient	Charges	Payments	Type/Check #	Adjustment	Balance
Total						

Exhibit 5.6
Sign-in sheet

WELCOME to our office!
PLEASE SIGN IN

DATE_____

TIME ARRIVED	PATIENT NAME	DATE OF BIRTH	TIME OF SCHEDULED APPT.	PHYSICIAN	NEW PATIENT? YES/NO

open a payroll account. The only purpose of this account is to deposit enough funds to allow the practice to accommodate its payroll on a timely basis without concerns for cash flow.

PURCHASING

The purchasing function in medical practices is usually not a very formalized process; consequently, it is another area that typically needs more controls. In most practices, routine office-related and administrative supplies and services are usually monitored and authorized for purchase by the practice administrator. The practice's routine clinical supplies and services are ordered by the clinical supervisor or coordinator.

When supplies are delivered to the practice, the way the delivery is checked and processed is often inconsistent. To institute a good internal control system, the staff member who orders supplies should not be the same individual who checks in and verifies the order received. Each item should be checked against the packing slip or invoice that accompanies the order. The packing slip should then be initialed and forwarded to the accounts payable, where it should be filed awaiting receipt of the invoice for the shipment.

ACCOUNTS PAYABLE

From an internal control standpoint, accounts payable should be another major area of concern for medical practices. Many medical practices lack proper controls with regard to cash disbursements. Too often, one staff member has too much control over check-writing and payment-approval functions. And too often, physicians find themselves in a position of not knowing what the practice's financial condition is, where the checkbook is kept, where the bank statements are mailed, and where the accounts payable invoices are. This is clearly unacceptable.

The rule of thumb for medical practices is that the only people who should have check-signing authority are the owner physicians—for larger practices, two to three physicians is an acceptable number. Many practices rotate this duty among the responsible physicians, while other practices instruct the staff to have checks signed by the physician who is present at the time. Either option works, and both provide for more than one eye on disbursements at all times.

When accounts payable are processed, it is important that invoices be researched and approved for payment, usually by the responsible physicians, prior to their signing the checks. Invoices should be matched to packing slips, where applicable, and when checks are prepared for signature, the invoices and packing slips should be submitted along with them. The physician who will be signing the checks should review the invoices for validity prior to signing. Finally, invoices should be initialed with date paid and check number, usually by the staff member who prepares the checks.

One problem occasionally seen in medical practices involves the maintenance of medical reimbursement plans—*reimbursement* being the operant word. Many times, rather than requiring the employee to prove payment, the practice simply repays the employees, some of whom find they can turn in duplicate bills and make some money.

ACCOUNTS RECEIVABLE WRITE-OFFS, PATIENT REFUNDS, AND CONTRACTUAL ADJUSTMENTS

Write-offs for bad debt accounts should always be approved by the attending physician, as should patient refunds. Contractual adjustments should also be monitored.

With computerized practice management systems, practice staff can easily make adjustments to patient accounts. When accounts receivable balances climb, there is a great tendency for staff to go into the system and offset old balances.

With regard to deceased patients, inactive accounts receivable balances are often overlooked. However, the appropriate billing action should still be taken on these accounts and the appropriate write-offs be made. Many practices leave these accounts as active balances, thus over-inflating or underestimating certain reporting totals. Additionally, account balances related to patients with hardship cases and no families to care for them still require appropriate billing actions and notations made in the accounts receivable records. Proper care should diligently be taken to document the reasons for waiving payment on hardship cases. Furthermore, the government requires providers to charge no more for Medicare patients than they do for their other patients. It is recommended that practices maintain proper controls to document and follow up on account balances such as these.

One area of accounts receivable that should be monitored and periodically reviewed by the physician is patient refunds, an area often seen as having potential for embezzlement and in many practices it has been. Practice staff are able to set up fictitious patients and generate refunds for which they cash the check and pocket the money. However, to reiterate the focus of this chapter, the more proper controls that are in place making it difficult for employees to bilk the system, the more the practice is protected from theft and embezzlement. Examples of patient refund requests and insurance refund requests are shown in Exhibits 5.7 and 5.8.

Bank Statements

Many loopholes are often found in bank statements and the handling of bank statements in medical practices. Some rules of thumb for bank statements follow.

First of all, ensure that the bank statements are reconciled each month; the sooner a discrepancy or error can be found, the easier it is to correct. When reviewing bank statements, look for large withdrawals and deposits that are out of the ordinary; these should be investigated immediately. A consistently decreasing balance where the practice has not experienced decreasing revenues should also be investigated.

A major rule of thumb for bank statements is that, if possible, they should be mailed directly to the practice's *outside accountant* and reconciled by the accounting firm. If they are mailed directly to the practice, they should subsequently arrive unopened at the accounting firm performing the bank reconciliations for the practice.

All checks should be examined for unauthorized signatures during the bank statement review. Many banks do not offer to return actual checks to businesses with their bank statements, but send only photocopies. It would be wise for physicians to request originals or to go to the bank and look at the backs of the original checks from time to time, especially if the practice disperses a lot of cash in the form of patient refunds. Also, the practice should pay attention to checks that have been used out of order; this is a classic way of hiding missing

Exhibit 5.7
Patient refund request

DATE: _____

Patient Name	Account Number	Amount	EOBs Reviewed?	Reason for Refund	Research Employee Initials	Refund Approved Initials	Adjustment to Computer System Initials

Exhibit 5.8
Insurance refund request

DATE: _____

INSURANCE PLAN: _____

PATIENT ACCOUNT NUMBER: _____

AMOUNT: _____

APPLICABLE EOBS ATTACHED?   Yes _____ No _____

REASON FOR REFUND:

_____ Wrong Patient

_____ Wrong Provider

_____ Duplicate Payment

_____ Overpayment

_____ Other _____

PHONE CALLS MADE TO PAYER
(DATE, CONTACT, RESULT): _____

LETTER PREPARED? (ATTACH COPY) Yes _____ No _____

RESEARCHED BY: _____

REFUND APPROVED BY: _____

ADJUSTMENT TO COMPUTER
SYSTEM MADE BY: _____

---

checks. The practice should also go through the original check forms to ensure that no checks are missing from the numerical sequence among the unused checks. Special attention should be paid to checks that have been ordered and have not been received to insure that these checks did not actually disappear after they arrived at the practice. Voided checks should also be investigated.

Fidelity Bonds

It is highly recommended that every medical practice carry a fidelity bond insurance policy on their employees. This is a business insurance policy that covers the practice and reimburses the owners of the practice in cases of theft and embezzlement by employees.

Employee Vacations

No matter how much the practice staff are trusted by the physicians, and no matter how diligently the staff perform their work, it is imperative that every employee take a vacation. An alarm should go off when an employee refuses to go on vacation; the refusal could be a sign that this employee is trying to hide something. It is often the case in embezzlement situations that the signs of theft are uncovered when the employee is on vacation. For this reason alone, medical practices are encouraged to cross-train employees as much as possible. If the practice staff know how to perform each other's tasks and responsibilities, then additional cross-checks can automatically be put in place as internal controls.

Human Resources

Many internal controls that are often overlooked concern the human resources function of the practice. Of particular concern should be the hiring process. Many practices do not perform background checks and employer verification on applicants, yet, if there is significant information to be gained about an applicant, much would be learned through this process. Background checks should always be performed when applicants are recommended by existing staff members. Our tendency is to let down our guard when it's a friendly interview. Many times an internal recommendation is viewed as, "Well, if she's a friend of Mary's, then she should be okay."

One real-life experience encountered in a medical practice was the case of an accounts receivable collections clerk who was very, very good at performing her job. She had previously worked with another collections clerk, and recommended that clerk for a new opening in the practice where she was currently employed. The practice failed to perform background checks and previous employer verification on this applicant, and only two weeks into his position, the new employee proved to be undependable. He left during the lunch hours and stayed gone for long periods, and at times did not show up on the job at all. The clerk was soon terminated. It was learned later that he had been facing charges for embezzlement from a previous employer, and that the employee who'd recommended him had been fully aware of those charges.

In today's business environment, it is understandable that we all want to trust everyone and hope that everyone is ethical and honest. However, as can be demonstrated in real life from some of these examples, such trust is not always wise. The only real protection for the medical practice or any other business is to implement internal controls to prevent acts of theft. It is much easier to protect the assets of a medical practice from the beginning than it is to pursue litigation and recourse at a later date.

Computer Security

A couple of other important issues with regard to tightening internal controls of a medical practice have to do with computer security, including the control of passwords and back-up tapes and processes.

With regard to passwords, some computer systems will allow passwords that will work for several users at a time. It is recommended, however, that a practice have only one user per password, and that passwords be changed periodically. Staff should be encouraged not to choose obvious subjects as passwords, such as a spouse's, child's, or pet's name, or a birthday or social security number. These subjects, if not already commonly known among staff, are easily obtained.

Computer back-up tapes are another area that practices do not always properly protect. For example, back-up tapes are often made diligently, then haphazardly thrown into someone's drawer, unlocked and unprotected. It is recommended that practices make daily back-up tapes that are kept in a safe overnight. Practices should also make monthly back-up tapes, which should be stored off-site. Depending on the size of the practice and whether it has electronic medical records, it may be beneficial and highly recommended that the back-up tape be taken off-site each day or at least weekly so that these types of records can be preserved in the event of a catastrophe.

Keys

Access and possession of keys to the practice, its safe, deposit boxes, desks, file drawers, narcotics cabinets, supplies, and so on should be safeguarded. All too often accessibility to some or all of these assets has gone unnoticed. Although it is recommended that if more than one employee or physician have access to a given entry, keys in general should be kept out of immediate reach or obvious storage places.

Unfortunately, there are numerous examples of why these safeguards are recommended. In the following case, practice staff tried to be diligent in performing their responsibilities, but were unsuccessful. Although they locked up undeposited checks and monies at night, every single staff member and physician in this practice had a key to the safe. So, what was protected in this case? It could be argued that no one from the outside could come into the practice and steal the money. However, such an act is not the only kind of theft a practice must prevent. Its primary concern, in fact, is to protect itself from its employees—those who have both immediate access and the opportunity to commit theft.

Cash Boxes

The same situation described regarding keys is often experienced with cash boxes. Two types of cash boxes are typically found in medical practices: the petty cash box and the change funds box. Smaller practices will usually only operate with one cash box that functions as both.

Medical practices usually house a petty cash box in the practice manager's office. Change fund boxes are often kept at the front desk because they are used to make change for patients who are making payments over the counter.

When too many employees have access to the cash boxes, having keys to the boxes is useless. In many practices keys aren't even used; the boxes are left unlocked because "it's too much trouble to get the key when we need it." Other practices have keys and keep their boxes locked when not in use. Two questions should be asked if this is the case:

1. Where is the key kept and who knows where it is? One such practice encountered had one key, which was kept hanging on a bulletin board in the break room. This is not a recommended internal control!

Exhibit 5.9
Petty cash log

Date	Item	Cost	Balance
Total:			

2. Can the box (even though it is locked) be easily picked up and carried out of the practice? The answer to this question, too often, is yes. This is especially true with change fund boxes that are kept on and around the front reception or checkout desks.

Change fund boxes have the most potential for theft. These boxes have been seen as open cash drawers, open boxes sitting on desks, and the like. Patients, suppliers, vendors, anyone can easily reach over desks and through windows to grab money. Practices should always count the money and balance at the end of each day. Large practices that have both a change fund and a petty cash fund should count and verify each day the receipts for monies used. Under no circumstances should a practice get into the routine of cashing personal checks for lunches or postage, or of paying for postage for employees, and so on.

Exhibit 5.10
Monthly log

Date	Total Charges	Total Payments	Total Deposits	Balance
Total:				

Many practices think this is okay, but it does loosen control over those funds and the creates a lax and too-trusting atmosphere.

The keeper of the petty cash fund should keep a log of monies spent along with the receipts. This should be kept until petty cash is replenished, and then filed, at which time a new log should be started. For an example of a petty cash log sheet, see Exhibit 5.9; for an example of a log of monies, see Exhibit 5.10.

CONCLUSION

Certainly, many of these recommendations would make a practice believe that it should operate like the Federal Reserve with triple-locked doors of six-inch steel. However, a substantial amount of money flows through a medical practice. For this reason, it should be reiterated that without these internal controls in place, the medical practice is ripe for theft.

In summary, it is recommended that medical practices conduct periodic internal control reviews designed to alert practice management and ownership to possible embezzlement. Reviews should be performed internally throughout the year. It is recommended that at least once a year, a preferably unannounced review be conducted by an independent third party.

Things to Look For

The following is a good checklist that practice management should use to review internal controls periodically. The list was taken from the American Institute of CPAs Consulting Services Practice Aid 97-1: Fraud Investigations in Litigation and Dispute Resolution Services.

Selected Indicia of Fraud

The following listing of selected indicia of fraud is presented for illustrative purposes only and is not exhaustive. The conditions listed do not necessarily indicate the existence of fraud; rather, each is an indication that fraud may be present. Many times legitimate activity or other reasons may explain the indicia of fraud. For example, an employee enjoying a lifestyle not readily explained by his or her current earnings may have previously inherited a substantial sum of money. As a result, the CPA should exercise appropriate caution in forming opinions before an adequate investigation. Even then, the CPA should avoid offering opinions about guilt or innocence since the ultimate conclusion of law is a matter for the tier of fact.

Lack of written corporate policies and standard operating procedures

Lack of interest in or compliance with internal control policies, especially division of duties

Disorganized operations in such areas as bookkeeping, purchasing, receiving, and warehousing

Unrecorded transactions or missing records

Bank accounts not reconciled on a timely basis

Continuous out of balance subsidiary ledgers

Continuous unexplained differences between physical inventory counts and perpetual inventory

Bank checks written to cash in large amounts

Handwritten checks in a computer environment

Continual or unusual fund transfers among company bank accounts

Fund transfers to offshore banks

Transactions not consistent with the entity's business

Deficient screening procedures for new employees

Reluctance by management to report criminal wrongdoing

Unusual transfers of personal assets

Employees living beyond their means

Vacations not taken

Frequent or unusual related-party transactions

Employees in close association with suppliers

Expense account abuse

Business assets dissipating without explanation

Inadequate explanations to investors about losses

If the medical practice will implement the proper internal controls as discussed in this chapter, the practice will be protecting itself from revenue loss through employee embezzlement and fraud. Although there are never any guarantees that embezzlement and fraud will be detected 100% of the time, establishing various internal controls will certainly make them more difficult.

CHAPTER SIX

Cost Accounting

OVERVIEW

Cost accounting in the medical practice is a relatively new phenomenon, although the rest of the business world has been taking advantage of this type of accounting for decades in order to determine their costs. This information allows them to take their products and services to market, and to have enough internal information to permit suitable decision making during negotiations. Medical practices have never really been included in that group of the business world, primarily because medical practices, physicians, and hospitals have always had the luxury of charging a fee for each service provided, then billing the insurance companies or patients. Most insurance companies would pay part or all of the "usual, customary, and reasonable" fee for a particular geographic area, type of service, and/or specialty, and it was left up to the provider entity to bill the patient for the remaining balance.

As the years have passed, the fees for services have risen; accordingly, the health care dollars covering these services have increased as well. As a result, insurance companies have requested more money from the employers who are paying most of the premiums. This rise in costs helped create managed care as a way to regulate the costs of services and the provision of unwarranted services to patients, in an effort to hold down the overall cost of health care. This brings us to where we are today, with medical practices fighting for a decent rate of reimbursement from insurance companies. However, in order to get a "decent rate," medical practices must first know what it costs them to provide the services. Most practices today do not have a good idea of the cost of the services they provide.

Definition of Cost Accounting

To relate the cost of providing services in a medical practice to cost accounting theory, let's use an example taken from the manufacturing world. Everyone can relate to a bag of chocolate chip cookies purchased at a grocery store. The price the customer pays for that bag of cookies includes the direct cost of manufacturing those cookies, that is, the sugar, butter, flour, chocolate chips, ovens, and labor. The price paid by the customer also includes costs that may not be directly related to the product (i.e., the manufacturing of the cookies) as much as they are to the process of delivering the product all the way to the retail store. These costs include, for example, trucks that deliver the product to warehouses or directly to the stores; the salespeople and their company-owned cars, laptop computers, and cell phones; advertising; the production and redemption of coupons; and the design and use of packaging.

When relating this concept to medical practices, physicians and those performing a cost accounting analysis should understand that providing a service to a patient includes not only expenses related directly to the visit or procedure—medical supplies, the exam room, physician and nurse time, and so on—but also includes the cost of the administrative business office, billing and collection, computer system usage, facility rent and equipment lease, malpractice insurance, and all of the other expenses that a medical practice typically incurs in the normal course of its business. These are *all* costs of doing business; therefore, when using cost data to negotiate rates with managed care companies, medical practices need to insure that at minimum they recoup their costs.

There are a variety of ways to analyze costs for medical practices. An analysis can be performed for different procedure codes within a practice, for different doctors, different locations, and so forth, depending on the information a medical practice needs to make decisions, and the information and data the practice needs to control.

Why a Medical Practice Should Perform a Cost Accounting Analysis

Three important reasons exist for a medical practice to perform a cost accounting analysis. The most obvious one is the ability to make cost-based decisions, an impossible task without the cost factor. In the world of managed care, there is absolutely no accurate and reliable way to measure the profitability of a contract without a good understanding of a practice's cost of doing business and providing services.

The second reason is the indirect but enormous benefit of performing a cost analysis: helping the practice increase efficiency. The practice must *know* its operations, and an analysis like this forces staff and physicians to look at operations in a different light. Just by virtue of going through this process, practice management will uncover previously unnoticed facts and details, such as the way certain tasks are performed, how certain forms are used; and what rules are in place, absent, or antiquated and in need of revision.

The third reason is the importance of the cost accounting system itself. Not only will a cost accounting analysis provide a medical practice with a method to determine its costs, it will also, once the framework is put into place, give the practice a system that can be used as an effective management tool on an ongoing basis. It can be used for budgeting, financial performance measurement, and many other managerial decisions.

Note that, when a practice is going through this exercise, the revenue source is unimportant in determining the cost. Not to say that revenue is unimportant, but when you are determining costs it must be remembered that everything a practice does, regardless of whether the practice is charging for the service, is costing the practice money. A prime example is an employee's vacation. Although the practice is paying the employee who is on vacation, the employee is not performing any services, treating any patients, processing any claims, sending out any bills, inputting any data, and so on. However, the fact that no services are being performed does not mean the practice is not incurring a cost, and it is important that all such hidden or obscure costs be taken into consideration. Once the practice has determined its costs, the revenue sources become very important and should be taken into consideration in analyzing and using the results of the analysis to make future decisions.

In order to make full use of the results of a cost analysis for managed care contracting purposes, a practice needs to get comparable information from managed care companies, which can be difficult to do. This information includes the expected utilization by CPT code of plan members, the number of enrollees in the plan for which the practice would be responsible, and patient demographic data such as age, sex, zip code, and so forth of the enrolled members. This information is needed for an "apples to apples" comparison between the productivity, level of illnesses, patient demographics, and so on in the practice's history, as compared to managed care actuarial expectations. Knowing your costs is only part of the managed care decision making process; the more information you can obtain from the managed care company, the more effectively those decisions can be made.

PRELUDE TO THE COST ACCOUNTING ANALYSIS

Performing a cost accounting analysis is not difficult, with the exception of a practice's first one, which may seem overwhelming given the large amount of data that must be processed for the first time. Furthermore, the first analysis will typically be performed in retrospect. This is usually where the difficulty arises because most practices will not always have been tracking and recording data in a manner conducive to performing a cost accounting analysis. Therefore, lots of information will need to be researched and dug out of records, since the general ledger and financial statements more than likely will not provide an appropriate breakdown and description of the practice's historical expenditures. Once the system is set in place, however, cost analysis becomes a revision process thereafter.

In the managed care environment in which physicians operate today, the best denominator to use in a cost analysis is a calculation of a practice's cost per CPT code using relative value unit scales. There are, however, other methods for performing analyses. One of the most common methods, used by large organizations, manufacturing companies and hospitals, is called "activity based costing," or more commonly, ABC. Activity Based Costing measures the drivers of each cost and follows each activity or process from beginning to end. This method tracks activities through time and motion studies to help determine a more accurate cost. "Accurate" is the operant word here—although ABC is a very good method and gets the most accurate type of data if enough sample analyses are taken for each activity, it is not the most cost-beneficial method for the medical practice. Not only are the results of the cost analysis obtained more slowly with ABC, but the difference between ABC and the types of analysis discussed elsewhere in this book are immaterial to medical practices. However, it is nonetheless important for the reader to understand the concept of ABC and to know that it is a very accurate way to perform a cost accounting analysis.

Medical practices should also beware of using cost averages, such as cost per visit, cost per patient, and cost per procedure, when making important managerial decisions. These types of costs may be advantageous if you need a very quick assessment or a good ballpark idea of what a particular cost is, especially within a department, specialty, or doctor. However, in making either important decisions with regard to reimbursement from managed care contracts, or decisions that you will be locked into for a year or more, it is important not to rely solely on costs such as these.

Understanding Cost Behavior

Understanding the behavior of costs in a medical practice is important in order to identify problems of overspending, opportunities for consolidation, and so on. Two terms that are needed in describing the behavior of costs are "fixed costs" and "variable costs." As a practice moves toward a capitated environment from a fee-for-service environment, the distinction between these types of costs becomes more important.

Fixed costs are defined as those costs that typically remain constant, within a relevant range of activity without regard to the level of performance in a practice, such as the number of patients seen, the number of dollars produced, and so on. Whether the practice sees any patients at all is irrelevant; these fixed costs will still be incurred. Examples of fixed costs in a medical practice are rent, malpractice insurance, taxes, and licenses. Staff salaries are typically included in this category as well.

Variable costs are the opposite of fixed costs. *Variable costs* are defined as those costs within the practice that fluctuate with the level of productivity, number of patients seen, and the like. Examples of variable costs in a medical practice are medical supplies, postage, and administrative supplies such as stationery, charge tickets, office supplies, and medical chart supplies.

In most medical practices, the larger amount of expenses are fixed costs, but it is important to understand the behavior of both fixed and variable costs. See Exhibit 6.1 for an illustration of fixed and variable cost behavior and how those in a 100% fee-for-service environment compare to those in a 100% capitated environment, and the difference in profitability and break-even points. Notice on this graph that, until the practice treats a patient in a fee-for-service environment, the practice does not get paid—and the more patients a practice sees, the more money the practice collects. (Remember, regardless of whether the practice treats any patients, the practice still incurs its fixed costs.) After the point at which the practice covers its fixed costs, it will make a profit provided variable costs are covered; see the fee-for-service break-even point on the graph.

Also illustrated on the graph is the break-even point in a capitated environment. The smaller the number of patients treated, the

Exhibit 6.1
Fixed and variable cost behavior

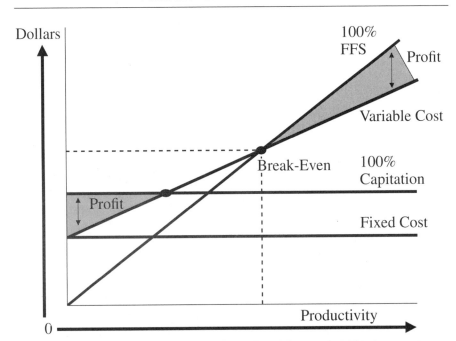

more profitable the practice. As patients are seen and treated, the practice incurs variable costs. Once the practice's level of capitated patients reaches the break-even point, however, the practice loses money on the next patient treated. This scenario for capitation is just the opposite as that for fee-for-service.

Revenue centers (also called profit centers) and cost centers are the next terms that a practice should understand when determining its costs. Before a cost analysis is performed, the first decision that must be made is what the practice will identify as its revenue and cost centers for the purpose of capturing cost data. In other words, how does the practice want to identify its costs (by what areas, locations, specialties, groups of codes, etc.)? This dictates how costs will be allocated.

Revenue centers are defined as those areas of the practice that contribute directly to the production of income. Examples of revenue-producing centers are office visits, surgery, radiology, laboratory, physical therapy, hand therapy, occupational therapy, pharmacy, audiology, allergy, EKGs, sonograms, mammograms, infusion therapy, nuclear medicine, lactation consulting, and immunizations. Other types of revenue centers can be delineated by practice or department location, by physician, by medical specialty, or by any other area of the practice that the physicians feel should be segregated to determine its costs.

Cost centers, on the other hand, are defined as those areas of the practice that, in and by themselves, are not directly related to the production of income, but taken as a whole, are an integral part of the practice. Examples of cost centers in a medical practice are the building or facility, the administration, medical records, reception and appointment scheduling, billing, housekeeping, and so forth. Any of these cost centers can be further broken down into other particular areas; however, the more cost centers a practice wants to identify, the less accurate will be the results in the cost allocation. Therefore, in making the decisions for revenue and cost centers, it is important to understand that *if you do not benefit* from compiling the data, then *do not do it.* In examining the mountain of data it would be possible to analyze, consider (1) whether that data is useful to the decisions you need to make, and (2) whether it is important for you to control that particular kind of data. If the data you want to analyze do not meet one or both of these criteria—if the analysis is not going to lead you to profitable decisions with regard to managed care and the future business of the practice—do not waste the time.

Exhibit 6.2
Direct costs and appropriate cost centers

Direct Cost	Revenue/Cost Center
Radiology technician	Radiology
Clinical Staff Salaries	Office Visits
X-ray Film	Radiology
Computer equipment	Administration
Transcription Services	Medical Records
Rent	Facility
Billing Clerk	Administration

Other cost centers that may be important are the process of pre-certification authorization, and practice staff who contribute almost 100% of their time to dealing with managed care issues. This can be effective information when negotiating with certain payers and illustrating to them the additional costs due to the administrative burden that your practice has experienced through the requirements of their extra paper work and so on.

Direct and Indirect Costs

Additional concepts the practice must also understand are those of direct costs and indirect costs, as mentioned in our earlier example of the production of cookies in a manufacturing environment. Direct costs are those costs that can be directly related to a particular revenue or cost center. When analyzing the practice, every revenue and cost center identified will have direct costs associated with each within its own category. When looking at the practice as a whole, there will be both direct and indirect costs, with the direct costs typically being the revenue centers and the indirect costs being the cost centers. But, again, in looking at each category separately, each revenue center and each cost center will have associated direct costs. Exhibit 6.2 gives examples of a practice's direct costs within each revenue and cost center.

Please note again the important distinction between the direct costs associated with each revenue and cost center and the direct costs

Exhibit 6.3
Indirect costs and appropriate cost centers

Indirect Cost	Cost Center
Billing Clerk	Administration
Business Insurance	Administration
Janitorial Service	Facility
Business Staff Salaries	Administration
Office Rent	Facilities
Office Supplies	Administration
File Clerk Salaries	Medical Records
Medical Chart Supplies	Medical Records

associated with the practice as a whole. Even though some of the cost centers in Exhibit 6.2 are indirect costs to the practice as a whole, each cost center will nonetheless have direct costs associated with it. This is important to the practice as its costs are initially recorded in the accounting records. The more of these costs that can be directly attributed at the time they are incurred to the appropriate revenue and cost center, the easier an analysis will be to perform. Exhibit 6.3 shows examples of a practice's indirect costs.

Also note again that the first decision that needs to be made in performing a cost analysis for a medical practice is the identification of the revenue and cost centers. Everything else in the analysis focuses on this decision. The next step is to begin the project; the following section lists and explains the data needed in order to begin.

Data Needed To Begin The Cost Accounting Analysis

- *Financial Statements.* Your financial statements will provide you with lump-sum information of each account's activity throughout the period. You will especially need detailed expense information.

- *Chart of Accounts.* Your chart of accounts may already be designed to help you, or it may need revisions once the analysis is performed. Again, the first time an analysis is performed it is likely that additional work must be done to obtain the information needed to separate costs into particular revenue and cost centers. Once this first analysis has been performed, it is recommended that the chart of accounts be redesigned to capture the data needed to perform an analysis as identified by revenue and cost centers, as illustrated in the cost study worksheets included with this chapter.

- *General Ledger.* Your general ledger should provide you with details of every expenditure; although the detailed general ledger is designed to do just that, medical practices and accounting firms alike often do not input detailed and informative descriptions. Many times the general ledger will be run for a medical practice and will merely result in a list of check numbers. Needless to say, with a lump-sum category called "supplies" or "repairs and maintenance," it is impossible to know what each expenditure was for, which revenue and cost center it applies to, to whom it should be allocated, and so on, without going back to review each and every check and invoice.

- *Payroll Register.* The payroll register provides an important set of data in performing a cost analysis, because you have a large expense related to salaries, and you want to analyze what each staff member is actually doing with time spent in the practice. A classic example is that of a full time nurse in the medical practice. The automatic assumption would be that that nurse spends 100 percent of his or her time performing patient services, but in most cases this assumption is found to be untrue. In very inefficient practices, the nurse may also be performing laboratory procedures, filing paperwork, making phone calls, answering telephones, scheduling appointments, and the like. It is important to determine, for cost allocation purposes, how the time is being spent by each staff member in order to get an accurate picture of where the resources are going for the services provided. This, in itself, is a very eye-opening exercise for a practice to perform.

- *Depreciation Schedule.* The depreciation schedule is needed to assign depreciation to each revenue and cost center. Typical depreciation schedules of medical practices do not break down specific assets as they should. Further work may be required to determine which asset should be in which revenue and cost center, and the current period depreciation associated with each.

- *Leases.* Lease paperwork will identify graduated lease payment schedules of rates that are planned to increase over the years. If you are performing a year-end cost analysis and negotiating managed care contracts for the following twelve-month period, it would benefit you to use the newly increased rate in the cost accounting model to get a more accurate picture of your future cost.

- *Productivity Report.* The productivity report reflects the frequency of use of each CPT code procedure during the period of the cost analysis. Most computer systems will print a CPT code frequency productivity report for each of its doctors, locations, and so forth.

From all of this data, everything but the productivity report will be included in the numerator of your final calculation of the cost analysis. The productivity report provides the information you will need for the denominator. Once all the information is collected, the cost accounting analysis will provide a division formula that will allow the practice to determine the final cost.

A very, very important point with regard to this list of data is that, when the information is gathered, the numerator data must be *for the same time period* as the denominator data. It is important to look at the cost of providing the services that were performed within the same time frame and to match those expenses with the services performed. It is also recommended that the medical practice's first analysis cover an entire twelve-month period or a calendar year. Most practices experience peaks and valleys in activity and productivity, and in certain costs that are incurred only once or twice a year. It is important to look at the entire cycle when performing an analysis. Realistically, although a practice can perform an analysis for a six-month period or a nine-month period, such frequency will require extra work and caution to prorate the expenses appropriately. It is never recommended that productivity be prorated or annualized.

Physician Compensation

Another matter that should be considered in performing a cost analysis is the level of physician compensation. In a fee-for-service environment, once the medical practice collects revenue and meets all of its operating expenses, the cash left over at the end of the period is typically physician compensation. It is recommended that the cost accounting analysis be performed using more than one level of physician compensation: the level at the time the analysis is performed, and also the desired compensatory levels for the future. For example, if a physician or group of physicians is compensated at market level or below market level and they would like to see an increase in compensation over the next few years, the analysis should be performed with above-market physician compensation levels. Likewise, if physicians are getting a relatively high compensation level and know that, in a particular market area, their reimbursement is going to be hit a little harder in the future, the analysis should be performed with the market level of physician compensation for an idea of what their costs will be. Obviously, a practice will want to negotiate for the highest rate obtainable, but it is good to have internal information of the profit margin ranges that are applicable to the practice. It may also be advantageous to perform the analysis with physician compensation at zero, if operating expense per CPT code is information that a practice needs to make viable decisions. Alternatively, it may be beneficial to perform the analysis by zeroing out operating expenses and plugging in physician compensation to review physician compensation costs per CPT code. Again, it depends on those two important factors of (1) decision making, and (2) the information the practice feels is most important to control.

PERFORMING THE ANALYSIS

The first step in performing a cost analysis is to allocate all of the expenses to each revenue and cost center—that is, to allocate the direct costs. Let's discuss an orthopedic practice by way of example. The expense category we'll consider is Salaries. Included in that expense category are salaries for physicians, x-ray technicians, athletic trainers, and business office personnel. Also within the Salaries category are physician salaries. We will assume that all staff are assigned 100 percent to their respective revenue and cost centers; that is, the expense of physician salaries would be assigned to Office Visits and Surgeries, x-ray technician salaries to Radiology, athletic trainer salaries to Physical Therapy,

Exhibit 6.4
Employee task list for cost accounting

Please describe your routine duties and job responsibilities below. Estimate the amount of time each week that you spend on each task. Your total number of hours should equal those you work during a typical week.

Description of Task	Number of Hours
Total Hours	

Employee Name _____
Date _____

and business office personnel salaries to Administration. (See Exhibit 6.4, "Employee Task List for Cost Accounting," for use in distributing staff salaries to the revenue and cost centers where they are utilized.)

Likewise, in an account called Supplies, office supplies would be allocated to Administration, injectables would be assigned to Office Visits and Surgeries, and patient chart files would be assigned to Medical Records. (See Worksheet 6.1 for a case example of this step.)

The following are examples of the types of costs that should be

Worksheet 6.1
Allocation of Operating Expenses to Revenue and Cost Centers

Operating Expenses	Totals	Office Visits/ Surgery	Radiology	Laboratory	Facility	Administrative	Medical Records	Totals
Lab Supplies	$ 66,849.90			$ 66,849.90				$ 66,849.90
X-Ray Supplies	38,820.85		38,820.85					38,820.85
Phamaceuticals	59,802.32	59,802.32						59,802.32
Medical Supplies	118,678.15	116,853.15	875.00	950.00				118,678.15
Office Supplies/Postage	84,102.51					74,145.51	9,957.00	84,102.51
Telephone	12,055.71					12,055.71		12,055.71
Electricity/Gas	21,606.61				21,606.61			21,606.61
Answering Service	3,272.80						3,272.80	3,272.80
Water & Trash P/U	4,134.37				4,134.37			4,134.37
Maintenance & Repairs (Equip.)	13,531.16	2,499.72	1,803.00	450.00		8,778.44		13,531.16
Repairs to Building	5,000.00				5,000.00			5,000.00
Maintenance Contracts	16,987.59		2,000.00	1,000.00		13,987.59		16,987.59
Laundry & Linens	3,690.95						3,690.95	3,690.95

Rent Expense	129,800.00				129,800.00			129,800.00
Building/Grounds Maintenance	5,576.29				5,576.29			5,576.29
Computer Lease	1,390.02					1,390.02		1,390.02
Travel/Entertainment	2,304.87					2,304.87		2,304.87
Dues/Books/Subscriptions	12,963.61	5,200.00				7,763.61		12,963.61
Advertising/Donations	3,734.74					3,734.74		3,734.74
Insurance	109,082.05	50,984.00	2,000.00	1,500.00		53,098.05	1,500.00	109,082.05
Flowers/Gifts	3,676.40					3,676.40		3,676.40
Uniforms	4,803.84		500.00	500.00		3,803.84		4,803.84
Profit Sharing Plan	99,472.66	70,850.00	1,322.45	3,515.93		20,639.72	3,144.56	99,472.66
Accountants Fee	8,975.00					8,975.00		8,975.00
Property Tax	5,833.52				5,833.52			5,833.52
Payroll—Physicians	650,000.00	650,000.00						650,000.00
Payroll—Staff	572,546.00	200,560.00	28,218.00	39,858.00		258,576.00	45,334.00	572,546.00
Payroll Taxes	64,905.93	34,449.00	2,158.68	3,049.14		21,781.06	3,468.05	64,905.93
Depreciation	13,921.00	2,600.00	2,777.00	501.00	144.00	6,036.00	1,863.00	13,921.00
Totals	$2,137,518.85	$1,193,798.19	$80,474.98	$118,173.97	$172,094.79	$500,746.56	$72,230.36	$2,137,518.85

captured under the three cost center categories used in this chapter's case study.

Examples of Facility Costs

- Building rent
- Janitorial service
- Repair and maintenance on building, such as minor construction, HVAC, and so on.
- Leasehold improvements
- Security systems and alarms
- Pest control
- Landscaping
- Outdoor maintenance

Examples of Administrative Costs

- Business staff salaries and benefits
- Computer system
- Computer system maintenance contract costs
- Office equipment
  —typewriters
  —calculations
  —telephones
  —fax machines
  —maintenance contracts on these assets, if applicable
- Office and administrative supplies and services
  —stationery
  —printing
  —postage

—answering service

—pagers

—bank charges

—billing and collection costs

—accounting

—legal

—telephone

—business insurance

Examples of Medical Records Costs

- Transcription fees

- Transcription staff salaries and benefits

- Dictation equipment

- Transcription equipment

- Supplies
  —dictation sticker labels
  —charts
  —files
  —dividers
  —metal storage files
  —off-site or on-site storage space

- File clerk salaries and benefits

Please note that once the cost accounting system is set up, Worksheet 6.1 can be used as a what-if scenario worksheet. Any of these items can be changed and calculated through the spreadsheets to determine what the cost will be in a given situation. The next step in performing an analysis is to allocate cost centers to revenue centers; in other words, allocate indirect costs to direct costs so that the cost analysis will provide not only the cost of directly treating a patient, but also all of the other practice costs that should be included in providing a particular service. Relating this task back to the cookie example at the beginning of this chapter, we are considering not only the direct costs associated with the package of manufactured cookies, but also all of the other costs within the retail price that you pay at the grocery store.

In order to allocate indirect costs to direct costs or cost centers to revenue centers, we must determine on what basis these costs should be allocated. In the example illustrated in this chapter on Worksheets 6.1–6.5, the cost centers are Facility, Administration, and Medical Records. Facility costs will be allocated on the basis of square footage that each revenue and cost center occupies within the practice. Administrative costs will be allocated on the basis of full-time equivalents of personnel in each of the revenue and cost centers of the practice. Medical Records costs will be allocated based on the number of relative value units worked in each of the applicable revenue and cost centers of the practice.

In another example, if the cost accounting analysis provides for a cost center called Reception and Appointments, an appropriate factor might be a per patient visit basis. If the practice were analyzing the cost of its Billing and Collection department, an appropriate factor might be based on the number of accounts. If it is found that costs will be allocated to the practice's chosen cost centers using all the same factors, it may be pointless to break out these cost centers at all. Again, what information is the practice trying to obtain?

Preferred Stepped-Down Allocation Order

In the second step it is important that the stepped-down allocation order chosen in cost analysis, allocation of indirect cost to direct cost, is logical. To illustrate using the example presented in this chapter, facility costs are stepped-down because it makes sense that each remaining cost and revenue center should be allocated its fair share of all the facility costs. It makes sense also because they are all utilizing space—they are all occupying and taking advantage of this cost center. In this same example, it also makes sense that medical records costs would be allocated last, because the only remaining revenue centers at this point in the calculation are the revenue centers of office visits and surgeries, laboratory, and radiology. Therefore, it makes sense because medical records costs should be attributable only to the services provided in the revenue centers. They should not be allocated to facility and administrative. By default, administration costs are stepped-down second and fall in the middle, because the logic behind facility and medical records is sound. The more cost centers an analysis has, the grayer these allocations can become. Ideally, the more expenses a practice can directly allocate through its chart of accounts to the appropriate revenue and cost center, the less allocation must be done in the analysis, thus providing cleaner and more accurate numbers. The preferred step-down order when using several cost centers would be as follows:

- Facility

- Housekeeping

- Security

- Administration

- Billing and Collection

- Appointment Scheduling

- Precertification Authorization

- Medical Records

Worksheet 6.2 is provided to illustrate this analysis. In a spreadsheet application this is merely a grid to provide the person performing the analysis with the information to make the allocation calculations.

However, it is not recommended that a practice use all of these cost centers to determine its cost. Again, two questions should be answered when identifying revenue and cost centers for a cost analysis: (1) What information is needed to make decisions? and (2) What data are needed from a control standpoint? Unless one or both questions receive substantial answers, it is not beneficial for the practice to analyze given cost center separately.

The third step in cost accounting analysis is to calculate the allocation of the indirect costs to the revenue centers. In performing the analysis based on the allocation factors determined in Step 2 on Worksheet 6.2, refer to "Allocation of Facility Costs" on Worksheet 6.3; notice that the percentage that applies to each revenue and cost center equals the percentage of square footage that these revenue and cost centers occupy in the practice. The direct costs of the Facility cost center are multiplied by this percentage in each of the remaining revenue and cost centers in

Worksheet 6.2

Allocation Factors for Allocating Cost Centers to Revenue Centers

	Total Direct Costs (from bottom of Wksht 1)	Facility: Total Square Footage	Administrative: No. of Full-Time Equivalent (FTE)	Medical Records: Total No. of Relative Value Units
Revenue Centers:				
Office Visits/Surgery	$1,193,798.19	4,500.0	8.0	42,523.86
Radiology	$ 80,474.98	200.0	0.8	6,043.72
Laboratory	$ 118,173.97	280.0	2.3	12,310.10
Cost Centers:				
Facility	$ 172,094.79	N/A	N/A	N/A
Administrative	$ 500,746.56	3,000.0	N/A	N/A
Medical Records	$ 72,230.36	300.0	2	N/A
Totals	$2,137,518.85	8,280.00	13.10	60,877.68

Worksheet 6.3
Step-Down Calculation for Allocating Cost Centers to Revenue Centers

	Direct			Indirect			Totals
	Office Visits/Surgery	Radiology	Laboratory	Facility	Administration	Medical Records	
Direct Costs (from bottom of Worksheet 1)	$1,193,798.19	$ 80,474.98	$118,173.97	$172,094.79	$500,746.56	$ 72,230.36	$2,137,518.85
Indirect Costs							
	54.35%	2.42%	3.38%		36.23%	3.62%	100.00%
Allocation of Facility Costs	$ 93,529.78	$ 4,156.88	$ 5,819.63	($172,094.79)	$ 62,353.18	$ 6,235.32	$0.00
	61.07%	6.11%	17.56%			15.27%	100.00%
Allocation of Administrative Costs	$ 343,877.71	$ 34,387.77	$ 98,864.84		($563,099.75)	$ 85,969.43	$0.00
	69.85%	9.93%	20.22%				100.00%
Allocation of Medical Records Costs	$ 114,860.08	$ 16,324.53	$ 33,250.49			($164,435.11)	$0.00
Total Allocated Indirect Costs	$ 552,267.57	$ 54,869.18	$137,934.96	$0.00			$ 745,071.72
Total Direct & Indirect Costs	$1,746,065.76	$135,344.16	$256,108.93	$0.00	$0.00	$0.00	$2,137,518.85

order to allocate the Facility cost. In essence, we are charging each revenue and cost center its "fair share" of occupying the space in the facility and the costs associated with the facility, such as rent, janitorial service, utilities, pest control, alarm system, and security.

The analysis is continued in this same manner until all cost centers have been allocated to the revenue centers. Once the analysis has made it through Worksheet 6.3, the required numerator information is completed. Notice the bottom right corner of Worksheet 6.3. The total cost should be the exact same as the total cost with which we started in the bottom right hand corner of Worksheet 6.1. Any adjustments or "what-if" calculations should be presented on Worksheet 6.1. Worksheets 6.2 and 6.3 provide support for the allocation of data on Worksheet 6.1. At the bottom of Worksheet 6.3, the indirect cost centers should be zero. All of those indirect costs have been shifted over to the revenue centers by your methods of allocation. However, the total cost for the practice has not changed, as is noted in the bottom of the last column on the right side of Worksheet 6.3.

Now that the numerator information is complete, the practice should calculate the total number of relative value units (RVUs) worked for each CPT code on its productivity frequency report. The Medicare Resource-Based Relative Value Scale (RBRVS) is the recommended scale for this type of analysis, as it has become the scale of choice by most managed care contracts. If practice management knows where the costs lie on this baseline, it is easy to make an "apples-to-apples" comparison when receiving contracts based on the RBRVS scale. See Worksheet 6.4 in this section for an example of this application. RBRVS scale was originally developed scaled to the CPT code 99213, which equaled 1.0 RVU. When RVUs were originally developed, things such as geographic area, physician time, malpractice insurance, educational and technical requirements, and practice operating expenses were considered.

Components of Relative Value Units under RBRVS

In the case example illustrated in this chapter the relative value units used are referred to as the "total RVU." The total RVU under the RBRVS is made up of three components: the first component represents the physician work expense, the second represents the practice's

Worksheet 6.4
Calculating Total Relative Value Units

CPT Code	RBRVS	Frequency	Total RVUs	Cost Per Procedure
Surgery				
10060	1.65	59	97.35	$ 67.75
10061	3.10	15	46.5	127.29
10120	1.73	27	46.71	71.04
10121	3.81	24	91.44	156.44
10140	2.06	9	18.54	84.59
10180	3.48	48	167.04	142.89
11000	1.04	3	3.12	42.70
11050	0.83	3	2.49	34.08
11200	1.24	18	22.32	50.92
11300	1.09	3	3.27	44.76
11305	1.24	42	52.08	50.92
11310	1.48	18	26.64	60.77
11400	1.49	21	31.29	61.18
11401	2.05	18	36.90	84.17
11402	2.59	3	7.77	106.35
11421	2.31	6	13.86	94.85
11422	2.80	3	8.40	114.97
11440	1.90	6	11.40	78.02
11602	4.07	3	12.21	167.12
11730	1.62	30	48.60	66.52
11750	4.15	42	174.30	170.40
11752	5.85	3	17.55	240.21
11765	1.25	96	120.00	51.33
12001	2.32	92	213.44	95.26
12002	2.72	90	244.80	111.69
12004	3.48	12	41.76	142.89

CPT Code	RBRVS	Frequency	Total RVUs	Cost Per Procedure
12011	2.56	9	23.04	105.12
12013	3.10	15	46.50	127.29
12051	3.58	3	10.74	147.00
13120	4.82	30	144.60	197.91
13131	6.00	15	90.00	246.37
13132	10.96	9	98.64	450.03
16000	1.27	3	3.81	52.15
16010	1.22	12	14.64	50.09
16030	2.68	3	8.04	110.04
17000	1.05	69	72.45	43.11
17002	0.30	3	0.90	12.32
17100	0.93	12	11.16	38.19
17110	1.08	15	16.20	44.35
17200	1.04	42	43.68	42.70
20220	2.67	12	32.04	109.63
20520	2.64	30	79.2	108.40
20550	1.28	18	23.04	52.56
20605	1.18	3	3.54	48.45
20610	1.29	12	15.48	52.97
26010	2.07	3	6.21	85.00
28190	2.53	3	7.59	103.88
29065	1.80	6	10.8	73.91
29075	1.48	6	8.88	60.77
29085	1.45	6	8.70	59.54
29105	1.45	3	4.35	59.54
29125	1.01	3	3.03	41.47
29425	2.12	6	12.72	87.05

CPT Code	RBRVS	Frequency	Total RVUs	Cost Per Procedure
29580	1.40	18	25.20	57.49
29705	1.16	3	3.48	47.63
36415	0.26	5017	1304.42	10.68
45330	2.31	123	284.13	94.85
46040	6.99	6	41.94	287.02
46083	2.11	17	35.87	86.64
53670	0.74	3	2.22	30.39
65205	1.10	18	19.8	45.17
69210	0.86	201	172.86	35.31
Total Surgery		**6,451**	**4,249.68**	
Radiology				
70150	1.20	27	32.40	26.87
70160	0.79	36	28.44	17.69
70200	1.23	3	3.69	27.54
70220	1.19	342	406.98	26.65
70250	1.00	24	24.00	22.39
70260	1.43	21	30.03	32.02
70360	0.69	24	16.56	15.45
71010	0.75	36	27.00	16.80
71020	0.96	2717	2608.32	21.50
71100	0.92	102	93.84	20.60
71110	1.22	9	10.98	27.32
71120	0.96	12	11.52	21.50
72010	1.72	123	211.56	38.52
72020	0.66	6	3.96	14.78
72040	0.94	3	2.82	21.05

continued

Worksheet 6.4 (Continued)

CPT Code	RBRVS	Frequency	Total RVUs	Cost Per Procedure
72050	1.38	157	216.66	30.90
72070	0.99	66	65.34	22.17
72074	1.26	33	41.58	28.22
72080	1.01	6	6.06	22.62
72100	1.01	39	39.39	22.62
72110	1.4	230	322.00	31.35
72170	0.78	24	18.72	17.47
72202	0.92	6	5.52	20.60
72220	0.84	12	10.08	18.81
73000	0.77	24	18.48	17.24
73030	0.85	200	170.00	19.04
73050	0.98	18	17.64	21.95
73060	0.84	45	37.80	18.81
73080	0.84	135	113.40	18.81
73090	0.77	55	42.35	17.24
73100	0.74	9	6.66	16.57
73110	0.80	188	150.40	17.92
73130	0.80	277	221.60	17.92
73140	0.63	116	73.08	14.11
73510	0.90	80	72.00	20.15
73550	0.84	9	7.56	18.81
73564	0.78	121	94.38	17.47
73590	0.78	55	42.90	17.47
73610	0.80	377	301.60	17.92
73630	0.80	395	316.00	17.92
73650	0.72	15	10.80	16.12
73660	0.63	29	18.27	14.11

Worksheet 6.4 (Continued)

CPT Code	RBRVS	Frequency	Total RVUs	Cost Per Procedure
74000	0.80	21	16.80	17.92
74020	1.05	71	74.55	23.51
Total Radiology		**6,298**	**6,043.72**	
Laboratory				
80006	0.23	24	5.52	4.79
80007	0.23	18	4.14	4.79
80019	0.31	293	90.83	6.45
80050	0.23	1,881	432.63	4.79
80058	1.14	75	85.50	23.72
80059	0.34	39	13.26	7.07
80061	1.92	170	326.40	39.95
80092	0.44	30	13.20	9.15
80156	0.86	6	5.16	17.89
80162	0.61	57	34.77	12.69
80168	0.61	30	18.30	12.69
80178	0.61	6	3.66	12.69
80184	0.76	12	9.12	15.81
80185	0.59	75	44.25	12.27
80194	0.78	3	2.34	16.23
81000	1.68	3363	5649.84	34.95
81025	0.15	51	7.65	3.12
85055	0.19	3	0.57	3.95
82150	0.61	51	31.11	12.69
82270	0.19	313	59.47	3.95
82310	1.09	213	232.17	22.68
82370	0.53	3	1.59	11.03

continued

CPT Code	RBRVS	Frequency	Total RVUs	Cost Per Procedure
82533	0.67	3	2.01	13.94
82607	0.71	27	19.17	14.77
82670	0.80	9	7.20	16.64
82746	0.74	15	11.10	15.40
82948	0.19	348	66.12	3.95
82952	0.40	27	10.80	8.32
83001	0.72	15	10.80	14.98
83002	0.71	6	4.26	14.77
83020	0.58	3	1.74	12.07
83036	0.27	104	28.08	5.62
83540	0.76	15	11.40	15.81
83718	0.90	33	29.70	18.72
83725	0.00	3	0.00	0.00
83735	0.76	12	9.12	15.81
84132	0.49	51	24.99	10.19
84146	0.67	3	2.01	13.94
84153	1.18	117	138.06	24.55
84155	0.87	101	87.87	18.10
84165	0.21	9	1.89	4.37
84403	1.24	6	7.44	25.80
84439	0.23	278	63.94	4.79
84443	0.46	335	154.10	9.57
84450	0.99	3	2.97	20.60
84550	0.32	36	11.52	6.66
84703	0.71	523	371.33	14.77
85014	0.11	158	17.38	2.29
85018	0.08	3	0.24	1.66

CPT Code	RBRVS	Frequency	Total RVUs	Cost Per Procedure
85024	0.40	6,308	2523.20	8.32
85610	0.84	695	583.80	17.48
85651	0.48	34	16.32	9.99
85730	0.34	5	1.70	7.07
86038	0.50	15	7.50	10.40
86039	0.53	9	4.77	11.03
86060	0.53	3	1.59	11.03
86287	0.27	18	4.86	5.62
86290	0.57	3	1.71	11.86
86291	0.61	36	21.96	12.69
86293	0.44	3	1.32	9.15
86295	0.48	3	1.44	9.99
86299	0.55	3	1.65	11.44
86302	0.51	21	10.71	10.61
86317	0.65	183	118.95	13.52
86403	0.44	1,265	556.60	9.15
86430	0.57	3	1.71	11.86
86431	0.23	30	6.90	4.79
86580	0.32	12	3.84	6.66
86585	0.26	147	38.22	5.41
86592	0.32	84	26.88	6.66
86644	0.57	3	1.71	11.86
86665	0.68	6	4.08	14.15
86671	0.46	6	2.76	9.57
86701	0.52	72	37.44	10.82
86762	0.57	18	10.26	11.86
86765	0.61	6	3.66	12.69

continued

CPT Code	RBRVS	Frequency	Total RVUs	Cost Per Procedure
86787	0.57	18	10.26	11.86
86900	1.58	6	9.48	32.87
87045	0.32	21	6.72	6.66
87070	0.23	33	7.59	4.79
87086	0.43	75	32.25	8.95
87177	0.46	36	16.56	9.57
87178	0.32	6	1.92	6.66
87205	0.51	3	1.53	10.61
87206	0.19	18	3.42	3.95
87220	0.17	3	0.51	3.54
87230	0.21	3	0.63	4.37
87252	0.57	3	1.71	11.86
88150	0.27	198	53.46	5.62
88312	0.10	18	1.80	2.08
Total Laboratory		**18,391**	**12,310.10**	
Office Visits/Medicine				
90703	0.62	176	109.12	25.46
90724	0.58	40	23.20	23.82
90732	0.93	6	5.58	38.19
90780	1.14	32	36.48	46.81
90781	0.57	3	1.71	23.40
90782	0.11	127	13.97	4.52
90784	0.49	3	1.47	20.12
92002	1.39	3	4.17	57.07
93000	0.80	453	362.40	32.85
93005	0.46	876	402.96	18.89

Worksheet 6.4 (Continued)

CPT Code	RBRVS	Frequency	Total RVUs	Cost Per Procedure
94650	0.40	666	266.40	16.42
94760	0.27	810	218.70	11.09
95115	0.39	174	67.86	16.01
99201	0.91	801	728.91	37.37
99202	1.44	3,433	4943.52	59.13
99203	1.99	821	1633.79	81.71
99204	2.96	143	423.28	121.54
99211	0.40	459	183.60	16.42
99212	0.79	3,322	2624.38	32.44
99213	1.13	5,501	6216.13	46.40
99214	1.71	2,289	3914.19	70.21
99215	2.70	165	445.50	110.86
99222	3.27	1,906	6232.62	134.27
99232	1.55	3,945	6114.75	63.64
99238	1.83	1,803	3299.49	75.14
Total Medicine/Office Visits		**27,957**	**38,274.18**	
Grand total		**59,097**	**60,877.68**	

overhead expense, and the third represents the practice's malpractice insurance expense. These three components together represent the total RVU, which is used in this type of analysis because it allows an "apples to apples" comparison when the numerator of the equation includes physician, overhead, and malpractice expenses. All of these expenses are necessary to generate the total amount of revenue that has been produced in treating the practice's patients.

If an RVU has a zero value, the physicians should help establish a close semblance of an RVU to a more accurate analysis. The fact that Medicare does not pay for a particular code and the RVU is zero does not mean that the medical practice didn't perform work and expend resources to perform the procedure.

Please notice that Worksheet 6.4 is categorized by the revenue centers chosen for the analysis, reiterating the importance of the practice's making these decisions *prior* to performing the analysis. Notice that at the end of each section the Total Relative Value Units are calculated. This total serves as the denominator in the first important calculation, which finds the Cost Per Relative Value Unit (or Cost Per RVU).

For example, the total direct and indirect costs from the bottom of Worksheet 6.3 for Radiology are $135,344.16. The Total Relative Value Units (RVUs) worked in Radiology, found on Worksheet 6.4, are 6,043.72. By dividing the total RVUs into the total costs, a Cost Per Relative Value Unit of $22.39 is calculated, as can be seen on Worksheet 6.5. The next step is to use the Cost Per RVU to determine the practice's cost per CPT code procedure, as seen in Worksheet 6.4 in the last column. These numbers are calculated by multiplying Radiology's Cost Per RVU, which is $22.39 as found on Worksheet 6.5, by the RVU for each CPT code. Let's take, for example, CPT code 71020. If the Cost Per RVU is $22.39 and the RVU for this CPT Code is .96, the practice's Cost Per Procedure for this CPT code is $21.50.

The important distinction to be made here is that this cost is based on the level of operations, productivity, and expenditures that are included in this cost analysis as well as on the level of physician compensation included in the analysis. It is very important to understand that these numbers are subject to change.

Again, it is *highly* recommended that this analysis be performed periodically. This is not something that can be performed once and thrown in a drawer, leaving the physicians to assume thereafter that their cost is always "X." Cost must, in fact, be monitored on an ongoing basis. The determination of the practice's Cost Per Procedure is only a first (though crucial) step. The results can be used in calculations of capitation examples and for comparison with managed care fee schedules by CPT code—underlining the importance of getting as much information as possible from the managed care companies. Costs form only one piece of the puzzle—albeit a big piece!

Cash versus Accrual Basis

Two types of analysis may be beneficial in performing a cost analysis for a business that keeps its books on the modified cash basis of ac-

Worksheet 6.5
Calculating Results Per Relative Value Unit

Revenue-Producing Centers	Office Visits/Surgery	Radiology	Laboratory	Totals
Total Direct and Indirect Costs (from bottom of Worksheet 3)	$1,746,065.76	$135,344.16	$256,108.93	$2,137,518.85
Total RVUs in Each Revenue Center (from Worksheet 4)	42,523.86	6,043.72	12,310.10	60,877.68
Total Cost per RVU (Total dir. & indir. cost divided by total RVUs in each revenue center)	$41.06	$22.39	$20.80	$35.11

counting, which includes most medical practices. In the first type, the analysis is performed on a true cash basis with adjustments made for items that are not reported on the cash basis, such as depreciation. The goal is to make the analysis on a true cash flow basis, which gives a realistic view of a practice's cost based on its current level of cash required to cover operating expenditures and debt repayment. For example, let's say a practice purchased a piece of medical equipment and financed it over three years. The equipment was fully depreciated in year one because of the practice's ability to take advantage of the tax law IRC Section 179, which allows depreciation for small businesses up to a certain amount each year. Financial statements in year two, however, will not reflect depreciation on this piece of equipment but *will* reflect principle and interest payments on the financing of the equipment. The point is that the lack of depreciation does not mean the practice had no cash outlay related to the equipment. It is assumed that the practice did incur interest expense, which would be reflected on its income statement for year two, and principal payments, which would be reflected as decreased liability balances on its balance sheet for year two.

In the second type of analysis, the cash basis financial statements are converted to the accrual basis. As is discussed elsewhere in this book, the accrual basis affords the practice a much more accurate picture of its true cost in that it matches the revenues produced during the period being analyzed with the expenses attributable to the production of those revenues during the same period. In the cash basis, for example, a malpractice insurance premium may be paid in July for the subsequent six-month period of coverage; however, under the accrual basis, even though the premium was paid in July, 1/6 of that premium would be accounted for in each month between July and December. The accrual basis would also include the accounts receivable balance with an estimated percentage of uncollectable accounts. The net revenue should be close to the amount that the practice actually shows as cash collection on the cash basis for its current level of operation. The accrual basis also shows depreciation and amortization expenses, as does the modified cash basis of accounting. The accrual basis financial statements also reflect accounts payable to vendors and suppliers that are yet to be paid. It should also reflect profit sharing contributions, accrued and not yet paid, as well.

Importance of Correct CPT Coding

Physicians' and other providers' CPT coding frequencies have a direct impact on the results of a cost analysis. Since the denominator used in the cost equation is made up of the Relative Value Units associated directly with the CPTs that were performed, coding must be as accurate as possible. Current Procedural Terminology coding should reflect the resources that were used in the practice to provide the services. The RVUs represent the work required and the resources expended that go into a particular procedure. Therefore, if CPT coding reflects lower than average frequency of code usage, the RVUs will likewise be lower than average, and when the cost analysis is performed it will result in an inflated cost. Similarly, if coding is skewed to the higher levels, the RVUs used in the cost analysis will be inflated and the result of the cost analysis will be lower is realistic. A practice would benefit from studying its coding frequencies and insuring that coding is as accurate as possible. (See the "Evaluation and management CPT review" chart, Exhibit 6.5.)

If a practice uses, for example, the resources to perform a 99213 office visit procedure but codes the procedure as 99212, it is doing itself an injustice, because although it is truly using the resources for a 99213 it is getting paid for only a 99212. It is recommended that practices have their coding and charts reviewed for accuracy. Obviously, not only does this affect the results of the cost analysis, but it is also important from a fraud and abuse standpoint to have proper documentation in the charts to support the codes used.

Multiple Surgeries

When multiple surgeries are billed to the insurance company, modifiers are used because payers believe that it costs less to perform a second and third procedure on a patient after the first procedure has been performed, due to the convenience and advantage of having the patient already in the hospital. Therefore, the payer may reimburse the second procedure at 75% of the allowable amount and the third procedure at 50% of the allowable amount. What this means from a cost analysis standpoint is that the second procedure realistically used only

Exhibit 6.5
Evaluation and management CPT review

PRACTICE NAME: _____

WORKSHEET PREPARATION DATE: _____

CPT Code	Frequency	Percentage
99201	_____	_____
99202	_____	_____
99203	_____	_____
99204	_____	_____
99205	_____	_____
Total		100%
99211	_____	_____
99212	_____	_____
99213	_____	_____
99214	_____	_____
99215	_____	_____
Total		100%
99221	_____	_____
99222	_____	_____
99223	_____	_____
Total		100%
99231	_____	_____
99232	_____	_____
99233	_____	_____
Total		100%
99241	_____	_____
99242	_____	_____
99243	_____	_____
99244	_____	_____
99245	_____	_____
Total		100%
99251	_____	_____
99252	_____	_____
99253	_____	_____
99254	_____	_____
99255	_____	_____
Total		100%
99291	_____	_____
99292	_____	_____
Total		100%

Exhibit 6.6
Summary of managed care reimbursement

PRACTICE NAME: _____
WORKSHEET PREPARATION DATE: _____

CPT Code	Current Fee	Plan___ Reimb	% Discount	Plan___ Reimb	% Discount	Plan___ Reimb	% Discount	Plan___ Reimb	% Discount	Plan___ Reimb

Exhibit 6.7
Estimating case scenario costs with drugs/pharmacy

CPT Code	Cost per RVU	Relative Value Unit	Cost per Procedure	Frequency	Total Cost
99204	$ 41.06	2.96	$ 121.54	1	$ 121.54
99212	$ 41.06	0.79	$ 32.44	8	$ 259.52
93000	$ 41.06	0.80	$ 32.85	2	$ 65.70
71020	$ 22.39	0.96	$ 21.49	2	$ 42.99
Subtotal					$ 489.75
Add Billable Drugs/Pharmaceutical:					
Drug Dosage A:					
Invoice Cost			$ 13.00	2	$ 26.00
Drug Dosage B:					
Invoice Cost			$ 34.00	1	$ 34.00
Total Case Cost					
(Including Drugs)					$ 549.75

75% of the resources that the first procedure used, because the patient was already in the hospital and prepared for the procedure.

The third procedure is assumed to have used only 50% of the resources of the first procedure. In a cost analysis, the same mathematical application should be made to the RVUs associated with the second and third procedures. A medical practice's software system should be able to track CPT codes that have modifiers by frequency; therefore, in the analysis multiply the RVU associated with the procedure that was performed second by 75% and the RVU for the procedure that was performed third by 50%. This will give the practice a close approximation of the resources that were actually consumed to perform the second and third procedures.

COST ACCOUNTING ANALYSIS RESULTS AND MANAGED CARE

Refer to Exhibit 6.6 "Summary of managed care reimbursement," for an example of how to apply the cost per RVU and the cost per procedure to managed care scenarios. The results of an analysis, along with further information and data obtained from managed care companies and other data sources, can help practice management make better informed decisions regarding the acceptance and negotiation of managed care contracts.

Inclusion and Exclusion of Drugs/Pharmaceuticals Costs

An added consideration in performing a cost analysis is whether to include certain pharmaceutical and drug costs. Notice in the case example presented in this chapter that Worksheet 6.1 depicts pharmaceutical costs. If the medical practice administers expensive drugs, such as those used in chemotherapy, or drugs given in different dosages than commonly packaged by the pharmaceutical company, and bills the patient for these drug costs as well as for the administration of these drugs, it may benefit the practice to initially pull these costs out of the equation on Worksheet 6.1. When the pharmaceuticals are left in the model, the cost per CPT code reflects a portion of these drug costs spread out according to the allocation factors—in other words, each CPT code reflects a piece of these costs (see the example regarding the drug cost scenario, Exhibit 6.5). Simply running the cost analysis without these costs included results in a cost per CPT code. Once the cost per CPT code is known, the specific drug cost associated with a particular routine visit or case can be added to those CPT code costs. This gives the physicians good information regarding a particular case or routine type of visit and helps them negotiate for case rate reimbursement as well as helping with other managerial decisions.

See Exhibit 6.7, "Estimating case scenario costs with drugs/pharmacy," which illustrates the use of analysis results that ignore the drug costs. Note how the applicable drug costs are then added back into the cost for the particular clinical case.

SUMMARY

In summary, it is imperative that medical practices use cost analysis for informed management decision-making. This chapter has illustrated many applications for this type of information. Recognize that in a managed care environment, a practice can ill afford to ignore the value of cost analysis.

Special Accounting Issues Related to Medical Practices

OVERVIEW

Throughout the 1980s and most of the 1990s, the pace at which medical practices have merged into larger groups and then been purchased by hospitals and health systems has been fast and furious. This pace has slowed down over the last few years, however, which can be attributed to several factors. First, the number of practices available for merging or acquisition is much smaller than it was even a few years ago. Second, the early buyers of practices encountered problems that have taught us both good ways and bad ways to acquire practices. And third, the efforts to develop fully-integrated delivery systems have met with limited success.

Regardless of the reasons behind a practice acquisition or merger, a practice valuation is always used to support the purchase price. Valuations are done both by accounting firms and by consulting firms that are independent of both the medical practice and the purchaser.

Entire books have been written on this subject, so the discussion here will focus on just some of the main pointers. Most transactions outside the health-care industry calculate a purchase price as simply the one agreed upon by both the buyer and the seller. Often such agreements are reached without an independent, fair market valuation report to back up the purchase price. In the health-care industry, the purchase price is often based solely on the fair market valuation report. The difference is that in health-care transactions, private inurement issues sometimes restrict the purchaser to paying no more than fair market value.

Valuation of Medical Practices

One may choose among several methods of valuing businesses. Since each method relies on different assumptions, it is rare that the different methods will arrive at identical values. The different valuation methods are as follows; the subsequent examples, for the sake of simplicity, will all assume that the same practice is being valued.

- Cost or asset approach

- Income approach using excess earnings

- Income approach using discounted cash flow

- Market approach

Cost or Asset Approach

The cost approach is the easiest method to calculate and can be thought of as either the cost of building the business from scratch (reproduction cost), the cost of replacing the business (replacement cost), or the value of the assets today (book value). It is appropriate to use the latter method for a business the majority of whose ability to generate a profit is based on tangible assets. For example, a manufacturing plant has high capital needs, and book value would be a reasonable valuation method for the plant. In the book value method, the balance sheet is examined and any appropriate adjustments are made to arrive at the valuation. Such adjustments usually account for inventory calculations, depreciation methods, and market prices for buildings and land. Medical practices usually have limited tangible assets, and thus have scant need for the book value method of valuation.

In Exhibit 7.1, "Cost Approach," the adjusted book value of the practice assets (assuming an asset acquisition) would be $204,000, and the adjusted book value of the stock (assuming a stock acquisition) would be $114,000. What this method does not take into consideration is the ability of the medical practice to generate cash flow into the future.

Exhibit 7.1
Cost approach

	Book Value	Adjustments	Adjusted Book Value
Cash and Cash Equivalents	12,000	0	12,000
Inventory	6,000	1,000	7,000
Accounts Receivable	25,000	(9,000)	14,000
Short Term Assets	43,000	(8,000)	33,000
Furniture, Fixtures, Equipment, net	29,000	5,000	34,000
Building	100,000	10,000	110,000
Land	10,000	15,000	25,000
Long Term Assets	139,000	30,000	169,000
Total Assets	**182,000**	**22,000**	**204,000**
Accounts Payable	5,000	0	5,000
Other Payables	1,000	2,000	3,000
Short Term Liabilities	6,000	2,000	8,000
Notes Payable	50,000	0	50,000
Shareholder Equity	10,000	0	10,000
Retained Earnings	116,000	20,000	136,000
Long Term Liabilities	176,000	20,000	196,000
Total Liabilities	**182,000**	**22,000**	**204,000**

Income Approach Using Excess Earnings

A better method of valuation for medical practices is the excess earnings method, which takes into consideration the practice's ability to generate a profit. In this methodology, the excess earnings of the practice are capitalized and risk factors are accounted for. This value is the estimated goodwill. Accounts receivable and other tangible assets are valued separately.

In most medical practices, all earnings are paid out at year end in order to avoid double taxation. Thus, unadjusted earnings are usually zero, which leaves no goodwill value. Adjustments must then be made to standardize the earnings, such that certain expenses that physicians have been allowed to run through the practice are usually excluded, and physician compensation is adjusted to an average physician salary. The purpose of the latter adjustment is to calculate the bonus or additional compensation that a practice has generated for being better than average.

In Exhibit 7.2, the income approach using excessive earnings

Exhibit 7.2
Income approach—excess earnings

	Prior Fiscal Year
Revenue, Cash Basis	600,000
Practice Expenses, Adjusted	(300,000)
Gross Profit before Physician Expense	300,000
Physician Expense (MGMA Standard)	(175,000)
Excess Earnings of Practice	125,000
Capitalization Rate	25%
Estimated Goodwill Value	**$500,000**

yields a total goodwill of $500,000. To this amount would be added the $14,000 in accounts receivable and $190,000 for all other assets.

Income Approach Using Discounted Cash Flow

The most popular method of valuation for medical practices is the discounted cash flow method, which takes into consideration the practice's ability to project both its revenue and its expenses into the future. The factors involved are projected earnings, projected overhead expenses, projected physician expenses, projected capital expenditures, and the risk involved in meeting cash projections. Considered together, these factors represent the estimated goodwill. Accounts receivable and other tangible assets are valued separately.

In order that projections may be made, the practice operations must be assessed and then a number of modifications made that assume what the future cash flow will be. These modifications include number of visits, patient mix, charges, collections, hours worked, rent and utilities, supplies, equipment, personnel costs, staffing ratios, physician compensation, inflation factors, direct competition, and any other issues that could impact the practice. Typically, these projections are made for five years. The terminal year represents year 6 and every year into the future; the capitalization rate is used to determine the terminal year cash flow. The present value of years 1 through 5 plus the terminal year are added to arrive at the value of the goodwill.

In Exhibit 7.3, the income approach using discounted cash flow yields a total goodwill of $655,059. To this amount would be added the $14,000 in accounts receivable and $190,000 for all other assets. Though

Exhibit 7.3
Income approach—discounted cash flow

	Base Year	Year 1	Year 2	Year 3	Year 4	Year 5	Terminal
Revenue	600,000	675,305	675,305	695,564	716,431	737,924	
Overhead	300,000	309,000	318,270	327,818	337,653	347,783	
Physician Expense	175,000	180,250	185,658	191,228	196,965	202,874	
Financing Expenses	0	57,305	38,764	39,927	41,124	42,357	
Net Cash	125,000	128,750	132,613	136,591	140,689	144,910	144,910
Capitalization Rate	100%	100%	100%	100%	100%	100%	20%
Cash Flow	125,000	128,750	132,613	136,591	140,689	144,910	724,550
Discount Rate		22%	22%	22%	22%	22%	22%
Present Value		105,533	89,098	75,222	63,507	53,617	268,083
Total, Years 1–5	386,976						
Terminal Year	268,083						
Total Goodwill	655,059						

somewhat simplified, the example does illustrate the more important points.

Market Approach

Another method of valuation for medical practices is the market approach method, which takes into consideration what other buyers are paying for similar practices. In this methodology, several factors are taken into consideration to determine a peer group on which to base the "going rate," or the market price estimate. These factors include the size of the practice in terms of revenue, FTE physicians, or both; the specialty or sub-specialties of the physicians; the geographic location; and the level of capitation in the market. The value derived is the estimated goodwill. Accounts receivable and other tangible assets are valued separately.

In Exhibit 7.4, the goodwill of the practice under the market approach would be $270,000. To this amount would be added the $14,000 in accounts receivable and $190,000 for all other assets.

Exhibit 7.5 shows which factors are taken into account in each methodology.

Weighted-Average Methodology

The weighted-average methodology, which takes several techniques into consideration, is appropriate when several different methods are

Exhibit 7.4
Market approach

	Prior Fiscal Year
Revenue, Cash Basis	600,000
Market Rate[1]	45%
Estimated Goodwill Value	**$270,000**

[1]Based on Goodwill Registry, as discussed on page 187.

Exhibit 7.5
Factors taken into account for each methodology

	Book Value	Excess Earnings	Market Price	Discounted Cash Flow
Revenue	No	Yes	Yes	Yes
Overhead	No	Yes	No	Yes
Physician Expense	No	Yes	No	Yes
Risk	No	Yes	No	Yes
Future Changes	No	No	No	Yes
Market Conditions	No	No	Yes	Yes
Easy to Calculate	Yes	Yes	Yes	No

used to determine the value of the medical practice. Each methodology is assigned a specific weight, the calculation for that method is multiplied by the weight, and then all the factors are summed to arrive at the final valuation. For example, the market approach recognizes what other similar practices are selling for. By incorporating this method, the buyer and seller are recognizing what is happening in the market place. The excess earnings method recognizes the historical performance of the practice; the discounted cash flow method recognizes what is expected in the future. Thus, the blend of these three approaches should be a fair representation of the value. In Exhibit 7.6, the goodwill value under the weighted-average methodology is $531,530. To this amount would be added the $14,000 in accounts receivable and $190,000 for all other assets.

Benchmarks for Goodwill

There are several sources for benchmarking goodwill in medical practice valuations. Not all have a comprehensive database for every type of transaction, so it may be necessary to check with several sources for

Exhibit 7.6
Weighted-average methodology

	Value	Weight Factor	Total
Market Approach	270,000	20%	54,000
Excess Earnings	500,000	30%	150,000
Discounted Cash Flow	655,059	50%	327,530
Total		100%	531,530

a given valuation. A number of sources are listed here; a few have an additional explanation.

- Goodwill Registry

- BoxComps

- Done Deals

- Mergerstat Review

- Robert Morris & Associates

- Institute of Business Appraisers

- The Center for Health Care Industry Performance Studies

- Proprietary databases

- Public databases

Goodwill Registry.   The most popular source of medical-practice acquisition data is the Goodwill Registry, a large database that is often purchased and used by consulting companies with valuation practices. This database of physician acquisitions can be used to determine what the market is paying for similar medical practices. The report can be sorted by practice specialty, practice location, or practice size (per physician or gross revenue), as well as by recent transactions.

Proprietary Databases.   Many valuation consultants keep a database of all of the valuations they perform. Their internal databases are proprietary and confidential and thus not for sale. Proprietary databases are maintained by valuation consultants in order to benchmark future valuations, often in conjunction with the Goodwill Registry.

These proprietary databases usually track the same data elements as the Goodwill Registry does.

Public Databases.   Purchases of physician practices that are subject to public scrutiny (as when the purchaser is a publicly held company) are reported through the Securities and Exchange Commission. While there is no formal database, purchases can sometimes be aggregated to form a reasonable benchmark.

GOODWILL AND OTHER INTANGIBLES IN MEDICAL PRACTICE ACQUISITIONS

Since a medical practice is a provider of services, the true value of the practice is its ability to generate cash flow. The value of the expected future cash flow, as mentioned earlier, is called goodwill; goodwill and other intangibles are an inevitable result of the valuation process. Depending on the methodology being used, the type of transaction, and the terms of the deal, the impact on accounting and tax issues will vary significantly. Please remember that the following discussion constitutes a business primer only; qualified business and legal advice should be sought in any medical practice acquisition.

Asset Classifications

Section 1060 (a) of the Internal Revenue Code provides the rules regarding allocations of asset purchase prices. A residual method is used to allocate the total purchase price among the five categories of assets, first to Class I, then to Class II, and so on. Any residual amount not falling in the first four classes is allocated to Class V. (Real estate is not typically included in the purchase of a physician practice.) A description of the categories of assets and their respective asset allocations follows.

Class I, "Cash and Cash Equivalents," includes checking and bank accounts. Cash and its equivalents are very easy to calculate. The only issue is whether cash is included in the purchase, and if not, that the seller not delay paying bills in order to keep the extra cash.

Class II, "Liquid Assets," includes highly liquid assets, such as certificates of deposit, easily marketable stock, and other securities. Like cash, liquid assets are easy to calculate. Potential problems could be non-liquid stock or similar vehicles for which a simple calculation of value is not available.

Included in Class III, "Non-Cash Assets," are all tangible and intangible assets not falling into Classes IV and V, such as equipment, supplies, furniture, and other items.

The first three classes contain essentially tangible assets, which include all assets on the balance sheet of the practice, such as cash (Class I); cash equivalents (Class II); and supplies (office, medical, lab, etc.), owned equipment (leased equipment is handled separately), furniture, and other miscellaneous assets such as prepaid expenses (Class III). These assets may be purchased at book value or, in some cases, valued separately. These values are relatively easy to calculate and the allocation is simple.

Problems may arise in two areas. The first area is that of equipment valuation—since used equipment prices can vary significantly, disagreement on the value may arise. It is advisable to use an independent firm to value the equipment when the amount is significant or the parties cannot agree. The second area of potential trouble is accounts receivable. The receivables of a medical practice are typically valued separately from the other tangible assets. Not all receivables on the books will be collected, and the purchaser will want to know how much cash should be collected from these receivables. This amount is found using an aging report with the receivables shown separately by payer and expected collection rates assigned to each age category for each payer. This report is often made as part of the overall valuation.

In many medical practice purchases the physician will attempt to sell the real estate (typically a hospital) to the purchaser. From the physician's perspective, it might make sense to sell everything, including real estate; however, from the purchaser's perspective, it may not make good business sense to get into the real estate business. Alternatively, the physician may want to keep the real estate and lease it to the purchaser, which happens when the physician is looking for passive income and when the purchaser wants to limit the cash outlay. Such leases tend to be long term (10–20 years). If the real estate is purchased, it is accounted for as any other real estate purchase. One caveat to remember: if future physician compensation is to be based on managing practice expenses, the fair market value of what the rent expense would have been if the real estate were leased rather than purchased should be included.

Items in Class IV, Section 197 Intangibles, are intangible assets (other than goodwill and going concern value) acquired after August 10, 1993, and used in a trade or business for the production of income. These assets may be amortized over a 15-year period. The code refers specifically to eight categories of assets that meet this definition:

1. Goodwill, going concern value, covenants not to complete (noncompetition agreements) entered into in connection with the acquisition of a trade or business

2. Workforce in place

3. Information base

4. Patents, copyrights, formulas, designs, or similar items

5. Customer-based intangibles

6. Any supplier-based intangibles

7. Licenses, permits, or other rights granted by a governmental unit or agency

8. Franchises, trademarks, and trade names

The code specifically excludes ten categories of assets from Section 197 eligibility:

1. Interests in a corporation, partnership, trust, or estate

2. Interests under certain financial contracts

3. Interests in land

4. Computer software not acquired in connection with the purchase of a business or that is readily available for purchase by the general public, is subject to a nonexclusive license, and has not been substantially modified

5. Certain separately acquired rights and interests, including an interest in a patent or copyright or in a film, sound recording, video tape, book, or similar property

6. Interests under existing leases of tangible property

7. Interests under existing indebtedness

8. Sports franchises

9. Residential mortgage servicing rights

10. Professional fees and transaction costs incurred in a corporate organization or reorganization

As can be seen from these lists, the assets most likely to be part of a medical practice purchase are goodwill, noncompetition agreements, workforce in place, trademarks, and trade names. Except for goodwill, these will be Class IV assets.

The final class of assets, Class V, contains goodwill and going concern value. Any remaining value not assigned to the other four classes is considered goodwill.

Accounting Implications

Stock Purchase

If the acquisition is a stock purchase, the purchaser will typically categorize the acquisition as an "investment in subsidiary," because the purchaser is buying stock like an investment. In this case, the seller will have capital gains on the value of the stock sold. The purchaser will not be able to amortize the purchase price and does not get the benefit of the "stepped-up" value of the practice until it is either sold, dissolved, or otherwise removed from the balance sheet. In this case, the advantage is usually to the seller. In addition to being able to avoid double taxation (i.e., taxation at both the corporate and individual levels), the seller recognizes the sale as a capital gain, and also is freed of all liabilities of the practice (except those specifically excluded in the purchase agreement). Thus, purchasers should be sure to perform their due diligence, as the liabilities of the practice are being purchased as well.

Asset Purchase

If the acquisition is an asset purchase, the acquisition must be expensed over time, according to asset classes. The tangible assets are usually amortized over the useful life of the asset. This period is often set at five years for the entire group of hard assets (for simplicity), although it is possible to do a breakdown of each asset and set up an itemized amortization schedule.

Accounts receivable are typically accounted for at face value, with an offsetting bad debt entry for the difference between the face value and the appraised value. As these old receivables are collected, they are strictly balance-sheet transfers and are not income to the purchaser. After a period of time (typically six to nine months) these receivables should be entirely written-off, but again, as a balance-sheet transfer and not as income or expense, except for the difference between the valuation amount and the amount actually collected.

Goodwill and other Section 197 intangibles are amortized over 15 years. The seller of the practice will need to account for the sale in the same manner as the purchaser will, so that their allocations of the purchase price among the various asset classes will match. Matching accounting is important because both parties must file Form 8594 with relevant tax implications, as we will now discuss.

Tax Implications

Stock Purchase

In a stock purchase, the buyer will carry the cost of the purchase price as an investment, and thus will have no tax implications until the practice is either sold, dissolved, or revalued. When one of these events occurs, there will be tax implications. The capital gains tax will be determined by the length of time the stock was held. In addition, the corporate structure of the buyer will be important. If the buyer is a C-corporation, there will be issues of double taxation (taxation at both the corporate and shareholder levels).

The seller's gain however, is subject to capital gains tax at the time of the sale, except for installment sales (which are not covered in this chapter). One should seek tax counsel familiar with these rules. Treating some or all of the purchase price as a capital gain rather than as ordinary income is preferable from the seller's point of view. If the seller is a corporation (as in the sale of a subsidiary), then the double-taxation issues are still present.

Asset Purchase

In an asset purchase, the buyer will be able to amortize each class of assets, as previously discussed. The amortization will be accounted for as an expense that lowers net income and therefore reduces the tax burden. Of course, if the acquiring entity is tax exempt, there are no tax savings.

The seller must recognize the gain on each class of assets according to the value assigned. The sale of tangible assets, if the price is different from book value, could represent either a tax gain or a loss. The entire amount of the receivables will be recognized as ordinary income, assuming the practice has not yet recognized the receivables (which is the case for practices using the cash basis of accounting). If the receivables have been recognized, any difference from book value must be recognized. The amounts of goodwill and intangibles must be recognized as ordinary income. As most physicians are in the top income tax bracket, the advantage of a stock sale versus an assets sale can be significant.

Impact of Section 338

In most stock transactions, the acquisition is treated as described previously. However, Section 338 of the Internal Revenue Code allows for a stock transaction to be treated as an asset acquisition. To take advantage of this opportunity, two criteria must be met: (1) the buyer must make a qualified stock purchase of the stock of the seller, and (2) the buyer must make an election to treat the transaction as an asset purchase.

A qualified stock purchase is defined as meeting two criteria: (1) the buyer acquires at least 80% of the total combined voting power of all classes of stock entitled to vote within 12 months, and (2) the buyer acquires at least 80% of the total number of shares of all other classes of stock (except nonvoting stock, which is limited and preferred to dividends).

The advantage of the 338 election to the buyer is that the buyer receives the stepped-up basis to fair market value. This is accomplished by treating the seller as a new corporation on the day after the transaction. The "new-seller" corporation buys the assets of the "old-seller" corporation and becomes a subsidiary of the buyer. The tax burden is shifted to the seller as a corporate-level tax, which is to be paid upon liquidation of the "old-seller" corporation. Care must be taken to avoid shifting the burden back to the buyer as a result of the sale. This is accomplished with a tax allocation clause in the stock purchase agreement with reference to the 338 election as part of the sale.

The election negatively impacts the seller because of the additional tax burden. Thus, such an election should be made only when there are significant net operating losses (NOLs) that can offset the additional tax burden. Four issues must be evaluated in determining whether to take the 338 election:

- The tax burden the seller faces in a stock sale (calculated as the difference between the basis and the purchase price and applying the capital gains tax rate)

- The tax burden the seller faces in an asset sale (calculated as the difference between the basis and the purchase price and applying the capital gains tax rate)

- The amount of NOLs that can be applied by the seller to offset other gains

- The tax situation of the seller (because the tax burden passes to the seller)

Impact of Depreciation Recapture

When assets are sold, the seller must take into consideration the depreciation expenses already claimed in prior years as well as any amortization of Section 197 intangibles. In general, the rule is that when depreciation has been taken as an ordinary expense, when it is recovered, it is considered a gain subject to ordinary income tax. Any gain above and beyond the original basis price is subject to capital gains tax. Exhibit 7.7 illustrates these rules. In Scenario 1, the ordinary gain is $20,000 (from the recapture) and the capital gain is $25,000. Assuming that the asset was held for more than one year, it would also qualify as a long-term capital gain. In Scenario 2, the ordinary gain is $20,000 and the capital gain is $5,000. In Scenario 3, the ordinary gain is $10,000,

Exhibit 7.7
Depreciation recapture

	Scenario 1	Scenario 2	Scenario 3
Cost of assets	50,000	50,000	50,000
Depreciation expenses claimed	20,000	20,000	20,000
Book value (adjusted basis)	30,000	30,000	30,000
Sales price / fair market value	75,000	55,000	40,000
Actual gain	45,000	25,000	10,000
Adjusted basis (after depreciation)	30,000	30,000	30,000
Depreciation recaptured	20,000	20,000	20,000
Recomputed basis	50,000	50,000	50,000
Fair market value	75,000	55,000	40,000
Lower of recomputed basis or fair			
market value	50,000	50,000	40,000
Adjusted basis	30,000	30,000	30,000
Ordinary gain	20,000	20,000	10,000
Actual gain	45,000	25,000	10,000
Ordinary gain	20,000	20,000	10,000
Capital gain	25,000	5,000	0

and there is no capital gain. Note that if the sale price is less than $50,000, then the entire gain would be ordinary gain and there would be no capital gain. If the sale price is below $30,000, then there is a capital loss.

Impact of Section 197

When assets are sold, the seller must take into consideration any amortization of Section 197 intangibles. No loss may be claimed for the unamortized portion of a Section 197 intangible upon sale of that intangible, if any other Section 197 intangible acquired in the same transaction is retained. The remaining basis (unamortized portion) is added to the basis of the retained Section 197 intangibles. Exhibit 7.8 illustrates these rules. Assume that Intangible 1 is goodwill and Intangible 2 is a noncompetition contract. The noncompetition contract is disposed of after year 5.

Exhibit 7.8
Impact of Section 197

	Section 197 Intangible 1	Section 197 Intangible 2
Basis, upon acquisition	30,000	12,000
Amortization, after five years	10,000	3,000
Unamortized portion	20,000	9,000
Adjusting entry	9,000	(9,000)
Adjusted basis, start of year 6	29,000	0
Annual amortization for each year through 15	2,900	N/A

Start-up Costs

The cost of developing a new joint venture or of acquiring an existing business is not deductible as are operating expenses. These expenditures, usually referred to as work in progress (WIP) or development costs, are capitalized until the transaction is completed. Once the transaction is completed, the capitalized expenditures are amortized over at least a five-year period in accordance with Section 195. This is accomplished on the first tax return for the new joint venture by completing Form 4562 (Depreciation and Amortization) and attaching the election statement. To qualify as an amortizable start-up cost, the cost must be incurred in connection with one of the following:

- Investigating the creation or acquisition of an active trade or business

- Creating an active trade or business

- Any activity engaged in for profit and for the production of income before the day on which the active trade or business begins, in anticipation of such activity's becoming an active trade or business

In addition, start-up costs must qualify as allowable business deductions, except that they were paid or incurred prior to the business's actually existing. Typical costs to be capitalized include:

- Legal fees associated with the transaction

- Feasibility studies

- Business consulting fees

- Valuation reports

- Appraisals and assessments

Cost excluded from start-up costs include:

- Interest on indebtedness (Section 163 [a])

- Taxes (Section 164)

- Research and experimental expenditures (Section 174)

If a business is sold or disposed of prior to the end of the amortization period, the remainder of the expenses may be deductible as a loss under Section 165.

TRANSACTIONS

Transactions include mergers and acquisitions, sometimes referred to as "M&A," as well as joint ventures. A *merger* is the coming together of multiple existing entities resulting in one surviving entity. An *acquisition* is the purchase of one entity by another entity. A *joint venture* is the development of a new entity that leaves the current entities intact. Transactions are an area of the business environment that, by definition, is constantly changing. All industries go through periods of high growth when new companies are being formed, periods of stability when the number of competitors remains constant, and periods of consolidation when the number of competitors is reduced. It is during a consolidation period that transaction activity is at a peak.

The health care industry has been undergoing rapid change for more than 30 years now, although each sector is affected differently at different times. The hospital sector was impacted by the Hill-Burton Act, which stimulated large growth in the creation of new hospitals; the creation of Medicare and Medicaid; and the implementation of prospective payment in 1983. It has recently experienced extreme pressure on reimbursement from the Balanced Budget Act of 1997 (BBA97). In the last 15 years about 16% of general acute-care hospitals in this country have closed and many more have either merged or changed to serve non-acute patients.

The health maintenance organization sector is currently in a period of consolidation: the number of HMOs, which had been increasing during the 1980s, is now declining as these companies try to grow larger in order to control more of the market. The physician sector is in a slow but steady consolidation period: fewer and fewer physicians want to "hang up a shingle," preferring instead to be employed. The home health care sector was in rapid growth during the 1990s, but now is in rapid consolidation following the enactment of BBA97. The latest sector to experience growth is ambulatory care centers, including ambulatory surgery centers (ASCs). Many of these ASCs are new joint ventures in which hospitals and physicians are coming together as partners.

The basics of transactions and a number of related definitions are given here. Keep in mind that essentially every concept listed here could fill a book on its own. This book is intended to be a primer and to illustrate the complexity, and sometimes confusion, of working in the health care industry. The best advice is to seek experienced business and legal experts to assist you through the process.

A *merger*, defined briefly already, is the consolidation of two or more legal entities that results in the creation of a single new entity. For example, Company A and Company B merge and the resulting legal entity is called Company C.

An *acquisition*, on the other hand, is the purchase of one company by another such that one company survives and the other does not. For example, Company A acquires Company B and the resulting legal entity is Company A. Sometimes the acquired company is absorbed into the acquiring company. Other times, the acquired company continues to operate as a business unit of the acquiring company.

Any business, new, merged, acquired, or otherwise, must have a prescribed legal structure. There are numerous types of legal structures, each having complex legal, business, tax, and accounting issues. The more common ones are outlined here; Exhibit 7.9 further illustrates the more popular structures and their differences.

The first of these legal structures is a *sole proprietorship*, which is an unincorporated business owned by a single individual. This structure is most commonly used by medical practices with one or only a few

Exhibit 7.9

Key characteristics of alternative forms of legal organization

Factor	C Corporation	S Corporation	Partnership (General and Limited)	Limited Liability Company
Ownership				
Limit on Number of Owners	None	Maximum of 75	Minimum of two; no maximum	Minimum of two; no maximum
Limit on Types of Owners	None	Limited to estates, individuals, and some trusts	None	None
Limit on Classes of Owners	Unlimited	One class; may have voting and non-voting	Unlimited	Unlimited
Liability				
Liability of Owners	Stockholders are generally not liable for any debts of a corporation. Thus, liability is limited unless loans or notes are guaranteed by the shareholders or the corporate veil is pierced.	Same as for a C-corp, unless liabilities arise from a shareholder's own actions.	General partners are usually jointly and severally liable for all debts of the entity. Conversely a limited partner is usually limited to the amount of capital contribution.	Same as a C-corp.

continued

Exhibit 7.9 (Continued)

Factor	C Corporation	S Corporation	Partnership (General and Limited)	Limited Liability Company
Control				
Management	Flexible. In a large corporation, control is often in the hands of top management. In a closely held corporation, management is often exercised by the owners.	Fairly flexible. Active participation is typical because the total number of shareholders can not exceed 75.	Usually, all general partners will actively participate in management activities. The partners can grant management control to certain partners in accordance with the partnership agreement. Limited partners are not allowed to have a significant role in management.	Flexible. Management structure is determined by members and detailed in the operating agreement.
Ease of Formation	Must meet state law requirements for incorporation. Expenses tend to be higher than those of a partnership.	Same as those for a C-corp. Because these entities are closely held, costs tend to be less than for a C-corp.	Few formal restrictions and normally a small expense. Limited partnership will be required to file a Certificate of Limited Partnership. Formation of a limited partnership and syndication cost can be expensive.	Must meet state law requirements for LLC status. Expenses similar to those for a C-corp.
Basis of Interest/ Stock upon Formation	Equal to money and adjusted basis of property. Share of corporation's liabilities does not increase basis. Not a pass-through entity.	Same as for a C-corp, except that the basis is an important consideration if losses are generated.	Equal to the amount of money and adjusted basis of property transferred to the partnership. Plus partner's pro rata share of partnership liabilities will increase basis.	Same as for a partnership.

Liquidation	Normally, shareholder approval is required.	Same as for a C-corp.	Ordinarily, agreement among the partners can cause liquidation, unless the partnership agreement provides otherwise.	Same as for a partnership.

Taxes

Who is Taxed on Income and Losses	Corporation is taxed on its taxable income, regardless of distribution to shareholders.	Shareholders are taxed on their shares of income, regardless of distributions. Losses can be deducted by shareholder to the extent of adjusted basis in stock.	Partners are taxed on their shares of income, regardless of distributions. Losses may be deducted to the extent of basis.	Same as for a partnership.
Interest of Partnership or Corporation Received Tax-free in Exchange for Property	Non-recognition treatment if 80% control requirement is satisfied after transfer. Liabilities attached to property transferred may limit tax-free treatment. Only a limited amount of stock can be transferred in exchange for services rendered upon incorporation.	Same as for a C-corp.	Non-recognition treatment of property in exchange for partnership interest. Significant liabilities transferred can pose a problem.	Same as for a partnership.
Consequences of Transferring Mortgage Property to an Entity	To the extent the liability exceeds the adjusted basis of property in the aggregate, the excess is considered a gain distributed.	Same as for a C-corp.	Gain recognized if other partners' pro rata shares of debt exceed transferring partner's basis in the partnership interest.	Same as for a partnership.

continued

Exhibit 7.9 (Continued)

Factor	C Corporation	S Corporation	Partnership (General and Limited)	Limited Liability Company
Limitation on Deductibility of Losses	Non-limitation on losses deducted by the separate entity. Losses may be carried over or back.	Losses limited to the shareholder's basis. As with a partnership, the carryover of losses to future years is allowed.	Losses are deductible by the partner to the extent of partnership basis. Non-deductible losses may be carried over indefinitely to future years.	Same as for a partnership.
Cash Distributions not in Liquidation or Redemption	Taxable as dividend income to the extent of earnings and profits. Distributions in excess of earnings and profits and stock basis can result in a capital gain.	Similar to that of a partnership. Tax-free to the extent of stock basis.	A distribution is tax-free to the extent of adjusted basis of the partnership interest.	Same as for a partnership.
Distribution in Redemption of Interest/Stock	Depending on requirements met, may be considered capital or dividend.	Tax-free distribution to the extent of stock basis. Any excess distribution may result in capital gain.	Taxability of withdrawing partners receiving payments in exchange for property, including goodwill if such allocation is made, are treated as a sale or exchange. All other payments are taxed as guaranteed payment of distributive share of income. Very attractive provision.	Same as for an S-corp.

Complete Liquidation	Gain recognized by a corporation on distributions of property. Shareholder is treated as having sold stock for distribution received in liquidation; therefore, gain is usually a capital gain. In complete liquidation, gain is taxed at both corporate and shareholder levels.	Similar to that of a C-corp, except gain at S-corp level increases basis of S-corp shareholders' stock.	Distribution is tax-free as long as money, inventory, and unrealized receivables distributed do not exceed adjusted basis.	Same as for a partnership.
Capital Gains and Losses	Capital gains are taxed to the corporation. Capital losses are not currently deductible, but may be carried over or back.	Capital gains and losses flow through to the shareholders.	Capital gains and losses flow through to the partners.	Same as for a partnership.
State Income Tax	Most states impose a tax on corporate earnings.	Income taxed imposed by some states.	No taxes imposed at the partnership level in most states.	Same as for a partnership; however, some states tax LLCs as C-corps.
Federal Income Tax	No filing necessary upon formation. Must file Form 1120 annually.	Must file Form 2553 to make S election. Must file Form 1120S annually and distribute K-1 forms to partners.	No filing necessary upon formation. Must file Form 1065 annually and distribute K-1 forms to partners.	Same as for a partnership.

continued

Exhibit 7.9 (Continued)

Factor	C Corporation	S Corporation	Partnership (General and Limited)	Limited Liability Company
Other Considerations				
Fringe Benefits	Fully deductible. Available to all shareholders and employees. Cannot be discriminatory in favor of highly compensated employees or may be taxable to those individuals.	Fully deductible. Available to shareholders owning 2% or less of stock. For owners with more than 2%, certain restrictions apply.	Partially deductible to partners.	Same as for a partnership.
Self-employment Taxes	Not applicable to corporate dividends; shareholder/employee is subject to employment tax on wages.	Non applicable to S-corp pass-through income.	General partners' share of partnership income is subject to self-employment tax. A limited partner's share is not, unless the income is a guaranteed payment for services.	Varies. Seek legal advice.
Retirement Plans	Shareholders and employees can be included in a corporation's regular, qualified plan.	Same as for a C-corp.	Partners may participate in self-employed qualified plans. Limitations are generally similar to those of C-corps.	Same as for a partnership.
Accounting Method	Must use accrual method if over $5 million in annual gross receipts.	May use cash method unless sells goods out of inventory.	May use cash method unless sells goods out of inventory. Limited partnerships may be subject to further restrictions.	Same as for a partnership.

providers. The owner typically uses his or her social security number for the business and must file a Schedule C as part of his or her personal income tax return.

A *partnership* is an unincorporated business owned jointly by two or more people. This structure is most commonly used by small businesses due to the simplicity and ease with which the partnership can be formed. In a partnership, both partners must report profits and losses annually on their respective individual income tax returns.

A *limited partnership* is the same as a regular partnership, except that there are two types of partners (owners). At least one partner is a general partner, and at least one other partner is a limited partner. General partners are differentiated from the limited partners by rights. A general partner is involved in the management of the partnership, while a limited partner cannot be. A general partner is liable for the business while a limited partner is not. Liability means that if the business loses money, the general partner is personally at risk for losses and may be sued as an individual by creditors of the business. All partners annually report distributions of profits (and losses) on their individual income tax returns. Essentially, limited partners are supplying capital to the business through the purchase of the partnership shares, but because they are not involved in the management of the partnership, are not held personally liable for any losses the business may incur.

A *limited liability partnership* (LLP) is a relatively new legal entity in which there are limits on the personal liability of each partner for business losses. The LLP is similar to the limited liability company described on page 206. Some states also recognize what is called a professional LLP, which parallels the professional corporation described in the next paragraph. Many law firms and accounting firms have converted from a partnership to an LLP or even a PLLP because of the attractiveness of the limited personal liability.

A *taxable corporation*, or C-corp, is a legal entity organized under Chapter C of the Internal Revenue Code. The owners of a C-corp purchase shares of the corporation in exchange for voting privileges and distribution of profits or dividends. The C-corp must file an annual income tax return and pay taxes. Any distribution of after-tax profits, or dividends, to the shareholders must be declared as income by the shareholder. Thus the profits of a C-corp are taxed twice (once at the corporate level and once at the individual level). However, the C-corp structure has a number of advantages, especially in terms of which tax deductions are allowed. A special type of C-corp, called a professional corporation, is recognized at the state level. This type of C-corp is available to professionals who must be licensed to practice in the state, such as physicians, dentists, lawyers, and accountants (PC or PA). Non-licensed entities (persons, corporations, trusts, etc.) are not eligible to own shares of a professional corporation.

An *S-corporation*, or S-corp, is a taxable entity organized under Chapter S of the Internal Revenue Code. It functions like a C-corp for accounting purposes, but is taxed like a partnership in that it must distribute profits and losses annually. However, the number of shareholders is limited to 75 and restrictions are placed on who can be a shareholder, which limits the S-corp's usefulness as a viable legal structure for large businesses.

A *non-profit taxable corporation* is the same as a C-corp in that it is taxable at the federal level. The difference is that it is non-taxable at the state level. The rules regarding the granting of non-profit status at the state level vary from state to state. Thus, multi-state companies desiring to take advantage of this special status will need to check state laws for each state in which they wish to operate. These types of companies typically feel they may not qualify for tax exempt status at the federal level (described in the following paragraph), but due to a less stringent qualifications, can qualify at the state level.

Several types of *non-profit tax exempt corporations* are organized under Section 501 of the Internal Revenue Code. Many people are familiar with 501(c)3, which is the most common tax exemption clause, but there are several others that cover professional associations, fraternal organizations, and the like.

Finally, a *limited liability company* (sometimes referred to as an LLC) is a relatively new type of corporation. It functions like a C-corp for accounting, operations, shareholder liability, and so forth, but it is taxed like a partnership. This tax status avoids the double taxation incurred by taxable corporations and has become the vehicle of choice for joint ventures in the health care industry.

Federal Legal Issues

The selection of a legal vehicle is often the easiest decision to be made in a health care transaction, although it is by no means always actually easy. There are always legal issues to resolve, preferably with the assistance of legal counsel specializing in health care transactions. The major issues are as follows.

Medicare and Medicaid Fraud and Abuse

Legislation has been enacted that attempts to limit the ability of providers to defraud or abuse the Medicare and Medicaid programs. *Fraud* is defined as gaining something of value through the intentional deception, misrepresentation, or concealment of material facts. *Abuse* is defined as a repeated or recurring practice inconsistent with rules, regulations, or ethical standards, which results in unnecessary financial loss to these governmental programs. An example of abuse is upcoding: although each individual case is not fraud per se, the practice demonstrates a consistent pattern of selecting a higher-than-necessary reimbursement code. Abuse is typically more difficult to prove than fraud.

Although it is not the only law of its kind, the False Claims Act may be the best known due to its recent press regarding both huge settlements and pending cases. The False Claims Act makes it a crime to submit a false claim to the government and to abuse the system in an attempt to increase unwarranted reimbursement. A provider risks exclusion from these governmental programs if the offences are serious enough. Because most providers depend on these programs for as much as 80% of their revenue, exclusion would effectively force a provider out of business.

Anti–Self-Referral

The Stark I and Stark II laws prohibit a provider's referring a Medicare or Medicaid patient to a facility in which the provider has an ownership or compensation interest, unless certain requirements (called safe harbors) are met. Under these laws, if a provider does make a prohibited referral, the penalty can be as severe as exclusion from the programs. These laws are so complex (Stark II takes 10 pages in the Federal Register plus another 60 pages to explain) that the interpretation and implementation of Stark II is still being discussed today, six years after it formally became law. Providers are going forward with their business plans and trying their best to be in compliance with the law, at least as it is currently understood. It is not unreasonable, however, to expect that there may still be some modifications to this particular law before it can be formally enforced. It is best to seek legal counsel familiar with this law.

Section 501(c)3

Eligible organizations are granted tax-exempt status under the Internal Revenue Code by meeting certain criteria. The provision of health care is recognized as a charitable activity; most hospitals and many other health care organizations gain tax exempt status simply by providing this service. To maintain tax-exempt status, the organization must meet further requirements. For example, in the case of a 501(c)3 organization, no assets of the organization may inure to private parties. The penalty for violation could be revocation of the tax-exempt status. In recent years, some of these tax-exempt organizations have been challenged, and some, including HMOs, have abandoned their tax-exempt status in order to free themselves of the restrictions.

Antitrust

In M&A, as well as in joint ventures, the resulting entity may run afoul of antitrust laws such as the Sherman Act or the Hart-Scott-Rodino Act. These laws attempt to maintain a level playing field by encouraging competition. When the contemplated M&A or joint venture may end up with a significant market share, the Department of Justice may legally prevent the deal. In antitrust analyses, two main factors are analyzed: first, what is the product; and second, what is the relevant service area. An antitrust analysis should be performed by legal counsel familiar with these laws.

State Legal Issues

State Laws

Many states have adopted fraud and abuse laws as well as anti–self-referral laws parallelling the federal laws. The state laws are enacted to cover the remainder of the population not covered by the governmental programs. Because some states have not enacted parallel laws, it is critical to examine state as well as federal law to ensure that the entity is in compliance.

Restrictive Covenants

Many transactions, especially medical practice purchases, include restrictive covenants, such as noncompetition agreements. The covenants restrict one or both parties from engaging in behavior or practices that may harm the new entity. Sometimes, a portion of the purchase price is allocated to the value of the restrictive covenant. This is important to keep in mind, as the buyer must amortize the purchase price properly and the seller must pay taxes accordingly.

Corporate Practice of Medicine

All states have enacted legislation requiring that an entity may practice medicine only if properly licensed to do so in that state. This is referred to as the corporate practice of medicine, since the courts initially interpreted this legislation to mean that a corporation would be practicing medicine if it both hired a physician to practice medicine and was paid for the services the physician provided. Most states have enacted exceptions to these laws, allowing certain types of legal entities, such as hospitals or HMOs, to hire physicians. Some states expressly allow professional corporations to exist. Other states have ignored this interpretation of the law and do not pursue cases, although another state with the exact same situation may pursue legal action.

Open Meetings and Records

Organizations that are public are subject to open-meeting laws, sometimes referred to as sunshine laws. These organizations must make all minutes of their meetings public and often must disclose contract documents. Such contracts could contain sensitive material (such as physician compensation packages). Entities subject to open meetings laws should take care to comply with them.

Bond Issues

Most hospitals and many other health-care organizations carry long-term debt as part of their capitalization. One issue they face is the accounting for interest and principal as they relate to reimbursement by the Medicare and Medicaid programs (certain interest expenses are excluded as reimbursable). Another issue is that most bonds are issued with restrictions on financial performance. The board and senior management should be aware of these restrictions and of the organization's position in relation to them. For example, a hospital may not have the capacity to take on any more debt (due to a bond covenant) and thus may have to seek alternative financing or abandon its intended project (including M&A or joint venture).

Documents Related to Mergers and Acquisitions

Articles of Incorporation, Bylaws, Operating Agreements, and Partnership Agreements

All legal entities are organized under state laws. These laws require certain documents to be filed. While some of these documents can be simple, like the Articles of Incorporation, others can be so complex as to take weeks of negotiation, like the Operating Agreement of an LLC. The source of this complexity is the fact that these documents, while full of legalese, contain clauses that can have a dramatic impact on the accounting and taxation of the owners. Such clauses include the mechanisms for issuing new shares, qualifications for ownership, valuation of shares, termination clauses, repayment agreements, and so on. If the parties cannot agree on these clauses, the deal may not be consummated.

Contribution and Purchase Agreements

The contribution agreement and purchase agreement serve the same purpose in that they allow the new entity to acquire assets (and sometimes liabilities). These documents always have tax and accounting effects. A contribution agreement allows a seller to exchange assets for shares of the acquiring entity. If assets are being sold, they must be accounted for correctly; if shares of an existing legal entity are being sold, a different mechanism is used to account for the transaction. Both mechanisms have tax implications for the seller.

A purchase agreement is similar to a contribution agreement except that the seller receives cash instead of equity. Numerous laws govern how purchases may take place, especially when a not-for-profit entity is involved, as is the case in many health care transactions. The method of valuation is one regulated area; the allocation of the purchase price to tangible and intangible assets is another. Both impact the amortization (if any) of the purchase price.

Valuation Report

All not-for-profit entities are required to pay fair market value for goods and services purchased. One mechanism for determining fair market value is an independent valuation. Numerous valuation techniques are accepted by the IRS, and the valuation report is part of the legal documents of a transaction.

Administrative Services Agreements

Many joint ventures include an agreement for administrative services, sometimes called a management agreement. An M&A transaction, because it has only one surviving entity, rarely needs this agreement, although there are exceptions. In a joint venture, administrative services may be provided by one of the existing entities or by an external organization. If a not-for-profit entity is part of the transaction, fair market valuation services may be needed. Accounting for management fees can impact both the income statement and the taxes.

Employment Agreements

Employment agreements are usually for physicians, although occasionally, related agreements are made for medical directorships. These agreements are usually subject to fair market valuation standards and can impact the accounting and taxation of an entity in the case of a guarantee.

Accounting Implications of Mergers and Acquisitions

The discussions regarding accounting implications and tax implications (see next section) refer to both stock purchases and asset purchases. In the present context, "stock" and "asset" will apply specifically to the medical practice as a whole rather than to individual items within the practice. In addition, in cases in which the medical practice is being contributed to a joint venture (a tax-free exchange for stock), the same rules apply to any cash received, while stock received is treated as an investment.

Buyer

The first accounting consideration is whether a stock or an asset purchase has taken place. In a stock purchase, there is no amortization, whereas in an asset purchase, there will be amortization. In a stock purchase, any acquisition costs are added to the basis calculation. In an asset purchase, the acquisition costs are amortized over a period, usually at least five years.

In an asset purchase, usually no liabilities are assumed. In a stock purchase, all liabilities are assumed unless they are specifically excluded or indemnified. Obviously, incorrectly determining the value of the liabilities can have a substantial impact on the acquiring organization's income statement.

Seller

In an asset sale, a capital gain or loss will be recognized. If the seller still has an organization, any gains within the corporation may be double taxed. When the organization is liquidated, there may be additional capital gains or losses, and the seller is responsible for any remaining liabilities. In a stock sale, there will be a gain or loss depending on the basis in the stock, and all liabilities are transferred to the buyer. Thus it is often to the advantage of the seller for the transaction to be a stock purchase and an advantage to the buyer for the transaction to be an asset purchase.

Tax Implications of Mergers and Acquisitions

Buyer

In an asset purchase, the buyer may depreciate the assets purchased and amortize the acquisition costs, creating a tax advantage for the buyer. Of course, if the assets are later sold, the basis has been reduced, possibly creating a substantial capital gain. In a stock purchase, the buyer does not have the advantage of depreciation or amortization expenses to reduce income and taxes, although if the asset is later sold, the basis will be higher and therefore potential capital gains reduced.

Seller

In both asset and stock purchases, there will be capital gains or losses to the seller, who will then owe taxes accordingly (either short- or long-term). However, in an asset purchase, there may be additional taxes depending on the status of the seller. For example, if a corporation sells assets, there will be a taxable transaction (gain or loss) within the corporation. If the corporation is subsequently liquidated, there will be another taxable transaction when the liquidating dividend is paid to the shareholders.

One Example

An interesting situation can occur when the seller has a significant note payable. In one case, the medical practice assets were valued at $1.5 million and the practice had a note payable for $650,000. If the assets were sold, then the cash received, less an assumed tax rate of 33.3%, would be $1 million. After paying off the note, the physician would have had $350,000. However, if the sale included the note, the physician would receive $566,666 ($1,5000,000 − $650,000 = $850,000 less the ⅓ tax burden); the physician obviously would come out ahead. At the same time, the buyer would have had to come up with only $850,000 rather than $1.5 million. In this particular case, the buyer would have had to go to the bank to finance the acquisition either way, so assumption of the note payable (and its favorable interest rate) simplified the whole transaction and favored *both* parties. As can be seen from even this simple situation, the specifics of every deal necessitate exploring the various alternatives, and the use of expert business and legal advisors cannot be overemphasized.

HOSPITAL INCOME GUARANTEES

A *hospital income guarantee* is usually made either as part of a physician employment agreement or in support of the start-up of a non-hospital physician who is moving into the hospital's service area. These agreements are complex legal documents with significant accounting and tax implications. The guarantee provides the physician security from the uncertainties of starting a new practice. It is often used in more rural areas (or in inner city locations) where physician recruitment and retention can be difficult.

The Income Guarantee Contract

Term

The length of the contract term, including provisions for renewal negotiations, should be detailed. It often includes the initial term, subsequent terms, and the means of formally initiating the negotiation process (often a written notification given to the other party 90 to 180 days prior to the expiration of the term).

Calculation Methodology

The method for calculation of the guarantee must be clearly delineated with all definitions clearly stated, including how to calculate revenue, what is included as revenue and excluded, what expenses are included and excluded, the frequency of payments (usually monthly), and so forth.

Revenue Ownership

If the physician remains a hospital employee, the physician will assign to the employer all rights to revenue generated while on the job. There may be certain activities the revenue from which the physician is allowed to keep, which should be explicitly stated in the methodology section. A non-employee physician keeps all revenue, and any payments to or from the physician are supplemental.

Payment Methodologies

How the physician submits a bill to the hospital and how the hospital pays the physician should be clearly defined. The physician should be required to submit documentation in support of any request for payment from the hospital; typically, a physician is required to submit a monthly statement to the hospital at the end of each month. The hospital then cuts a check within the stipulated time frame. If guarantees are being repaid, the physician should remit a check to the hospital with the monthly statement.

Repayment Clauses

The physician should understand that all the obligations of the contract must be fulfilled or the guarantee amounts paid will have to be returned to the hospital. Such repayment can include signing bonuses, relocation expenses, and any other payments made on behalf of the physician, as long as they are detailed in the contract as having to be repaid. The obligations can include taking all coverage, serving on committees, maintaining at least a minimum number of office hours, providing charity care, and any other types of obligations. Such activity allows the hospital to demonstrate community benefit and justify why the physician is receiving the guarantee.

Termination Rights

All contracts should spell out the termination rights of both parties, and hospital guarantee contracts are no exception. They must define breach of contract, mechanisms for curing a breach, how to give notices to other parties, and how to unwind the deal if a termination is effected.

Treatment of Guarantee

The guarantee can be treated in one of two ways by the hospital—as an expense or as a loan. If the contract calls for repayment of the guarantee amounts at any point in the future, all payments to the physician should be treated as a loan and carried on the balance sheet as such. Repayments will then reduce the loan. In many cases, when the term of the contract is reached the physician will not have repaid the full loan amount. In these cases, if the physician remains in the area and maintains a full practice, the loan will be forgiven over a period of years. Of course, there are tax and accounting implications as to how the guarantee is handled.

Accounting Implications of a Hospital Income Guarantee

To the Hospital

The hospital has two options when paying out income guarantees. The first option is to treat the payments as an expense. This reduces income for the hospital and could have an impact on the income statement, and when the physician pays back the guarantee, the repayment must be treated as income. The second option is to treat the payments as a loan, thus moving the impact to the balance sheet. Any repayments then become a reduction of the outstanding debt. If any loan amounts are later forgiven, these amounts must be treated as an expense at the time of the forgiveness. A hospital entering into an income guarantee situation should estimate the impact to the income statement and balance sheet, and should check bond covenants to make sure that the hospital remains in compliance. A hospital with a tenuous bottom line can benefit from classifying such payments as a loan until they are either repaid or amortized at a later date. The advantage to this treatment is that, theoretically, the physician will be providing a much greater benefit to the hospital once the practice is up and running, and thus any expenses incurred in forgiveness will be offset by the benefits of the physician's full practice.

To the Physician

The physician receiving income guarantee payments will want to know how the hospital is treating these payments. If the hospital is treating them as expenses, then the physician will want to declare the payments as income. If the hospital is treating the payments as a loan, then the physician should, too.

Tax Implications of a Hospital Income Guarantee

To the Hospital

The tax implications to the hospital apply only if the hospital is subject to paying tax in the first place. If it is, the hospital may want to account for the payments as an expense and reduce its current tax burden. Any repayment of the guarantee will have to be declared as income. If the payments are treated as a loan, then as the loan is forgiven, the hospital will be required to send the physician a Form 1099 for the amount of forgiveness for each and every calendar year in which forgiveness occurs.

To the Physician

The physician receiving income guarantee payments will want to account for the payments as a loan. This reduces the current tax burden, although it increases the amount of debt the physician owes. When the hospital begins forgiving the loan, the physician must account for the forgiveness as income. The advantage of this is the postponement of income tax and, theoretically, assistance cash flow, as the physician will be better able to afford the tax burden after the practice is up and running.

EXIT STRATEGIES AND LIQUIDATIONS

Exit strategies are set forth in most investment vehicles such that the investor knows how he or she can leave, or exit, from the investment. In some cases, the exit is easy, although it is more likely that it will be quite complicated. Several issues need to be addressed concerning exit strategies: the valuation of shares, the payment of certain liabilities, the receipt of cash, taxation issues, and in some cases, noncompetition agreements and other agreements that survive the exit of a shareholder or partner.

Liquidation occurs when a corporation formally ceases to exist or when a partnership formally dissolves. In the latter case, the shareholders or partners must formally dissolve the organization and go through the process of liquidating all assets, paying all liabilities, allocating closing expenses, calculating final dividends, and of course settling any tax issues. There may be certain clauses of agreements that survive the dissolution of the organization as well, such as noncompetition clauses, indemnity clauses, and tail coverage insurance issues.

Exit Strategies

Exit strategies are an integral part of the original deal. It is well documented that not every business venture survives; thus, even though it may seem like a negative way to approach a joint venture, exit strategies must be discussed and agreed upon prior to entering a deal. In a physician acquisition, there is typically an employment contract for the physician, usually with clauses that allow the employer to terminate the contract when certain circumstances occur. There are also clauses that allow the physician to terminate the contract. At some point, all physicians will want to retire!

Triggering Events

When the physician is an investor in a joint venture, he or she typically must fulfill certain requirements. Shareholder agreements should require the physician to sell any interest in the joint venture when these requirements are no longer being met or when certain other events occur. These are called triggering events and include the loss of medical license, loss of DEA license, relocation from the service area, conviction of a felony, retirement, permanent disability, and more. When a triggering event occurs, the physician will be required to exit.

Valuations

When the exit occurs, the shares are repurchased by the organization. This repurchase includes a valuation of the shares and a cash payment plan. The valuation methodology should be described in the bylaws, partnership agreement, or operating agreement, as should be a prescribed payment plan. For small joint ventures, a triggering event can put a severe cash strain on the organization. In order to mitigate this strain, payments are often spread over a five-year period and usually carry a market interest rate on the balance due.

Installment payments must be accounted for properly because of the tax implications. The recipient does not recognize the cash until it is actually received. If interest is included, it must be accounted for properly so that the physician knows how each installment payment should be taxed (as capital gains versus ordinary income).

Repayment Clauses and Liquidated Damages

In addition, there may be repayment issues. For example, when a physician has sold a practice to the organization, the physician may have to repay some or all of the purchase price under certain circumstances. Such repayment obligations will be fully described in the purchase agreement (or contribution agreement if the practice was contributed in exchange for equity) and should be netted against any proceeds due from the sale of the stock. These repayment obligations also have tax implications for both parties.

In addition, the physician may be subject to liquidated damages, as occurs when a violation of the noncompetition agreement occurs. While it is difficult to enforce these agreements in some states, the agreement does give the organization some recourse in those situations in which the organization's business is being harmed.

The Importance of Exit Clauses

It is important that the previous situations are all described in detail in the transaction documents. Discussing such "negative issues" when the parties are trying to form a working relationship can seem like a hindrance to the process. However, not only is it far less expensive to decide on these strategies before the deal is signed, the negotiations give a good indication of whether the parties can work together on difficult issues and come to a mutual agreement.

Liquidation

At some point, an organization may dissolve, and a number of issues above and beyond those of an exit must be accounted for. In this scenario, the corporate structure itself may dictate how the liquidation is handled. In general, the purpose of liquidation is to dissolve the business entity and restore the owners to their previous positions. For example, if a physician practice was contributed to a joint venture group practice, then upon liquidation the physician will have the same assets returned. The difficulty, of course, is in taking into account any changes in value since formation, and resolving liabilities and other obligations.

General Method of Liquidation

The general method of liquidation is covered in IRC Section 331. This transaction is in effect the stockholder's selling shares back to the corporation, so the sale is treated as a capital gain (either short or long term). However, when the final distribution includes assets, the complicated depreciation recapture rules apply. It is best to have an accountant familiar with these rules make the calculations.

Just as in an exit scenario, liquidation distributions may be made in installments. For a cash basis stockholder (such as a physician), the capital gain or loss is recognized when the cash is received. However, a stockholder on an accrual basis (such as a hospital) must recognize the gain when it is determined.

Net Fair Market Value

The calculation of the value of the stock is simple: the fair market value of the assets less the liabilities equals the net fair market value. The determination of gain or loss is the difference between the net fair market value and the cost basis of the stock. Whether the gain or loss is short or long term depends on how long the shares were held.

Of course, the difficulty is in determining the value of the assets. When a medical practice is contributed in exchange for stock, a valuation is performed; likewise, when the practice is sold back to the physician, another valuation must be performed. The second valuation of the practice will not be any easier than the first. The same data must be collected and the same calculations must be performed. Hopefully, however, the process will be quicker, as the parties should be familiar with the process.

All other assets must be valued as well, such as land, buildings, leaseholds, new equipment, and so forth. In addition, there may be unamortized startup costs that must be written off, repayment obligations that may need to be collected, and liabilities that must be resolved.

Accounts Receivable

One area that needs special attention is accounts receivable. The receivables, upon dissolution, should be valued and distributed as part of the dividend. Once the receivables have been distributed, they must be accounted for by the recipients; upon receipt, they should be offset against the basis of the stock (along with any other assets received). Once the receivables are either collected or written off, there may be additional gains or losses. Whether the gains and losses are short- or long-term capital gains depends on how long the stock was held.

Legal and Business Assistance with the Process

Liquidations are as difficult, if not more so, than formations, because liquidation normally occurs when the business has not turned out as the parties anticipated. Tempers are usually short, and there is plenty of blame for everyone. It is strongly advised to retain legal counsel as well as business consultants familiar with unwinding procedures to assist in and de-personalize the process so that it can get done.

ADVANCES AS LOANS OR INCOME

Compensation, dividends, advances, and loans are funded and recognized for income tax and book reporting in many different ways. Adding to the complexity is the fact that the presentation may be different for a sole proprietorship, partners in a partnership, S Corporations, and C Corporations. Each entity generally has a set of guidelines that governs the way in which these items are considered. The special interests of the individual as compared to the business should also be considered. Therefore, it becomes extremely critical that we verify the way in which a loan is presented on the balance sheet. A transaction that appears to be a loan to a partner may be considered gross income if the Internal Revenue Service has the opportunity to recast the note in the context that best suits it. The following sections will examine these transactions as they are presented in the Internal Revenue Code.

Deciding Criteria

Funds paid to an individual (other than direct compensation or dividends) may be classified as either a loan or an advance. A *loan* is defined as an amount received with the intent to repay. An *advance* is generally an amount received against future earnings. A loan, unlike an advance, is not included in the income of the borrower. Following are several examples of transactions and their classification of loan or net income.

- An advance is considered a loan if it is made with a written promissory note documenting the intention to repay. In certain circumstances, however, an advance can be considered a bona fide loan without written documentation. What this means is that although written documentation is not required, the argument that a true lender/borrower relationship exists is easier to support with written documentation.

- To prevent a loan from being recharacterized as an advance, the method of repayment must be reasonably certain. Imagine, for example, that a partner with a direct interest in a business borrows cash from his or her percentage of the year-end net profits. When the net profits for the business are disbursed at year-end, the partner who borrowed the funds uses his or her share to pay on the loan. The loan repayment is not so uncertain that it is considered to be invalid; there was a reasonable likelihood that the partnership would generate a profit.

- Business withdrawals not formally structured as loans may be classified as below market interest loans, and can include any withdrawal of business funds by an owner for personal purposes. These types of transactions are subject to the provisions in Internal Revenue Code §7872. An explanation of this section of the code as it refers to the treatment of this type of loan will be discussed later.

- An amount advanced to a corporate employee but not deducted from compensation paid is considered a loan. The method of payment of the loan is not considered uncertain in this circumstance.

- If a company eliminates a loan as a dividend distribution, that loan is included as income for the individual.

- If the loan is discharged or written off by the company and is no longer recognized as an outstanding loan, the amount discharged becomes taxable income for the borrower at the time the write-off was recorded.

- An expense advance paid to an employee but used for personal purposes must be included in the income of the employee unless an enforceable right exists for the employee to repay the amount.

Types of business entities must also be considered, as transactions are treated differently for each different type of business structure. The following section will outline some of the issues relating to the treatment of loans and income for some different types of business forms to determine which loans are subject to IRC §7872, and how to properly record the loan or income for tax purposes.

Sole Proprietorships

The issue of withdrawals or loans from a company to an officer or employee stems from the separation of the individual from the entity.

Since there is no separate entity in a sole proprietorship, there are no special accounting or tax considerations for loans from a sole proprietorship to its owner.

Partnerships

A partnership, as defined in a previous section, is the next simplest form of business entity. A partnership is an unincorporated entity with at least two members. The members of the partnership are acting jointly in business transactions and retaining property. A partnership can be a group, joint venture, or any other unincorporated entity that conducts a business venture. A partnership entity does not pay federal income tax, but is required to file a tax return for the partnership. This is what is known as a *pass-through entity:* the income, loss, and credits are "passed through" to the partners for inclusion on their personal returns. Although the partnership itself does not pay income tax and is not a separate entity, the treatment of loans from the partnership to its members is different than that of a sole proprietorship.

The net income or loss is distributed to each partner based upon the amount of his or her share in the partnership. This amount is reported on the partner's personal tax return. The net income of a partner with an outstanding loan to the partnership is netted against that outstanding balance before any distribution of income as compensation.

For example, a partnership reports a net income for the year ending 1999 of $30,000.00. The partnership has three equally sharing members, so the net income for each partner would be $10,000.00. If Partner A borrows $25,000.00 from the partnership on January 1, 1999, Partner A would report the $10,000.00 as gross income for 1999 and the balance of $15,000.00 would remain as a receivable on the partnership's balance sheet (see Exhibit 7.10).

The net income reported on each partner's personal income in Exhibit 7.10 would be $10,000.00. Disbursements of net income as compensation to the partners will be as follows:

Partner A	$0
Partner B	10,000
Partner C	10,000

Exhibit 7.10
Partnerships

S Corporation
Statement of Revenue and Expenses
Year 1999

Total Revenue	$100,000.00
Total Expenses	70,000.00
Net Income	$30,000.00

Partner A's compensation of $10,000 for the year ending December 31, 1999, has been applied to his outstanding loan balance to the partnership for $25,000. Partner A's new loan balance for the year 2000 will be $15,000.

Under Internal Revenue Code §7872, Partner A would owe interest to the partnership at the statutory federal rate of interest that was in effect as of the date of the origination of the loan. The interest would accumulate on the balance sheet for the year 2000 or until the loan has been paid in full. If the loan should reach a point at which the total on the balance sheet falls below $10,000.00, the Internal Revenue Code §7872 would not apply. Therefore, interest would not be required on the remaining balance.

S-Corporations

Although the S corporation is a separate entity, each partner of an S-corporation reports his or her percentage of the corporation's income and expenses on his or her personal tax return. An S-corp is then a pass-through entity; therefore, a loan from an S-corp is similar to borrowing from the other partners. If the previous example were an S-corp, however, some special considerations would apply.

For example, the provisions for interest under IRC Section 7872 would still apply if the example were an S-corp instead of a partnership. If the S-corporation reported a loss instead of a gain, the entire $25,000.00 would remain on the balance sheet and would accumulate interest based on IRC Section 7872.

However, careful consideration must be made in the documentation of advances from an S-corp. Distributions of funds from an S-corp to its partners must be as either compensation or dividends because it is a separate entity. Compensation and dividends received by a partner are included in his or her personal income.

In order to classify an advance as a loan, an S-corp must have the written promissory note to document the loan. Without this appropriate documentation, a loan to a partner can be construed by the IRS to be a dividend. Dividends in an S-corp must be distributed equally. Considering a loan to one partner to be dividends paid may cause inequality in dividends paid, and the IRS could declare the S-corp invalid.

C-Corporations

The characteristics (outlined earlier in this chapter) of a C-corporation show that this type of entity is completely separate from the owners or shareholders. Any distribution of funds from a C-corporation to an individual is either a dividend or compensation and must be treated as income for the recipient.

Internal Revenue Code Section 7872

As stated previously, withdrawals of funds not formally structured as loans can be classified as arm's-length transactions and must be given special consideration. These transactions, in addition to loans with low stated interest rates and below–market interest loans, are governed by the Internal Revenue Code Section 7872.

This section states that a loan containing little or no interest is considered an arm's-length transaction and is subject to a statutory federal rate of interest. In other words, these loans are subject to the federal interest rate in effect on the date of the transaction, regardless of the interest rate stated on the note. The borrower is obligated by this rule to pay interest at the effective rate on these types of loans. This rule is in effect for corporation-shareholder loans, gift loans, compensation loans from an employer to an employee, and any loan that has an effect on either party's tax liability.

There is, however, a $10,000.00 exception to Internal Revenue Code Section 7872, called the *de minimus* exception. This is the minimum amount for which the arm's-length transaction rules apply. Any loan above this amount may be subject to interest. This limit is not based on current-year activity, but on the total accumulated amount of the loan outstanding on the entity's balance sheet date. However, this limitation does not apply if the principle purpose of the loan is determined to be tax avoidance.

CHAPTER EIGHT

Tax Issues Affecting Medical Practices

Numerous tax issues can impact a medical practice; this chapter summarizes the most common subject areas. For a more detailed discussion, please refer to the Internal Revenue Code Regulations. The non-CPA reader should contact a tax accountant experienced in working with medical practices.

FORMATION OF A PERSONAL SERVICE CORPORATION

A corporation is a *personal service* corporation if all the following conditions are met:

1. The corporation is a C-corporation.

2. The corporation's principal activity during the testing period is the performance of personal services.

3. Owner-employees of the corporation perform a substantial part of the services during the testing period (generally, the testing period for a tax year is the prior tax year).

4. Owner-employees own more than 10% of the corporation's stock on the last day of the testing period.

Any activity that involves the performance of services in the fields of health, veterinary services, law, engineering, architecture, accounting, actuarial science, performing arts, or certain consulting services is considered to be the *performance of personal services*. In order to be considered a *principal activity*, the performance of personal service activities must provide the corporation with more than 50% of its total compensation costs. The *owner-employee* in the previous criteria is a person who, on any day of the testing period, is both an employee of the corporation and owns any outstanding stock of the corporation. This rule applies even if the legal form of the person's relationship to the corporation is such that the person would be considered an independent contractor for other purposes.

Determining the Corporation's Fiscal Year

A personal service corporation must use a calendar year as its fiscal year, unless it can establish a business purpose for a different period or it makes a Section 444 election (discussed later). For example, Corporation A has been in existence since 1980. It has always used a January 31 fiscal year for its accounting period. To determine whether A is a personal service corporation for its tax year beginning February 1, 1996, the testing period is A's tax year ending January 31, 1996.

The testing period for the first tax year of a new corporation, on the other hand, starts with the first day of the tax year and ends on the earlier of (1) The last day of its tax year, or (2) The last day of the calendar year in which the tax year begins. For example, Corporation B's first tax year begins June 1, 1996. B wants to use a September 30 fiscal year for its accounting period. B's testing period for its first tax year is from June 1, 1996, through September 30, 1996. If B wants to use a March 31 fiscal year, the testing period is from June 1, 1996, through December 31, 1996.

SECTION 444 ELECTION

A personal service corporation can elect under Section 444 of the IRC to use a tax year different from the one it would normally be required to use. Certain restrictions do apply to this election: it is not allowed for a personal service corporation that establishes a business purpose for a different period, and the personal service corporation must meet all of the following requirements to qualify for the election:

1. It is not a member of a tiered structure (see Section 1.444-2T of the regulations).
2. It has not previously had a Section 444 election in effect.
3. It elects a year that meets the deferral period requirement.

The determination of the deferral period depends on whether the personal service corporation is retaining its current tax year, or changing or adopting a new tax year with a Section 444 election. Generally, a personal service corporation can make a Section 444 election to retain its tax year only if the deferral period of the new tax year is three months or less. The deferral period in this case is the number of months between the beginning of the retained year and the close of the first required tax year. If the personal service corporation is changing to a tax year other than its required year, the deferral period is the number of months from the end of the new tax year to the end of the required tax year. The IRS will allow a Section 444 election only if the deferral period of the new tax year is less than the shorter of (1) three months, or (2) the deferral period of the tax year that is being changed (the tax year immediately preceding the year for which the personal service corporation wishes to make the Section 444 election). If the personal service corporation's tax year is the same as its required tax year, the deferral period is zero.

For example, Partnership BD uses a calendar year, which is also its required tax year. BD cannot make a Section 444 election because the deferral period is zero.

On the other hand, Partnership E, a newly formed partnership, began operations on December 1, 1997. E is owned by calendar-year partners. E wants to make a Section 444 election to adopt a September 30 tax year. E's deferral period for the tax year beginning December 1, 1997, is three months, the number of months between September 30 and December 31.

Filing Form 8716, "Election To Have a Tax Year Other Than a Required Tax Year," with the Internal Revenue Service Center, is the method by which a Section 444 election is made. Form 8716 must be filed by the earlier of (1) the due date (not including extensions) of the income tax return resulting from the Section 444 election; or (2) the 15th day of the 6th month of the tax year for which the election will be effective. For this purpose, the month in which the tax year begins is counted, even if it begins after the first day of that month. A copy of Form 8716 must be attached to Form 1065 or to the appropriate Form 1120 for the first tax year for which the election is made. (There is an automatic extension of 12 months to make this election; see the form instructions for more information.)

For example, Partnership AB began operations on September 11, 1999, and is qualified to make a Section 444 election to use a September 30 tax year for its tax year beginning September 11, 1999. AB must file Form 8716 by January 15, 2000, which is the due date of the partnership's tax return for the period from September 11, 1996, to September 30, 1999.

Imagine, however, that AB had begun operations on October 21, 1999. AB would now be required to file Form 8716 by March 15, 2000, the 15th day of the 6th month of the tax year for which the election would first be effective.

Another example is that of Corporation BA, which first becomes a personal service corporation for its tax year beginning September 1, 1999. BA qualifies to make a Section 444 election to use a September 30 tax year for its tax year beginning September 1, 1999. BA must file Form 8716 by December 16, 1999, the due date of the income tax return for the short period from September 1, 1996, to September 30, 1999.

Note that a partnership or an S-corporation that makes a Section 444 election must make certain payments, and a personal service corporation must make certain distributions. A partnership or an S-corporation must make a "required payment" for any tax year in which the Section 444 election is in effect, and the required payment for that year (or any preceding tax year) is more than $500. Any tax year in which a Section 444 election is in effect, including the first year, is called an "applicable election year." The required payment represents the value of the tax deferral the owners receive by using a tax year different from the required tax year.

Form 8752, "Required Payment or Refund Under Section 7519," must be filed each year in which the Section 444 election is in effect, even if no payment is due. If the required payment is more than $500 (or the required payment for any prior year was more than $500), the payment must be made when Form 8752 is filed. If the required payment is $500 or less, and no payment was required in a prior year, Form 8752 must be filed showing a zero amount.

Form 8752 must be filed and the required payment made (or zero amount reported) by May 15 of the calendar year following the calendar year in which the applicable election year begins. For example, if a partnership's applicable election year begins July 1, 1996, Form 8752 must be filed by May 15, 1997.

The preceding rules apply to a partnership or an S-corp; a personal service corporation with a Section 444 election in effect must distribute certain amounts to owner-employees by December 31 of each applicable year. If it fails to make these distributions, it may be required to defer certain deductions for amounts paid to owner-employees. The amount deferred is treated as paid or incurred in the following tax year. For information on the minimum distribution, see the instructions for Part I of Schedule H (Form 1120), Section 280H, "Limitations for a Personal Service Corporation (PSC)."

A partnership, S-corp, or personal service corporation can file a back-up Section 444 election if it requests (or plans to request) permission to use a business-purpose tax year, discussed on page 232. If the request is denied, the back-up Section 444 election must be activated, provided the partnership, S-corporation, or personal service corporation otherwise qualifies.

The general rules for making a Section 444 election apply to filing a back-up Section 444 election. When Form 8716, is filed, "BACK-UP ELECTION" must be typed or printed at the top of the form. However, if Form 8716 is filed on or after the date Form 1128 is filed, "FORM 1128 BACK-UP ELECTION" must be typed or printed at the top of Form 8716.

A partnership or S-corp activates its back-up election by filing the return required, making the required payment with Form 8752, and printing at the top of the form, "ACTIVATING BACK-UP ELECTION." The due date for filing Form 8752 and making the payment is the later of (1) May 15 of the calendar year following the calendar year in which the applicable election year begins, or (2) 60 days after the partnership or S-corp has been notified by the IRS that the business-year request has been denied.

A personal service corporation activates its back-up election by filing Form 8716 with its original or amended income tax return for the tax year in which the election is first effective, and printing on the top of the income tax return, "ACTIVATING BACK-UP ELECTION."

The Section 444 election remains in effect until it is terminated. If the election is terminated, another Section 444 election cannot be made for any tax year. The election ends when the personal service corporation does any of the following:

- Changes its tax year to a required tax year

- Liquidates

- Willfully fails to comply with the required payments or distributions

- Becomes a member of a tiered structure

The election will also end if:

- An S-corporation's S election is terminated. However, if the S-corp immediately becomes a personal service corporation, it can continue the Section 444 election of the S-corp.

- A personal service corporation ceases to be a personal service corporation. If the personal service corporation elects to be an S-corporation, it can continue the election of the personal service corporation.

Business-Purpose Tax Year

A business-purpose tax year is an accounting period that has a substantial business purpose for its existence. In considering whether there is a business purpose for a tax year, significant weight is given to tax factors. A prime consideration is whether the change to a different tax year would create a substantial distortion of income, such as the following:

- Deferral of substantial income or the shifting of substantial deductions from one year to another to reduce tax liability

- A similar deferral or shifting for any other person, such as a partner or shareholder

- The creation of a short period in which there is a substantial net operating loss

The following nontax factors, which are based on the convenience of the taxpayer, are generally not sufficient to establish a business purpose for a particular tax year:

- Use of a particular year for regulatory or financial accounting purposes

- Use of a particular hiring pattern, such as typically hiring staff during certain times of the year

- Use of a particular year for administrative purposes, such as admission or retirement of partners or shareholders, promotion of staff, or compensation or retirement arrangements with staff, partners, or shareholders

- Use of a price list, model year, or other item that changes on an annual basis

- Deferral of income to partners or shareholders

For examples of situations in which a substantial business purpose has (and has not) been established, see Revenue Ruling 87-57, 1987-2 C.B. 117.

One nontax factor that may be sufficient to establish a business purpose for a tax year is an annual cycle of business activity called a "natural business year." A natural business year exists when a business has a peak and a nonpeak period. The natural business year is considered to end at or soon after the end of the peak period. (A business whose income is steady from month to month all year would not have a natural business year as such.) A natural business year is considered a substantial business purpose for an entity's changing its accounting period. The IRS will ordinarily approve this change unless it results in a substantial deferral of income or another tax advantage.

The IRS provides a procedure for a partnership, an S-corporation, or a personal service corporation to retain or automatically change to a natural business year as determined by the 25% test, which uses the method of accounting used for the tax returns for each year involved. To apply the 25% test:

1. Total the gross sales and services receipts for the most recent 12-month period that includes the last month of the requested fiscal year. Figure this for the 12-month period that ends before

the filing of the request. Also total the gross sales and services receipts for the last two months of that 12-month period.

2. Determine the percentage of the receipts for the 2-month period by dividing the total of the last 2-month period by the total for the 12-month period. Carry the percentage to two decimal places.

3. Figure the percentage following steps 1 and 2 for the two 12-month periods *just preceding* the 12-month period used in step 1.

If the percentage determined for each of the three years equals or exceeds 25%, the requested fiscal year is the natural business year.

A few special rules do apply to the use of the 25% test:

- If the partnership, S-corp, or personal service corporation qualifies for more than one natural business year, the fiscal year producing the highest average of the three percentages is the natural business year.

- If the partnership, S-corp, or personal service corporation does not have at least 47 months of gross receipts (which may include a predecessor organization's gross receipts), it cannot use this automatic procedure to obtain permission to use a fiscal year.

- If the requested tax year is a 52–53-week tax year, the calendar month ending nearest the last day of the 52–53-week tax year is treated as the last month of the requested tax year for purposes of computing the 25% test.

The IRS also allows an S-corp or a corporation electing to be an S-corp to adopt, retain, or change to a fiscal year that satisfies the requirements of the "ownership tax year test." The corporation qualifies for automatic approval if it is adopting, retaining, or changing to a tax year and shareholders holding more than 50% of its issued and outstanding shares of stock on the first day of the requested tax year have, or are all changing to, the same tax year. Shareholders desiring to change to the same tax year should follow Section 1.442-1(b)(1) of the regulations when requesting permission. If, on the first day of any tax year, the S-corp no longer meets the ownership tax year test, the corporation must change its tax year to a permitted year.

To get the automatic approval, the qualifying partnership, S-corp, or corporation electing to be an S-corporation, must file a tax return for the short period by the due date, including extensions.

Furthermore, the organization must file Form 1128 by the 15th day of the second calendar month following the close of the short period with the director of the Internal Revenue Service Center where the entity normally files its tax return. The envelope should be marked "Attention: ENTITY CONTROL." The applicant must type or print "FILED UNDER REV. PROC. 87-32" at the top of Form 1128.

In some cases, a late-filed Form 1128 may be accepted. However, applications the IRS receives 90 days after the due date will not be approved, except in very unusual and compelling circumstances.

A corporation that elects to be an S-corp and requests to adopt, retain, or change its tax year must file Form 2553, "Election by a Small Business Corporation." This form must be filed when the election request is made. No extension of time can be granted for filing Form 2553. The user fee is not due with the form; the IRS will notify the applicant when the fee is due.

For more information, see Revenue Procedure 87-32, 1987-2 C.B. 396.

AMORTIZATION OF INTANGIBLE ASSETS

Section 197 Intangibles

A company must amortize over 15 years the capitalized costs of "Section 197 intangibles" that were acquired after August 10, 1993. The company must amortize these costs if it holds the Section 197 intangibles in connection with its trade or business or in connection with an activity in which it is engaged for the production of income. The deduction each year is the part of the adjusted basis (for purposes of determining gain) of the intangible that is amortized ratably over a 15-year period, beginning with the month acquired. The company is not allowed any other depreciation or amortization deduction for a Section 197 intangible.

We will review here those assets that are Section 197 intangibles, as previously discussed in chapter 7:

1. Goodwill

2. Going concern value

3. Workforce in place, including its composition and the terms and conditions (contractual or otherwise) of its employment

4. Business books and records, operating systems, or any other information base, including lists or other information concerning current or prospective customers

5. A patent, copyright, formula, process, design, pattern, know-how, format, or similar item

6. A customer-based intangible

7. A supplier-based intangible

8. Any item similar to items 3–7

9. A license, permit, or other right granted by a governmental unit or agency (including renewals)

10. A covenant not to compete entered into in connection with the acquisition of an interest in a trade or business

11. A franchise, trademark, or trade name (including renewals)

Amortization of any of the intangible in items 1–8 that was created by the owner/shareholder is not deductible, unless it was created in connection with the acquisition of assets constituting a trade or business or a substantial part of a trade or business.

Goodwill is the value of a trade or business based on expected continued customer patronage due to its name, reputation, or any other factor. *Going concern value* is the additional value of a trade or business that attaches to property because the property is an integral part of a going concern. It includes value based on the ability of a business to continue to function and generate income even though there is a change in ownership.

The *workforce in place* includes the composition of a workforce (for example, its experience, education, or training). It also includes the terms and conditions of employment, whether contractual or otherwise, and any other value placed on employees or any of their attributes. For example, a company must amortize the part of a purchase price of a trade or business that is based on the existence of a highly skilled workforce. It must also amortize the cost of acquiring an existing employment contract or relationship with employees or consultants as part of the acquisition of a trade or business.

The *business books and records* category includes the cost of technical manuals, training manuals, or programs, data files, and accounting or inventory control systems. It also includes the cost of customer lists, subscription lists, insurance expirations, patient or client files, and lists of newspaper, magazine, radio, or television advertisers.

The *patents and copyrights* category includes package designs, computer software, and any interest in a film, sound recording, videotape, book, or other similar property, except as discussed on page 239.

A *customer-based intangible* is the composition of market, market share, and any other value resulting from the future provision of goods or services because of relationships with customers in the ordinary course of business. The company must amortize that part (if any) of the purchase price of a trade or business that is for the following intangible:

- Customer base

- Circulation base

- Undeveloped market or market growth

- Insurance in force

- Mortgage servicing contract

- Investment management contract

- Any other relationship with customers that involves the future provision of goods or services

Note that accounts receivable or other similar rights to income for goods or services provided to customers before the acquisition of that trade or business are not Section 197 intangibles.

A *supplier-based intangible* is the value resulting from the future acquisition of goods or services because of relationships in the ordinary course of business with suppliers of goods or services. These goods and services must be used or sold by the business. For example, the company must amortize the part of the purchase price of a trade or business that is based on the existence of any one of the following:

- A favorable relationship with distributors (such as favorable shelf or display space at a retail outlet)

- A favorable credit rating

- A favorable supply contract

Any license, permit, or other right granted by a governmental unit or an agency or instrumentality of a governmental unit is a Section 197 intangible. For example, a company must amortize the capitalized costs of acquiring (including issuing or renewing) a liquor license, a taxicab medallion or license, or a television or radio broadcasting license.

A *covenant not to compete* (or similar arrangement) entered into in connection with the acquisition of an interest in a trade or business or in a substantial portion of a trade or business, is a Section 197 intangible. An interest in a trade or business includes an interest in a partnership or stock in a corporation engaged in a trade or business.

If an amount is paid or incurred under a covenant not to compete (or similar arrangement) after the year in which the covenant (or similar arrangement) was entered into, the company must amortize that amount over the months remaining in the 15-year amortization period. Amounts paid under a covenant not to compete (or similar arrangement) that represent additional consideration for the purchase of stock in a corporation cannot be amortized. They must be added to the basis of the acquired stock.

A *franchise, trademark, or trade name* is a Section 197 intangible. A company can deduct amounts paid or incurred on the transfer, sale, or other disposition of a franchise, trademark, or trade name if all of the following apply to the amounts.

- They are contingent on the productivity, use, or disposition of the franchise, trademark, or trade name.

- They are part of a series of payments payable at least annually throughout the term of the transfer agreement.

- They are part of a series of payments that are substantially equal in amount or payable under a fixed formula.

A company must amortize any other amount, whether fixed or contingent that they paid or incurred because of the transfer of a franchise, trademark, or trade name.

Assets That Are Not Section 197 Intangibles

The following assets are not Section 197 intangibles:

1. Any interest in a corporation, partnership, trust, or estate

2. Any interest under an existing futures contract, foreign currency contract, notional principal contract, or similar financial contract

3. Any interest in land

4. Most computer software

5. Any of the following not acquired in connection with the acquisition of a trade or business or a substantial part of a trade or business:

   a. An interest in a film, sound recording, videotape, book, or similar property

   b. A right to receive tangible property or services under a contract or granted by a governmental agency

   c. An interest in a patent or copyright

   d. A right under a contract (or a right granted by a governmental agency) if the right:

      i. Has a fixed life of less than 15 years, or

      ii. Is of a fixed amount that, except for the section 197 intangible provisions, would be recoverable under a method similar to the unit-of-production method of cost recovery

6. An interest under either:

   a. An existing lease or sublease of tangible property, or

   b. A debt that was in existence when the interest was acquired

7. A professional sports franchise and any item acquired in connection with the franchise

8. A right to service residential mortgages unless the right is acquired in the acquisition of a trade or business or a substantial part of a trade or business

9. Certain transaction costs under a corporate organization or reorganization in which any part of a gain or loss is not recognized

Computer software includes all programs designed to cause a computer to perform a desired function. It also includes any database or similar item in the public domain and incidental to the operation of qualifying software.

Section 197 intangibles do not include computer software that is readily available for purchase by the general public, subject to a nonexclusive license, and not substantially changed.

Software that is not acquired in the acquisition of a substantial part of a business is not a Section 197 intangible. If a company is allowed to depreciate any computer software that is not a Section 197 intangible, it must use the straight line method with a useful life of 36 months.

Certain amounts that are taken into account in determining the cost of nonsection 197 property are not considered Section 197 intangibles. These amounts are added to the basis of the property. For example, none of the costs of acquiring real property held for the production of rental income are considered goodwill, going concern value, or any other Section 197 intangible.

Disposition of Section 197 Intangibles

A section 197 intangible is treated as depreciable property used in the company's trade or business. If property held for more than one year is disposed of, any gain on the disposition, up to the amount of allowable amortization, is ordinary income (Section 1245 gain). Any remaining gain, or loss, is a Section 1231 gain or loss. If the property is held one year or less, any gain or loss on its disposition is an ordinary gain or loss.

If more than one Section 197 intangible is acquired in a transaction (or series of related transactions) and one of them is later disposed of or becomes worthless, a loss on the intangible cannot be recognized.

Instead, the company must increase the adjusted basis of each remaining amortizable Section 197 intangible by the part of the loss not recognized. The increase is figured by multiplication of the loss not recognized on the disposition by the following fraction:

- The numerator is the adjusted basis of that remaining intangible as of the date of its disposition.

- The denominator is the total adjusted basis of all retained amortizable Section 197 intangibles as of the date of the disposition.

A covenant not to compete, or similar arrangement, is not considered disposed of or worthless before the disposition of the entire interest in the trade or business for which the parties entered into the covenant.

Furthermore, if one section 197 intangible is disposed of and another acquired in a nonrecognition transfer, the company must treat the part of the adjusted basis of the acquired intangible that is not more than the adjusted basis of the transferred intangible as the transferred Section 197 intangible. This includes the continuing amortization of the part of the adjusted basis treated as the transferred Section 197 intangible over its remaining amortization period. Nonrecognition transfers include transfers to a corporation, partnership contributions and distributions, like-kind exchanges, and involuntary conversions.

For example, the company owns a Section 197 intangible that it has amortized for four full years, with a remaining unamortized basis of $30,000. The company exchanges the asset plus $10,000 for a like-kind Section 197 intangible. The nonrecognition provisions of like-kind exchanges apply. The company amortizes $30,000 of the basis of the acquired Section 197 intangible over the 11 years remaining in the original 15-year amortization period for the transferred asset and the other $10,000 of adjusted basis over 15 years.

Anti-Churning Rules

A company cannot amortize certain Section 197 intangible over 15 years. Special rules prevent the conversion of Section 197 intangibles from property that does not qualify for amortization to property that would qualify for amortization.

The company cannot use 15-year amortization for goodwill, going concern value, or any intangible for which it cannot claim a depreciation deduction and for which an amortization deduction is only allowable under Section 197 if it meets both of the following criteria:

1. The company acquired the goodwill, going concern value, or other intangible after August 10, 1993.

2. Any of the following conditions apply:

    1. The company or a related person (defined shortly) held or used the intangible at any time from July 25, 1991, through August 10, 1993.

    2. The company acquired the intangible from a person who held the intangible at any time from July 25, 1991, through August 10, 1993, and as part of the transaction, the user does not change.

    3. The company grants the right to use the intangible to a person (or a person related to that person) who held or used the intangible at any time from July 25, 1991, through August 10, 1993.

Note that the anti-churning rules do not apply to an intangible acquired from a decedent if the property's basis is stepped up to fair market value.

Related Persons

For purposes of the anti-churning rules, the following are *related persons:*

- Members of a family, including only brothers, sisters, half-brothers, half-sisters, spouse, ancestors (parents, grandparents, etc.), and lineal descendants (children, grandchildren, etc.)

- An individual and a corporation when the individual owns, directly or indirectly, more than 20% in value of the corporation's outstanding stock

- Two corporations that are members of the same controlled group as defined in section 1563(a) of the Internal Revenue Code, except that "more than 20%" is substituted for "at least 80%" in that definition and the determination is made without regard to subsection (a)(4) and (e)(3)(C) of Section 1563

- A trust fiduciary and a corporation when the trust or grantor of the trust owns, directly or indirectly, more than 20% in value of the corporation's outstanding stock

- A grantor and fiduciary, and the fiduciary and beneficiary, of any trust

- Fiduciaries of two different trusts, and the fiduciary and beneficiary of two different trusts, if the same person is the grantor of both trusts

- A tax-exempt educational or charitable organization and a person who, directly or indirectly, controls the organization, or a member of that person's family

- A corporation and a partnership if the same persons own more than 20% in value of the outstanding stock of the corporation and more than 20% of the capital or profits interest in the partnership

- Two S-corporations if the same persons own more than 20% in value of the outstanding stock of each corporation

- Two corporations, one of which is an S-corporation, if the same persons own more than 20% in value of the outstanding stock of each corporation

- Two partnerships if the same persons own, directly or indirectly, more than 20% of the capital or the profits interests in both partnerships

- A person and a partnership when the person owns, directly or indirectly, more than 20% of the capital or profits interests in the partnership

The company must treat these persons as related if the relationship exists immediately before or immediately after the company acquired the intangible.

Ownership of Stock

In determining whether an individual owns, directly or indirectly, any of the outstanding stock of a corporation, the following rules apply:

- *Rule 1.* Stock owned, directly or indirectly, by or for a corporation, partnership, estate, or trust is considered owned proportionately by or for its shareholders, partners, or beneficiaries.

- *Rule 2.* An individual is considered as owning the stock that is owned, directly or indirectly, by or for his or her family. Family includes only brothers and sisters, half-brothers and half-sisters, spouse, ancestors, and lineal descendants.

- *Rule 3.* An individual owning (other than by applying Rule 2) any stock in a corporation is considered to own the stock owned, directly or indirectly, by or for his or her partner.

- *Rule 4.* For purposes of applying Rule 1, 2, or 3, the company should treat stock constructively owned by a person under Rule 1 as actually owned by that person. It should not treat stock constructively owned by an individual under Rules 2 or 3 as owned by the individual for reapplying Rule 2 or 3 to make another person the constructive owner of the stock.

Exception. An exception to the anti-churning rules applies if the company acquires an intangible from a person related by more than 20%, but not more than 50%, under both of the following conditions: (1) the seller recognizes gain on the disposition of the intangible; and (2) the tax the seller pays on the gain plus any other federal income tax imposed on the gain equals tax on the gain at the highest tax rate. If this exception applies, the anti-churning rules apply only to the amount of the adjusted basis in the intangible that is more than the gain recognized by the seller.

Note that the seller reports any additional tax under this exception on line 40 of the seller's Form 1040. On the dotted line next to line 40, the seller should also write "197."

Anti-Abuse Rule

The company cannot amortize any Section 197 intangible acquired in a transaction if the principal purpose was either to avoid the requirement that the intangible be acquired after August 10, 1993, or to avoid any of the anti-churning rules.

Incorrect Amount of Amortization Deducted

If the company did not deduct the correct amount of amortization for a Section 197 intangible in any year, it may be able to make a correction for that year by filing an amended return, as explained later in this section. If the company is not allowed to make the correction on an amended return, it can change its accounting method to claim the correct amount of amortization, also to be discussed shortly.

Even if the company does not claim amortization it is entitled to deduct, it must reduce the basis of the Section 197 intangible by the full amount of amortization it was entitled to deduct. If it deducts more amortization than it should, it must decrease its basis by any amount deducted from which it received a tax benefit.

Amended Returns

If the company did not deduct the correct amount of amortization, it can file an amended return to make any of the following three corrections.

- Correction of a mathematical error made in any year

- Correction of a posting error made in any year

- Correction of the amount of amortization for section 197 intangibles for which you have not adopted a method of accounting

If the company did not deduct the correct amount of amortization for the Section 197 intangible on two or more consecutively-filed tax returns, it has adopted a method of accounting for that property. If it has adopted a method of accounting, it cannot change the method by filing amended returns.

If an amended return is allowed, it must be filed by the later of (1) three years from the date the company filed its original return for the year in which it did not deduct the correct amount, or (2) two years from the time the company paid its tax for that year. A return filed early is considered filed on the due date.

Changing the Accounting Method

If the company did not deduct the correct amount of amortization for the Section 197 intangible on any two or more consecutively-filed tax returns, it has adopted a method of accounting for that property. It can claim the correct amount of amortization only by changing its method of accounting for amortization; the company will then be able to take into account any unclaimed or excess amortization from years before the year of change.

The company must first have the consent of the Commissioner of Internal Revenue to change its method of accounting. The Commissioner's consent may be obtained by following the instructions in Revenue Procedure 97-27, which is in Internal Revenue Bulletin (IRB) 1997-21. Internal Revenue Bulletins are available at many libraries and IRS offices. To get the consent, the company must file Form 3115 requesting a change to a permissible method of accounting for amortization. It cannot use Revenue Procedure 97-27 to correct any mathematical or posting error, as mentioned under Amended Returns.

In some instances, the company can receive automatic consent from the Commissioner if it deducted *less* than the allowable amount of amortization for the Section 197 intangible in at least two years immediately preceding the year of change. Instead of following the instructions in Revenue Procedure 97-27, the company can receive an automatic consent by following the instructions in Revenue Procedure 97-37 and Section 2.01 of the Appendix of Revenue Procedure 97-37, which are in Internal Revenue Bulletin (IRB) 1997-33. These procedures will enable the company to change its accounting method to take into account previously unclaimed allowable amortization. To get the consent, the company must file Form 3115 requesting a change to a permissible method of accounting for amortization.

This procedure can generally be used for property that meets all of the following three conditions.

- It is property for which the company computes amortization under Section 197 of the Internal Revenue Code.

- It is property for which, under the company's present accounting method, it claimed less than the amount of amortization allowable in at least the two years immediately preceding the year of change. (The year of change is the year the company designates on the Form 3115 and for which it has timely filed the Form 3115.)

- It is property the company owned at the beginning of the year of change.

However, a company generally *cannot* use the automatic consent procedure if any of the exceptions listed in section 2.01(2)(b) of the Appendix of Revenue Procedure 97-37 apply. The automatic consent procedure also is generally not all under any of the following situations:

- The company's federal income tax return is under examination.

- The company is before a federal court or an appeals office for any income tax issue and the method of accounting to be changed is an issue under consideration by the federal court or appeals office.

- The company changed the same method of accounting (with or without obtaining the consent of the Commissioner) during the four years before the year of change.

- The company filed a Form 3115 to change the same method of accounting during the four years before the year of change but did not make the change because the Form 3115 was withdrawn, not perfected, denied, or not granted.

For more information on how to get this automatic consent to change the method of accounting in order to claim previously unclaimed allowable amortization and on when it may and may not be used, see Revenue Procedure 97-37 and section 2.01 of the Appendix of Revenue Procedure 97-37, Internal Revenue Bulletin 1997-33.

Recapture of Amortization

Amortization claimed on Section 197 property is subject to the recapture rules of Section 1245 of the Internal Revenue Code. For more information on these rules, see Chapter 3 in IRS Publication 544.

AMORTIZATION OF START-UP COSTS

When a company goes into business, it must treat all costs it incurs to get the business started as capital expenses. Capital expenses are part of the company's basis in the business. Generally, costs for particular assets are recovered through depreciation deductions. However, the owners generally cannot recover other costs until they sell the business or otherwise go out of business.

The company can elect to amortize certain costs for setting up business. To be amortizable, the cost must qualify as either a business start-up cost, an organizational cost for a corporation, or an organization cost for a partnership.

Business Start-up Costs

Start-up costs are costs for setting up an active trade or business, or for investigating the possibility of creating or acquiring an active trade or business. Start-up costs include any amounts paid or incurred in connection with any activity engaged in for profit and for the production of income before the trade or business begins, in anticipation of the activity's becoming an active trade or business.

To be amortizable, a start-up cost must be one that could be deducted if it was paid or incurred to operate an existing active trade or business; it also must have been incurred before the day that active trade or business began.

Start-up costs include what the owners pay for investigating a prospective business and getting the business started. They may include costs for the following items:

- A survey of potential markets

- An analysis of available facilities, labor, supplies, and so forth

- Advertisements for the opening of the business

- Salaries and wages for employees who are being trained, and for their instructors

- Travel and other necessary costs for securing prospective distributors, suppliers, or customers

- Salaries and fees for executives and consultants, or for other professional services

Start-up costs *do not include* deductible interest, taxes, and research and experimental costs (discussed later in this chapter).

Any remaining deferred start-up costs for the business can be deducted if the business is completely disposed of before the end of the amortization period. However, these deferred start-up costs can be deducted only to the extent that they qualify as a loss from a business.

Costs of Organizing a Corporation

The costs of organizing a corporation are the direct costs of creating the corporation. The costs can be amortized only if they meet all three of the following tests:

- The costs must be for the creation of the corporation.
- The costs must be chargeable to a capital account.
- The business could amortize the costs over the life of the corporation, if the corporation had a fixed life.

Furthermore, the corporation must have incurred the costs before the end of the first tax year in which it was in business. A corporation using the cash method of accounting can amortize organizational expenses incurred within the first tax year, even if it does not pay them in that year.

Examples of organizational costs are:

- Expenses of temporary directors
- The cost of organizational meetings
- State incorporation fees
- Accounting services for setting up the organization
- The cost of legal services (such as drafting the charter, bylaws, terms of the original stock certificates, and minutes of organization meetings)

Costs that *cannot* be amortized include costs for issuing and selling stock or securities, such as commissions, professional fees, and printing costs, because they are not organizational costs. Also, a corporation cannot amortize costs associated with the transfer of assets to the corporation; these costs must be capitalized.

Costs of Organizing a Partnership

Partnership organizational costs are the direct costs of creating a partnership, and can be amortized only if they meet all three of the following tests:

- The costs must be for the creation of the partnership and not for starting or operating the partnership trade or business.
- The costs must be chargeable to a capital account.
- The costs could be amortized over the life of the partnership if the partnership had a fixed life.

Organizational costs include the following fees:

- Legal fees for services incidental to the organization of the partnership, such as negotiation and preparation of the partnership agreement
- Accounting fees for services incidental to the organization of the partnership
- Filing fees

Expenses *cannot* be amortized if they are connected with any of the following activities:

- Acquiring assets for the partnership or transferring assets to the partnership
- Admitting or removing partners, other than at the time the partnership is first organized

- Making a contract concerning the operation of the partnership trade or business (including a contract between a partner and the partnership)

- Syndication fees

Syndication fees are costs for issuing and marketing interests in the partnership (such as commissions, professional fees, and printing costs). Syndication fees must be capitalized. They cannot be depreciated or amortized.

The Amortization Process

The company must deduct start-up and organizational costs in equal amounts over a period of 60 months or more. The chosen period for start-up costs may be different from that for organizational costs, as long as both are 60 months or more. Once elected, the duration of an amortization period cannot be changed. The amortization period actually starts with the month in which business operations began.

The company's deduction is figured by dividing its total start-up or organizational costs by the months in the amortization period; the result is the amount the company can deduct each month.

A partnership using the cash method of accounting cannot deduct an expense it has not paid by the end of the tax year. However, any expense the partnership could have deducted as an organizational expense in an earlier tax year can be deducted in the tax year of payment.

Once company management decides to amortize costs, they must complete Part VI of Form 4562 and attach it to the company's income tax return. They must also attach one or more statements to this return; if the company has both start-up and organizational costs, a separate statement for each type of cost must be attached to the return. Each statement should have the following information:

- The total start-up or organizational costs to be amortized

- A description of what each cost is for

- The date each cost was incurred

- The month active business began (or the month the business was acquired)

- The number of months in the amortization period (not less than 60)

Included in these required attachments are Form 4562 and the accompanying statements for the first tax year the company is in business. The return must be filed by the due date (including any extensions).

Note that, if the company is organized as a corporation or partnership, only the corporation or partnership can elect to amortize its start-up or organizational costs—in other words, a shareholder or partner alone cannot make this election.

Furthermore, the shareholder or partner cannot amortize any costs incurred in setting up the corporation or partnership. The corporation or partnership can amortize these costs, but only if it reimburses the shareholders or partners for them. These costs then become part of the basis of the shareholder or partner's interest in the business, and can be recovered only when that person sells his or her interest in the business.

INDEPENDENT CONTRACTORS VERSUS EMPLOYEES

Medical practices frequently contract with companies or individuals on an independent contractor basis. However, many times these individuals are in fact employees of the medical practice. Whether such people are employees or independent contractors depends on the facts in each case. The general rule is that an individual is an independent contractor if the payer has the right to control or direct only the result of the work and not the means and methods of accomplishing the result.

Furthermore, an employer must generally withhold income taxes, withhold and pay social security and Medicare taxes, and pay unemployment tax on wages paid to an employee, but does not generally have to withhold or pay any taxes on payments to independent contractors.

Common-Law Rules

To determine whether an individual is an employee or an independent contractor under the common law, the relationship of the worker to the business must be examined. All evidence of control and independence must be considered. In any employee-independent contractor determination, all information that provides evidence of the degree of control and the degree of independence must be considered. Facts that provide evidence of the degree of control and independence fall into three categories: behavioral control, financial control, and the type of relationship of the parties as shown below.

Behavioral Control

Facts that show whether the business has a right to direct and control how the worker does the task for which the worker is hired include the type and degree of:

- Instructions the business gives the worker. An employee is generally subject to the business's instructions about when, where, and how to work. Even if no instructions are given, sufficient behavioral control may exist if the employer has the right to control how the work results are achieved.

- Training the business gives the worker. An employee may be trained to perform services in a particular manner. Independent contractors ordinarily use their own methods.

Financial Control

Facts that show whether the business has a right to control the business aspects of the worker's job include:

- The extent to which the worker has unreimbursed business expenses. Independent contractors are more likely to have unreimbursed expenses than employees. Fixed ongoing costs that are incurred regardless of whether work is currently being performed are especially important. However, employees may also incur unreimbursed expenses in connection with the services they perform for their business.

- The extent of the worker's investment. An independent contractor often has a significant investment in the facilities he or she uses in performing services for someone else; however, a significant investment is not required.

- The extent to which the worker makes services available to the relevant market.

- How the business pays the worker. An employee is generally paid by the hour, week, or month. An independent contractor is usually paid by the job, although it is common in some professions, such as law, to pay independent contractors hourly.

- The extent to which the worker can realize a profit or incur a loss. An independent contractor can make a profit or loss.

Type of Relationship

Facts that reveal the type of relationship between the parties include:

- Written contracts describing the relationship the parties intended to create.

- Whether the business provides the worker with employee-type benefits, such as insurance, a pension plan, vacation pay, or sick pay.

- The permanency of the relationship. If the company engages a worker with the expectation that the relationship will continue indefinitely, rather than for a specific project or period, it is generally considered to be evident that the company's intent was to create an employer-employee relationship.

- The extent to which services performed by the worker are a key aspect of the regular business of the company. If a worker provides services that are a key aspect of regular business activity, it is more likely that the employer will have the right to direct and control his or her activities. For example, if a law firm hires an attorney, it is likely that it will present the attorney's work as its own and would have the right to control or direct that work. This would indicate an employer-employee relationship.

Common-Law Employees

Under common-law rules, anyone who performs services for the employer is an employee, if the employer can control what will be done and how it will be done—even when the employee has considerable freedom of action. What matters is that the employer has the right to control the details of how the services are performed.

In an employer-employee relationship, the label makes no difference. The *substance* of the relationship, not the *label*, governs the worker's status. Nor does it matter whether the individual is employed full time or part time.

For employment tax purposes, no distinction is made between classes of employees. Superintendents, managers, and other supervisory personnel are all employees. An officer of a corporation is generally an employee, but a director is not. An officer who performs no services (or only minor ones), and neither receives nor is entitled to receive any pay, is not considered an employee.

Leased Employees

Under certain circumstances, a corporation furnishing workers to various professional people and firms is the employer of those workers for employment tax purposes. For example, a professional service corporation may provide the services of secretaries, nurses, and other similarly trained workers to its subscribers.

The service corporation enters with the subscribers into contracts under which the subscribers specify both the services to be provided and the fee to be paid to the service corporation for each individual furnished. The service corporation has the right to control and direct a worker's services for the subscriber, including the right to discharge or reassign the worker.

The service corporation hires the workers, controls the payment of their wages, provides them with unemployment insurance and other benefits, and is the employer for employment tax purposes.

Statutory Employees

Four categories of workers who are independent contractors under the common law are treated by statute as employees, and are called, quite logically, "statutory employees." These categories are illustrated as follows:

1. A driver who distributes beverages (other than milk) or meat, vegetable, fruit, or bakery products; or who picks up and delivers laundry or dry cleaning, if the driver is an agent of the employer or is paid on commission.

2. A full-time life insurance sales agent whose principal business activity is selling life insurance or annuity contracts, or both, primarily for one life insurance company.

3. An individual who works at home on materials or goods supplied by the employer, which must be returned to the employer or an individual the employer names (if the employer also furnishes specifications for the work to be done).

4. A full-time traveling or city salesperson who works on the employer's behalf and turns in orders to the employer from wholesalers, retailers, contractors, or operators of hotels, restaurants, or other similar establishments. The goods sold must be merchandise for resale or supplies for use in the buyer's business operation; the work performed must be the salesperson's principal business activity.

Social Security and Medicare Taxes.   The employer must withhold social security and Medicare taxes from statutory employees' wages if all three of the following conditions apply:

- The service contract states or implies that substantially all the services are to be performed personally by them.

- They do not have a substantial investment in the equipment and property used to perform the services (other than an investment in transportation facilities).

- The services are performed on a continuing basis for the same payer.

Federal Unemployment (FUTA) Tax.   For FUTA tax, the term employee means the same as it does for social security and Medicare taxes, except that it does not include statutory employees in Categories 2 and 3. Thus, any individual who is an employee under Category 1 or 4 is also an employee for FUTA tax purposes and subject to FUTA tax.

Income Tax.   The employer does not withhold income tax from the wages of statutory employees.

Reporting Payments to Statutory Employees.   The employer must furnish a Form W-2 to a statutory employee, and check "statutory employee" in box 15. Payments to the employee must be shown as other compensation in box 1. Social security wages are shown in box 3, social security tax withheld in box 4, Medicare wages in box 5, and Medicare tax withheld in box 6. The statutory employee can deduct his or her trade or business expenses from the payments shown on Form W-2. He or she reports earnings as a statutory employee on line 1 of Schedule C or C-EZ (Form 1040). (A statutory employee's business expenses are deductible on Schedule C or C-EZ [Form 1040] and are not subject to the reduction by 2% of his or her adjusted gross income that applies to common-law employees.)

Statutory Nonemployees

Statutory nonemployees fall into two categories: direct sellers and licensed real estate agents. They are treated as self-employed for all Federal tax purposes, including income and employment taxes, if both of the following criteria are met:

- Substantially all payments for their services as direct sellers or real estate agents are directly related to sales or other output, rather than to the number of hours worked.

- Their services are performed under a written contract providing that they will not be treated as employees for Federal tax purposes.

Misclassification of Employees

If an employer classifies an employee as an independent contractor without reasonable basis for doing so, the company may be held liable for employment taxes for that worker (the relief provisions that follow will not apply); see Internal Revenue Code section 3509 for more information.

If, however, the employer does have a reasonable basis for not treating a worker as an employee, the company may be relieved from having to pay employment taxes for that worker. To get this relief, the employer must file all required federal information returns on a basis consistent with its treatment of the worker. Neither present nor former management may have treated any worker that holds a substantially similar position as an employee for any periods beginning after 1977.

BELOW–MARKET INTEREST RATE LOANS

A *below-market loan* is a loan from the medical practice to the physician on which the practice charges no interest, or on which the interest rate is below the applicable federal rate. A below-market loan generally is treated as an arm's-length transaction in which the physician, the borrower, is treated as having received both a loan in exchange for a note that requires the payment of interest at the applicable federal rate, and an additional payment.

The additional payment is treated as a gift, dividend, contribution to capital, payment of compensation, or other payment, depending on the substance of the transaction. In the case of a demand loan covered by the below-market loan rules, two transactions are assumed to have taken place: (1) a transfer of forgone interest from the corporation to the physician, and (2) a retransfer of the forgone interest from the physician to the corporation. For any period, *forgone interest* is: the amount of interest that would be payable for that period if interest accrued at the applicable federal rate and was payable annually on December 31, minus any interest actually payable on the loan for the period.

Applicable federal rates are published by the IRS each month in the Internal Revenue Bulletin. The Internal Revenue Service office may also be contacted for these rates. How the physician treats the forgone interest depends on the type of loan he or she has. The following is a discussion of the various loans and the respective types of treatment of forgone interest.

Gift and Demand Loans

A *gift loan* is any below-market loan the forgone interest on which is in the nature of a gift. A *demand loan* is one payable in full at any time upon the lender's demand. If the physician receives a below-market gift loan or a demand loan, he or she is treated as having received an additional payment (as a gift, dividend, etc.) equal to the foregone interest on the loan. This amount is then treated as being transferred back to the corporation as interest. The physician may be entitled to deduct that amount as an interest expense, if it qualifies. The corporation must report this amount as interest income. These transfers are considered to occur annually, generally on December 31.

Term Loans

If the physician receives a below-market *term loan* (a loan that is not a demand loan), he or she is treated as having received a cash payment (as a gift, dividend, etc.) on the date the loan is made. This payment is equal to the loan amount minus the present value of all payments due under the loan. This excess amount is also treated as original issue discount on the loan; the original issue discount rules apply.

General Rules

The rules for below-market loans apply to:

- Gift loans

- Compensation-related loans (any below-market loans between an employer and an employee, or between an independent contractor and the person for whom the contractor provides services)

- Corporation-shareholder loans

- Tax avoidance loans

- Loans to qualified continuing care facilities (made after October 11, 1985)

- Other below-market loans to the extent provided in the Regulations

The rules for below-market loans do not apply to certain loans on days on which the total amount of outstanding loans between the borrower and lender is $10,000 or less. This exception applies only to:

- Gift loans between individuals, if the gift loan is not directly used to buy or carry income-producing assets

- Compensation-related loans or corporation-shareholder loans, if the avoidance of federal tax is not a principal purpose of the loan

For gift loans between individuals, if the outstanding loans between the lender and borrower total $100,000 or less, the forgone interest included in income by the lender and deemed paid by the borrower is limited to the borrower's net investment income for the year. This limit does not apply to a loan if the avoidance of federal tax is one of the main purposes of the interest arrangement (resulting in what is called, simply, a "tax avoidance loan"). Additionally, if the borrower's net investment income is $1,000 or less, the borrower's net investment income is treated as zero.

Some loans are specifically exempted from the rules for below-market loans, such as:

- Loans made available by lenders to the general public consistent with and on the same terms and conditions as the lender's customary business practices

- Loans subsidized by a federal, state, or municipal government that are made available under a program of general application to the public

- Certain employee-relocation loans

- Certain loans to or from a foreign person, unless the interest income would be effectively connected with the conduct of a U.S. trade or business and not exempt from U.S. tax under an income tax treaty

- Any loan for which the taxpayer can show the interest arrangement has no significant effect on the federal tax liability of the lender or the borrower (see "Significant Effect on Federal Tax Liability," discussed later in this chapter)

PERSONAL USE OF A MEDICAL PRACTICE–OWNED VEHICLE

General Valuation Rule

The corporation generally must include in the physician's wages the amount by which the fair market value of the fringe benefit is more than the sum of any amount the employee paid for the benefit, plus any amount the law excludes from income.

Fair market value is the price at which the property would change hands between a buyer and a seller, neither having to buy or sell, and both having reasonable knowledge of all the necessary facts. Sales of similar property around the same date may be helpful in figuring the fair market value of the property.

However, the corporation and the physician may use special rules to value certain fringe benefits. If the law excludes a fringe benefit cost from gross income, the difference between the fair market value and the excludable cost of that fringe benefit is not included in the physician's wages. If the law excludes only a limited amount of the cost, however, the fair market value of the fringe benefit that is due to any excess cost is included.

In general, the *fair market value* (FMV) of a fringe benefit is determined on the basis of all the facts and circumstances. The FMV of a fringe benefit is the amount the physician would have to pay a third party in an arm's-length transaction to buy or lease the particular fringe benefit. Neither the amount the physician considers to be the value of the fringe benefit nor the cost the corporation incurs to provide the benefit determines its FMV.

Employer-Provided Vehicles

The value of an employer-provided vehicle generally is the amount the physician would have to pay a third party to lease the same or a similar vehicle on the same or comparable terms in the same geographic area where the physician uses the vehicle. A comparable lease term would be the amount of time the vehicle is available for the physician's use, such as a one-year period. The value should not be determined by multiplying a cents-per-mile rate times the number of miles driven, unless the physician can prove the vehicle could have been leased on a cents-per-mile basis.

For the remainder of this discussion, a *vehicle* or *automobile* is any motorized four-wheeled vehicle manufactured primarily for use on public streets, roads, and highways.

Special Valuation Rules

The corporation may be able to use special valuation rules instead of the general valuation rule to value the use of any vehicle provided. The special valuation rules include the automobile lease rule, the vehicle cents-per-mile rule, the commuting rule, and the unsafe conditions commuting rule.

When reporting fringe benefits, the corporation can choose to use any of the special rules. However, neither the company nor the physician may use a special rule to value any benefit, unless one of the following conditions is met:

1. The corporation treats the value of the benefit as wages for reporting purposes by the due date of the return (including extensions) for the tax year the benefit was provided.

2. The physician includes the value of the benefit in income by the due date of the return for the year he or she received the benefit.

3. The physician is not a control employee (see page 271 for criteria).

4. The corporation demonstrates a good faith effort to treat the benefit correctly for reporting purposes.

The following are mandates for the use of the special rules.

- If the corporation uses one of the special rules to value a benefit it provides to the doctor, the doctor can use that special rule. If the company does not use one of the special rules, the doctor can use a special rule only if the company does not treat the value of the benefit as wages for reporting purposes by the due date of the return (including extensions) and any one of items 2 through 4 in the conditions just listed are met. In any case, the physician can always use the general valuation rule discussed earlier.

- If the corporation and the physician use a special rule properly, the physician must include in gross income the value the corporation determines under the rule, minus any amount he or she paid the corporation and any amount excluded by law from gross income. If the corporation also properly determines the amount of the physician's working condition fringe benefit (explained later under "Exclusion of Certain Fringe Benefits"), the physician must include in gross income the net value determined by the corporation, minus any amount he or she paid the corporation. The corporation and the physician can use the special rule to determine the amount the physician owes the company.

- If the company provides vehicles to more than one physician, it does not have to use the same special rule for each physician. If the company provides one vehicle for use by more than one physician (for example, an employer-sponsored van pool), it can use any special rule; however, the company must use that rule for all physicians who share use of the vehicle.

- The company must use the formulas in the special rules with only those rules. When the company properly applies a special rule to a fringe benefit, the IRS will accept its value for that fringe benefit. However, if the company does not properly apply a special rule, or if it uses a special rule but is not entitled to do so, the IRS will use the general valuation rule to value the fringe benefit.

Automobile Lease Rule.   If the company provides a physician or an employee with an automobile for an entire calendar year, it can use the automobile's annual lease value to derive the value of the benefit. If the company provides a physician with an automobile for less than an entire calendar year, the value of the benefit is either a prorated annual lease value or the daily lease value (see page 268). The lease value is included in the physician's wages unless it is excluded from gross income by law.

If the doctor uses the automobile for business, he or she may qualify to exclude part of the lease value as a working-condition fringe benefit. The company may reduce the amount of the lease value by the working-condition fringe benefit and include the net amount in the doctor's wages, or may choose to include the entire lease value.

Generally, the company can figure the *annual lease value* of an automobile as follows:

1. Determine the FMV of the automobile on the first date the automobile is available to any physician for personal use.

2. Using the following Annual Lease Value Table, read down column 1 to find the dollar range within which the FMV of the automobile falls. Then read across to column 2 to find the annual lease value.

Exhibit 8.1 is an example of the Annual Lease Value Table; the IRS is the source for the current table. The FMV of the automobile is the amount a person would pay to buy it from a third party in an arm's length transaction, in the area in which the vehicle is bought or leased. That amount includes all purchase expenses, such as sales tax and title fees.

A company with 20 or more automobiles should refer to Section 1.61-21(d)(5)(v) of the Income Tax Regulations. If the corporation and the physician own or lease an automobile together, they should both see Section 1.61-21(d)(2)(ii) of the Income Tax Regulations. The company does not have to include the FMV of a telephone or of any specialized equipment added to, or carried in, the automobile if the equipment is necessary for its business. However, it must include the value of specialized equipment in the FMV if the physician to whom the automobile is available uses that equipment in a trade or business other than the company's.

The corporation may be able to use a safe-harbor value as the FMV. For an automobile bought at arm's length, the *safe-harbor value* is the company's cost, including tax, title, and other purchase expenses. The company cannot have been the manufacturer of the vehicle. For a leased automobile, the safe-harbor value is one of the following:

- The manufacturer's invoice price (including options) plus 4%

- The manufacturer's suggested retail price less 8% (including sales tax, title, and other expenses of purchase)

Exhibit 8.1
Annual lease value table

Annual Automobile Lease			
Fair Market Value	**Value**	**Fair Market Value**	**Value**
$0–999	$ 600	22,000–22,999	6,100
1,000–1,999	850	23,000–23,999	6,350
2,000–2,999	1,100	24,000–24,999	6,600
3,000–3,999	1,350	25,000–25,999	6,850
4,000–4,999	1,600	26,000–27,999	7,250
5,000–5,999	1,850	28,000–29,999	7,750
6,000–6,999	2,100	30,000–31,999	8,250
7,000–7,999	2,350	32,000–33,999	8,750
8,000–8,999	2,600	34,000–35,999	9,250
9,000–9,999	2,850	36,000–37,999	9,750
10,000–10,999	3,100	38,000–39,999	10,250
11,000–11,999	3,350	40,000–41,999	10,750
12,000–12,999	3,600	42,000–43,999	11,250
13,000–13,999	3,850	44,000–45,999	11,750
14,000–14,999	4,100	46,000–47,999	12,250
15,000–15,999	4,350	48,000–49,999	12,750
16,000–16,999	4,600	50,000–51,999	13,250
17,000–17,999	4,850	52,000–53,999	13,750
18,000–18,999	5,100	54,000–55,999	14,250
19,000–19,999	5,350	56,000–57,999	14,750
20,000–20,999	5,600	58,000–59,999*	15,250
21,000–21,999	5,850		

*For vehicles with an FMV of more than $59,999, the annual lease value equals $(0.25 \times FMV) + \$500$.

- The retail value of the automobile reported by a nationally recognized pricing source, if that retail value is reasonable for that automobile

Each annual lease value in the table (Exhibit 8.1) includes the FMV of maintenance and insurance services for the automobile; this value must not be reduced by the FMV of any of these services that the company did not provide. For example, the annual lease value shouldn't be reduced by the FMV of a maintenance service contract or insurance the company did not provide.

The annual lease value does not include the FMV of fuel the company provided to a physician for personal use, regardless of whether the company provided it, reimbursed its cost, or had it charged to the company. The company must include the value of the fuel separately in the physician's wages. The company can value fuel provided at FMV or at 5.5 cents per mile for all miles driven by the physician. However, the company cannot value at 5.5 cents per mile fuel provided for miles driven outside the United States (including its possessions and territories), Canada, and Mexico.

If the company reimburses a physician for the cost of fuel, or has it charged to the company, the fuel is generally valued at the amount the company reimbursed, or the amount charged to the company if it was bought at arm's length. If the company has 20 or more automobiles, the requirements in Section 1.61-21(d)(3)(ii)(D) of the Income Tax Regulations will apply.

If the company provided any service other than maintenance and insurance for an automobile, the FMV of that service must be added to the annual lease value of the automobile in determining the value of the benefit.

If a corporation does adopt the automobile lease rule for an automobile, the following rules apply:

1. It must be adopted by the first day the automobile is available to any physician for personal use, with the following exceptions:
   a. If the commuting rule is adopted when the automobile is first made available to any physician for personal use, the company can change to the automobile lease rule on the first day for which the commuting rule is not used.
   b. If the vehicle cents-per-mile rule is adopted when the automobile is first made available to any physician for personal use, the company can change to the automobile lease rule on the first day on which the automobile no longer qualifies for that rule.

2. The company must use the rule for all later years in which the automobile is made available to any physician, except that, for any year during which use of the automobile qualifies, the company can use the commuting rule.

3. The company must continue to use the rule if it provides a replacement automobile to the physician and the company's primary reason for the replacement is to reduce federal taxes.

4. The physician can use the automobile lease rule only if he or she uses the rule beginning with the first day on which the automobile is made available for personal use (and he or she does not use the commuting rule).

The annual lease values in the table are based on a four-year lease term. These values will generally stay the same for the period that begins with the first date the company uses this special rule for the automobile and ends on December 31 of the fourth full calendar year following that date.

The annual lease value for each later four-year period is figured by determining the FMV of the automobile on January 1 of the first year of the later four-year period and selecting the amount in column 2 of the table that corresponds to the appropriate dollar range in column 1.

If the company uses the special accounting period rule discussed earlier, it can figure the annual lease value for each later four-year period at the beginning of the special accounting period that starts immediately before the January 1 date described in the previous paragraph. For example, assume that the company uses the special accounting period rule and that, beginning on November 1, 1997, the special accounting period is November 1 to October 31. The corporation elects to use the automobile lease valuation rule as of January 1, 1998, and may refigure the annual lease value on November 1, 2001, rather than on January 1, 2002.

For various reasons, the company may sometimes transfer an automobile from one physician or employee to another. Unless the primary purpose of the transfer is to reduce federal taxes, the annual lease value may be refigured based on the FMV of the automobile on January 1 of the calendar year of transfer.

However, if the company uses the special accounting period rule, it can refigure the annual lease value (based on the FMV of the automobile) at the beginning of the special accounting period in which the transfer occurs. If the company does not refigure the annual lease value, the physician cannot refigure it.

If an automobile is provided to a physician for continuous periods of 30 or more days but less than an entire calendar year, the corporation can prorate the annual lease value. Figure the prorated annual lease value by multiplying the annual lease value by a fraction, using the number of days of availability as the numerator and 365 as the denominator.

If an automobile is provided continuously for at least 30 days, but the period covers two calendar years (two special accounting periods if the corporation is using the special accounting period rule, discussed earlier), the corporation may prorate the annual lease value or the daily lease value. If the company has 20 or more automobiles, Section 1.61-21(d)(6) of the Income Tax Regulations will apply.

If an automobile is unavailable to the physician because of his or her personal reasons (for example, if the physician is on vacation), the company cannot take into account the periods of unavailability when a prorated annual lease value is in use. Furthermore, the company cannot use a prorated annual lease value if the reduction of federal tax is the main reason the automobile is unavailable.

If an automobile is provided for continuous periods of one or more but less than 30 days, its value is figured using the daily lease value: the annual lease value is multiplied by a fraction, using four times the number of days of availability as the numerator and 365 as the denominator.

However, the company can apply a prorated annual lease value for a period of continuous availability of less than 30 days by treating the automobile as if it had been available for 30 days. The company should use a prorated annual lease value if it would result in a lower valuation than would applying the daily lease value to the shorter period of availability.

Vehicle Cents-per-Mile Rule.   Under this rule, the company determines the value of a vehicle provided to a doctor for personal use by multiplying the standard mileage rate by the total miles the doctor drives the vehicle for personal purposes. The company may use the vehicle cents-per-mile rule if it provides a physician with a vehicle that the company reasonably expects will be regularly used in its trade or business throughout the calendar year (or for a shorter period during which it owns or leases it), or that meets the mileage rule requirements discussed later.

The company *cannot* use the vehicle cents-per-mile rule for an automobile first made available to a physician for personal use in 1998 if the FMV of the automobile is more than $15,600. If the corporation and the physician own or lease the automobile together, Section 1.61-

21(e)(1)(iii) of the Income Tax Regulations will apply and should be consulted.

The company must, in using the cents-per-mile rule, apply the standard mileage rate only to personal miles, and must disregard business miles. For example, if the physician drives 20,000 personal miles and 35,000 business miles in 1998, the personal use value of the vehicle is $6,500 (20,000 × 0.325). (*Personal use* is any use of the vehicle other than use in the company's trade or business.)

Whether a vehicle is regularly used in the company's trade or business must be determined on the basis of all the facts and circumstances. A vehicle is regularly used in the company's trade or business if it meets one of the following safe-harbor conditions:

- At least 50% of the vehicle's total annual mileage is for the company's trade or business.

- The company sponsors a commuting pool that generally uses the vehicle each work day to drive at least three employees to and from work.

Infrequent business use of the vehicle, such as for occasional trips to the airport or between the company's multiple business premises, is not regular use of the vehicle in the company's trade or business.

If the company provides a physician with a vehicle that it does not expect the physician to use regularly in its trade or business but that meets the mileage rule, the company can use the cents-per-mile method to value the benefit. A vehicle meets the mileage rule for a calendar year if it meets both of the following conditions:

- It is actually driven at least 10,000 miles in that year.

- It is used during the year primarily by the physician or employee.

The vehicle is being used primarily by the physician if he or she uses it consistently for commuting. For example, if only one physician uses a vehicle during the year and drives that vehicle at least 10,000 miles in that calendar year, the vehicle meets the mileage rule even if all miles driven by the physician are personal. (Mileage due to use of the vehicle by an individual other than the physician must be excluded.) If the company owns or leases the vehicle only part of the year, the 10,000 mile requirement should be reduced proportionately.

The cents-per-mile rate includes the FMV of maintenance and insurance for the vehicle; the company must not reduce the rate by the FMV of any service included in the rate that the company did not provide. (The company may take into account the services actually provided for the vehicle by using the general valuation rule, discussed earlier.)

For miles driven in the United States (including its territories and possessions), Canada, and Mexico, the cents-per-mile rate includes the FMV of fuel the company provides. If the company did not provide fuel, it may reduce the rate by no more than 5.5 cents.

For special rules that apply to fuel the corporation provides for miles driven outside the United States, Canada, and Mexico, the company should refer to Section 1.61-21(e)(3)(ii)(B) of the Income Tax Regulations.

If the company does adopt the cents-per-mile rule for an automobile, the following rules apply:

1. The company must adopt the rule by the first day the automobile is made available to any physician for personal use. However, if the company adopts the commuting rule when the automobile is first made available to any physician for personal use, it may change to the cents-per-mile rule on the first day for which the commuting rule is not used.

2. The company must use the cents-per-mile rule for all later years in which it makes the automobile available to any physician and in which the automobile qualifies, except that, for any year during which use of the automobile qualifies for the commuting rule, the company can use the commuting rule. However, if the vehicle does not qualify for the cents-per-mile rule during a later year, it may adopt for that year and thereafter any other special rule for which the vehicle then qualifies.

3. The company must continue to use the rule if it provides a replacement automobile to the physician and the primary reason for the replacement is to reduce federal taxes.

4. The physician may use the vehicle cents-per-mile rule only if he or she uses the rule beginning with the first day on which

the automobile is made available to him or her for personal use (and the company does not use the commuting rule).

Commuting Rule.   Under this rule, the value of the commuting use of a company-provided vehicle is $1.50 per one-way commute (that is, from home to work or from work to home) for each physician who commutes in the vehicle. The corporation may use this special rule to figure commuting value if both it and the employee meet all the following requirements.

1. The company owns or leases the vehicle and provides it to one or more doctors for use in the company's trade or business.

2. For bona fide noncompensatory business reasons, the company requires the physician to commute in the vehicle.

3. The company established a written policy under which it does not allow the physician to use the vehicle for personal purposes, other than for commuting or de minimis personal use (such as a stop for a personal errand on the way between a business delivery and the physician's home).

4. The physician does not use the vehicle for personal purposes, other than commuting and de minimis personal use.

5. If this vehicle is an automobile, the physician who must use it for commuting is not a control employee (defined in the next paragraph).

A company-provided vehicle generally used each workday to carry at least three employees to and from work in an employer-sponsored commuting pool meets requirements 1 and 2.

A *control employee* of a nongovernment employer is any employee who meets at least one of the following criteria:

- The employee is a board- or shareholder-appointed, confirmed, or elected officer of the corporation and whose pay for 1999 is $100,000 or more.

- The employee is a director of the corporation.

- The employee owns a 1% or more equity, capital, or profits interest in the corporation.

Any individual who owns (or is considered to own under section 318(a) of the Internal Revenue Code or principles similar to section 318(a) for entities other than corporations) 1% or more of the FMV of an entity (the "owned entity") is considered a 1% owner of all other entities grouped with the owned entity under the rules of section 414(b), (c), (m), or (o). A physician who is an officer or director of the corporation is considered an officer or director of all entities treated as a single corporation under section 414(b), (c), (m), or (o). Instead of using any previous criteria, however, the company can choose to treat as control employees all of its highly compensated employees.

Qualified Transportation Fringe

The company may exclude qualified transportation fringe benefits from the wages of physicians, up to certain limits. The following benefits, which the company may provide in any combination at the same time to a physician, are qualified transportation fringe benefits:

- A ride in a commuter highway vehicle if the ride is between the employee's home and work place

- A transit pass

- Qualified parking

Amounts the company can give to an employee for these expenses under a bona fide reimbursement arrangement are also excludable. Cash reimbursements for transit passes qualify only if a voucher or a similar item that the employee can exchange only for a transit pass is not readily available for direct distribution by the company or its employee.

The company may provide qualified transportation fringe benefits only to employees. The definition of "employee" includes common-law employees and other statutory employees, such as officers of corporations. Self-employed individuals, including partners, two-percent shareholders in S-corporations, sole proprietors, and other independent contractors are not employees for purposes of this fringe benefit.

For tax years beginning after 1997, a company may exclude qualified transportation fringe benefits from a doctor's wages even if the company provides them in place of pay.

The company cannot exclude a qualified transportation fringe benefit under the de minimis or working condition fringe benefit rules. However, if the company provides a local transportation benefit other than by transit pass or commuter highway vehicle, or to a person other than an employee as defined earlier, it may be able to exclude all or part of the benefit under other fringe benefit rules (de minimis, working condition, etc.).

A *commuter highway vehicle* is any highway vehicle that seats at least six adults (not including the driver). In addition, the company must reasonably expect that at least 80% of the vehicle mileage will be for transporting employees between their homes and work place, with the employees occupying at least one-half of the vehicle's seats (not including the driver's).

A *transit pass* is any pass, token, farecard, voucher, or similar item entitling a person, free of charge or at a reduced rate, to ride mass transit or in a vehicle that seats at least six adults (not including the driver), if a person in the business of transporting persons for pay or hire operates it. Mass transit may be publicly- or privately-operated and includes bus, rail, or ferry.

Qualified parking is parking the company provides to its employees on or near the business premises. It also includes parking on or near the location from which the employees commute to work using mass transit, commuter highway vehicles, or carpools. It does not include parking at or near the employee's home.

Exclusion Limits

For 2000, a company may exclude from the wages of each employee up to $65 per month for combined commuter highway vehicle transportation and transit passes, and $175 per month for qualified parking.

Furthermore, if for any month the fair market value of a benefit is more than its limit, the employer must include in the employee's wages only the amount over the limit, minus any amount paid for the benefit by or for the employee.

For example, imagine that each month, a certain company provides a transit pass valued at $70 to its employee, Tom Travis, who does not pay for any part of the pass. Because the value of the transit pass exceeds the limit, for each month the company provides this pass, $5 must be included in Tom's wages for income and employment tax purposes.

Imagine that the company also provides qualified parking each month for a value of $180 to Travis Ramon, who also does not pay for any part of the parking. Because the value of the parking exceeds the limit, for each month the company must include $5 in Travis's wages for income and employment tax purposes.

Now imagine another company, which provides qualified parking with a fair market value of $200 per month to all its employees, but charges them $25 per month. The value of the parking exceeds the limit by $25. The company must reduce that excess benefit by the amount its employees paid ($25), and must not include any amount in the employees' wages.

Withholding and Reporting for Taxable Benefits

The company must treat taxable transportation fringe benefits as wages subject to employment taxes. When and how the company withholds reports and on the value of qualified transportation fringe benefits that must be included in an employee's wages depends on whether the benefits are cash reimbursements or noncash benefits.

Cash Reimbursements. For employment tax purposes, the company must treat taxable cash reimbursements as paid when they are made available to the employee. The company must deposit and report amounts withheld along with its FUTA tax and its part of the social security and Medicare taxes.

Noncash Benefits. Even though a company includes an amount for noncash fringe benefits in an employee's wages, it cannot deduct that amount as wages. It may, however, be able to take an expense or depreciation deduction for its costs to provide the benefit. For example, if a noncash fringe benefit provided to an employee is the use of property leased by the company, the company must include the amount (value) of the benefit in the employee's wages but cannot deduct that amount as wages. However, it may be able to deduct the rent as a business expense.

A company may choose to treat certain taxable noncash fringe benefits (other than benefits provided as nonemployee compensation) as paid by the pay period, or by the quarter, or on any other basis as long as it treats the benefits as paid at least as often as once a year. However, this choice does not apply to fringe benefits that involve the transfer of personal property normally held for investment or the transfer of real property. The company should treat these benefits, and taxable cash fringe benefits, as paid when they are made available to the employee.

LEASING AN AUTOMOBILE

If a company leases a car for use in its business, it may use the standard mileage rate or actual expenses to figure the deductible car expense. This section explains how to figure actual expenses for a leased car.

A company may deduct the part of each lease payment that is for the use of the car in its business. It may not deduct any part of a lease payment that is for personal use of the car, such as commuting.

The company must spread any advance payments over the entire lease period. It may not deduct any payments made to buy a car, even if the payments are called lease payments.

If the company leases a car that is used in its business for a lease term of 30 days or more, it might have to figure an inclusion amount in income for each tax year the car is leased. An inclusion amount is not added to income; instead, it reduces the deduction for the lease payment. (This reduction has an effect similar to the limit on the depreciation deduction on an owned car.) The tables used to calculate the inclusion amount can be found in IRS Publication 463.

The inclusion amount is a percentage of part of the fair market value of the leased car multiplied by the percentage of business and investment use of the car for the tax year. It is prorated for the number of days of the lease term in the tax year. The inclusion amount applies to each tax year that car is leased if the fair market value of the car when the lease began was more than the amounts shown in the Exhibit 8.2. The company should figure the fair market value on the first day of the lease term. If the capitalized cost of a car is speci-

Exhibit 8.2
Leasing an automobile

Year Lease Began	Fair Market Value*
1999	$15,300/15,500
1997–1998	15,800/15,800
1995–1996	15,300/15,500
1994	14,800/14,600
1993	14,300/14,300
1992	13,800/13,700
1991	13,300/13,400
1987–1990	12,800

*These amounts are higher for electric cars.

fied in the lease agreement, that amount should be used as the fair market value.

If a car is leased for business use and, in a later year, changed to personal use, the company should follow the rules for figuring the inclusion amount. For the tax year in which the car is no longer used for business, the dollar amount for the previous tax year should be used, and the dollar amount should be prorated for the number of days in the lease term that fall within the tax year.

If, on the other hand, a car was originally leased for personal use and, in a later year, changed to business use, the car's fair market value must be determined on the date of conversion.

RECORDKEEPING

Well-organized records will make it easier to prepare the company's tax return and will help answer questions if the return is selected for examination, or if the company is billed for additional tax. Records such as receipts, canceled checks, and other documents that support an item of income or a deduction appearing on the return should be kept until the statute of limitations expires for that return. Usually this is three years from the date the return was due or filed, or two years from the date the tax was paid, whichever is later. There is no statute of limitations when a return is fraudulent or when no return is filed. The company should keep some records indefinitely, such as property records; it may need them to prove the amount of gain or loss if the property is sold. Generally, income tax returns should be kept for three years. They could help in preparing future tax returns or in amending a return.

All employment tax records must be retained for at least four years after the tax is due or paid, whichever is later.

There is no particular method of bookkeeping a company must use. However, it must use a method that clearly reflects its income and expenses, such as expenses for travel, entertainment, gifts, and cars. The records should substantiate the expenses.

Good records will help company management do the following:

- *Monitor the progress of the business.* Good records are needed to monitor the progress of business. Records can show whether a business is improving, which items are selling, or what changes need to made. Good records can increase the likelihood of business success.

- *Prepare financial statements.* Good records are needed to prepare accurate financial statements. These include income (profit and loss) statements and balance sheets. These statements can help in dealing with banks or creditors.

- *Identify the source of receipts.* A company may receive money or property from many sources, and its records can identify the source of receipts. This information is needed to separate business from nonbusiness receipts and taxable from nontaxable income.

- *Keep track of deductible expenses.* Expenses may be forgotten when the tax return is prepared unless records of them were kept when they occurred.

- *Prepare the tax returns.* Good records are needed to prepare the tax return. These records must support the income, expenses, and credits reported. Generally, these are the same records used to monitor business and prepare financial statements.

- *Support items reported on tax returns.* Business records must be available at all times for inspection by the IRS. If the IRS examines any of the tax returns, they may ask for an explanation on the items reported. A complete set of records will speed up the examination.

Necessary Types of Records

Except in a few cases, the law does not require any special kind of records; any recordkeeping system may be chosen that best suits the business and clearly reflects its income.

Supporting Documents

Purchases, sales, payroll, and other transactions in business will generate supporting documents. Sales slips, paid bills, invoices, receipts, deposit slips, and canceled checks are all supporting documents used to record the books. It is important to keep these documents after they've served their immediate purpose, because they support both the entries in the books and on the tax return. They should be kept in an orderly fashion—for instance, organized by year and type of income or expense—and in a safe place.

Gross receipts are the income received from business. Supporting documents showing the amounts and sources of gross receipts should be kept. Such documents include the following:

- Cash register tapes
- Bank deposit slips
- Receipt books
- Invoices
- Credit card charge slips
- Forms 1099–MISC

Purchases are the items bought and re-sold to customers. Supporting documents should show both the amount paid and the fact that the amount was for purchases. Documents for purchases include the following:

- Canceled checks
- Cash register tape receipts
- Credit card sales slips
- Invoices

Expenses are the costs incurred (other than purchases) to carry on business. Supporting documents should show the amount paid and that the amount was for a business expense. Documents for expenses include the following:

- Canceled checks

- Cash register tapes

- Account statements

- Credit card sales slips

- Invoices

- Petty cash slips for small cash payments

Note that a petty cash fund allows small payments to be made without the need for checks written for small amounts. Each time a payment is made from this fund, a petty cash slip should be filled out and attached to the receipt as proof of payment.

Travel, Transportation, Entertainment, and Gift Expenses. Documentary evidence such as receipts, canceled checks, or bills is generally required to support these expenses, unless any of the following conditions apply:

- The employee has meals or lodging expenses while traveling away from home for which they account to the company under an accountable plan, and the company uses a per diem allowance method that includes meals and/or lodging.

- The employee's expense, other than lodging, is less than $75.

- The employee has a transportation expense for which a receipt is not readily available.

The documentary evidence ordinarily will be considered adequate if it shows the amount, date, place, and essential character of the expense.

Assets. Assets are property, such as machinery and furniture, that a company owns and uses in its business. The company must keep records to verify certain information about its business assets, and needs records to figure the annual depreciation and the gain or loss when it sells the assets.

Their records should show the following information:

- When and how the asset was acquired

- Purchase price

- Cost of any improvements

- Section 179 deduction taken

- Deductions taken for depreciation

- Deductions taken for casualty losses, such as losses resulting from fires or storms

- How the asset was used

- When and how the asset was disposed of

- Selling price

- Expenses of sale

Documents that may show this information include the following:

- Purchase and sales invoices

- Real estate closing statements

- Canceled checks

GENERAL RULE FOR METHODS OF ACCOUNTING UNDER SECTION 446

It is important for a medical practice to select the correct method of accounting for its particular situation. The general rule outlined in Section 446(a) is that taxable income shall be computed under the method of accounting on the same basis as that on which the taxpayer regularly computes his or her income in keeping the books. Such an inclusive statement generates its own exceptions. Section 446(b) states that if no method of accounting has been regularly used by the taxpayer, or if the method used does not clearly reflect income, the computation of taxable income shall be made under such method as, in the opinion of the Secretary, does clearly reflect income. Clearly it is important that practitioners select the appropriate method for their circumstances.

Subject to the provisions stated above, Section 446(c) lets a taxpayer compute taxable income under any of the following methods of accounting:

- The cash receipts and disbursements method

- An accrual method

- Any other method permitted by this section

- Any combination of the foregoing methods permitted under regulations prescribed by the Secretary

It's also important to note that a taxpayer engaged in more than one trade or business may, in computing taxable income, use a different method of accounting for each trade or business.

Although there may be situations in which the accrual basis of accounting may be deemed beneficial, the selection of accrual accounting should not be done without proper planning. The lag between service delivery and cash deposited could put a great strain on a medical practice. The accrual basis would tend to inflate taxable income in the first year and during years of growth and expansion when the practitioner typically has the least amount of cash to pay taxes. As a general rule, medical practices use the cash basis of accounting for tax purposes.

With proper planning, the practitioner could adopt a method that includes the best of both accrual and cash basis accounting. In Hospital Corp. of America and Subsidiaries v. Comr., T.C. Memo 1996-105, the Tax Court ruled that a hybrid cash-accrual accounting method reflected income, and pointed out the IRS's acquiescence to its use during previous audits of the hospital, as well as the extensive and pervasive use of the cash method in the health care industry in general, as grounds for ruling in the taxpayer's favor.

GENERAL RULE FOR TAXABLE YEAR OF DEDUCTION UNDER SECTIONS 267 AND 461

Along with choosing a method of accounting, all medical practitioners should be familiar with the rules governing the year of inclusion or deductibility of items. Many medical practices eventually develop a sophisticated delivery system using multiple entities. Operating within one separate entity may be a wholly-owned equipment company, a billing and collections company, or other specialties. These related entities present special accounting needs and problems—for example, an equipment company may need to be on the accrual basis because of financing needs.

Under the cash receipts and disbursements method of accounting, amounts representing allowable deductions shall, as a general rule, be taken into account for the taxable year in which they are paid. Further, a taxpayer using this method may be entitled to certain deductions in the computation of taxable income that do not involve cash disbursements during the taxable year, such as the deductions for depreciation, depletion, and losses under Sections 167, 611, and 165, respectively. If an expenditure results in the creation of an asset having a useful life that extends substantially beyond the close of the taxable year, such an expenditure may not be deductible, or may be deductible only in part, for the taxable year in which the asset was made. An example is an expenditure for the construction of improvements by the lessee on leased property where the estimated life of the improvements is in excess of the remaining period of the lease. In such a case, in lieu of the allowance for depreciation provided by Section 167, the basis shall be amortized ratably over the remaining period of the lease. Section 178 and the regulations thereunder govern the effect to be given renewal options in determining whether the useful life of the improvements exceeds the remaining term of the lease in which a lessee begins improvements on the leased property after July 28, 1958 (other than improvements which on such date and at all times thereafter, the lessee was under a binding legal obligation to make). Section 263 and the regulations thereunder should be consulted for rules relating to capital expenditures, and Section 467 and the regulations thereunder should be consulted for rules under which a liability arising out of the use of property pursuant to a section 467 rental agreement is taken into account.

Often under an accrual method of accounting, an incurred liability (as defined in Section 1.446-1[c][1][ii][B]) generally is taken into account for Federal income tax purposes in the taxable year in which (1) all the events have occurred that establish the fact of the liability, (2) the amount of the liability can be determined with reasonable accuracy, and (3) economic performance has occurred with respect to the liability. (See paragraph [a][2][iii][A] of this section for examples of liabilities that may not be taken into account until a taxable year subsequent to the taxable year incurred, and see Sections 1.461-4 through 1.461-6 for rules relating to economic performance.)

Applicable provisions of the Code, the Income Tax Regulations, and other guidance published by the Secretary prescribe the manner in which an incurred liability is taken into account. For example, Section 162 provides that a deductible liability generally is taken into account in the taxable year incurred through a deduction from gross income. As a further example, under Section 263 or 263A, a liability that relates to the creation of an asset that has a useful life extending substantially beyond the close of the taxable year must be taken into account in the taxable year during which the liability was incurred through capitalization (within the meaning of section 1.263A-1[c][3]); this liability may later affect the computation of taxable income through depreciation or otherwise over a period including subsequent taxable years, in accordance with applicable Internal Revenue Code sections and guidance published by the Secretary. The principles of this paragraph (a)(2) also apply in the calculation of earnings and profits and accumulated earnings and profits.

While no liability shall be taken into account before both economic performance and all of the events that fix the liability have occurred, the fact that the exact amount of the liability cannot be determined does not prevent a taxpayer from taking into account that portion of the amount of the liability that can be computed with reasonable accuracy within the taxable year. For example, A renders services to B during the taxable year for which A charges $10,000. B admits a liability to A for $6,000 but contests the remainder. B may take into account only $6,000 as an expense for the taxable year in which the services were rendered. (1.461-1[a][2][ii])

The Section 267 Rule

Under the rules mentioned in Section 267, the accrual-basis medical practitioner must be attentive. Entities will not be allowed a deduction for ordinary and necessary business expenses if (1) the amount accrued remains unpaid after two and one-half months of the close of the year of inclusion; (2) the payee is on the cash receipts and disbursements method of accounting, with respect to gross income for the taxable year in which (or with which) the taxable year of accrual by the debtor-taxpayer ends; and (3) the amount of such items is not otherwise (under the rules of constructive receipt) included in the gross income of the payee. These rules are designed to put both entities, in effect, on the cash basis.

For example, imagine that Dr. A is the holder and owner of an interest-bearing note of the M Corporation, all the stock of which was owned by him on December 31, 2000. Dr. A and the M Corporation make their income tax returns for a calendar year. The M Corporation uses an accrual method of accounting; Dr. A uses a combination of accounting methods permitted under section 446(c)(4) in which he uses the cash receipts and disbursements method with respect to items of gross income. The M Corporation does not pay any interest on the note to Dr. A during the calendar year 2000 or within two and one-half months after the close of that year, nor does it credit any interest to Dr. A's account in such a manner that it is subject to his unqualified demand and thus is constructively received by him.

M Corporation claims a deduction for the year 2000 for the interest accruing on the note in that year. Since Dr. A is on the cash receipts and disbursements method with respect to items of gross income, the interest would not normally be included in his return for the year 2000. Under the provisions of section 267(a)(2) and this paragraph, no deduction for such interest is allowable in computing the taxable income of the M Corporation for the taxable year 2000 or for any other taxable year. However, if the interest had actually been paid to Dr. A on or before March 15, 2000, or if it had been made available to Dr. A before that time (and thus had been constructively received by him), the M Corporation would be allowed to deduct the amount of the payment in computing its taxable income for 2000.

Other Section 461 Considerations

If any provision of the Code requires a liability to be taken into account in a taxable year later than the taxable year provided in paragraph (a)(2)(i) of this section, the liability is taken into account as prescribed in that Code provision (1.461-1[a][2][iii][A]) as, for example, in Section 267 (transactions between related parties) and section 464 (farming syndicates).

If the liability of a taxpayer is subject to Section 170 (charitable contributions), Section 192 (black lung benefit trusts), Section 194A (employer liability trusts), Section 468 (mining and solid waste disposal reclamation and closing costs), or Section 468A (certain nuclear decommissioning costs), the liability is taken into account as determined under that section and not under Section 461 or the regulations thereunder (1.461-1[a][2][iii][B]).

Section 461 and the regulations thereunder do not apply to any amount allowable under a provision of the Code as a deduction for a reserve for estimated expenses.

Except as otherwise provided in any Internal Revenue regulation, revenue procedure, or revenue ruling, the economic performance requirement of Section 461(h) and the regulations thereunder is satisfied to the extent that any amount is otherwise deductible under Section 404 (employer contributions to a plan of deferred compensation), Section 404A (certain foreign deferred compensation plans), or Section 419 (welfare benefit funds), as shown in section 1.461-4(d)(2)(iii).

Effect in Current Taxable Year of Improperly Accounting for a Liability in a Prior Taxable Year

Medical practitioners need to ascertain the facts necessary to file a correct return. Under Section 1.461-1(a)(3), each year's return should be complete in itself. The expenses, liabilities, or losses of one year generally may not be used to reduce the income of a subsequent year. In a return for a subsequent taxable year, one may not take into account liabilities that, under the company's current method of accounting, should have been taken into account in a prior taxable year. If the company finds that a liability should have been taken into account in a prior taxable year, it should file a claim for credit or refund of any overpayment of tax arising therefrom, provided the period of limitation has not elapsed. Similarly, if a company finds that a liability was improperly taken into account in a prior taxable year, it should, if within the period of limitation, file an amended return and pay any additional tax due. However, except as provided in Section 905(c) and the regulations thereunder, if a liability is properly taken into account in an amount based on a computation made with reasonable accuracy and the exact amount of the liability is subsequently determined in a later taxable year, the difference, if any, between such amounts shall be taken into account for the later taxable year.

RETIREMENT PLANS AND EMPLOYEE LEASING

Congress enacted Section 414(n) of the Internal Revenue Code because of perceived abuses in the use of leased employees to circumvent certain retirement plan rules. The new rules treat the employees of certain leasing organizations as being employees of the business that is leasing their services for purposes of the rules governing qualified retirement plans. Under these rules, the employer business includes all entities required to be aggregated under Section 414(b), (c), and (m). When these rules apply, the leased employees are treated as employees of the leasing business organization for purposes of the following requirements:

- The minimum participation standards of Sections 401(a)(3) and 410

- The Section 401(a)(4) nondiscrimination rules for contributions and benefits

- The minimum standards for vesting under Sections 401(a)(7) and 411

- The limits on compensation and benefits under Sections 401(a)(16) and 415

- The Section 401(a)(17) limitations on compensation taken into account

- The Section 401(a)(26) minimum participation standards

- The Section 408(k) provisions for SEPs

- The Section 408(p) provisions for SIMPLE plans

- The top-heavy rules of Section 416

- The Section 4980B rules on failure to satisfy the health care continuation requirements for group health plans

Employees of an Affiliated Service Group

In general, all employees of the members of an affiliated service group shall be treated as employed by a single employer. This makes it difficult for the medical practitioner to tailor retirement plans for different groups of employees.

A *service organization* is an organization the principal business of which is the performance of services. An *affiliated service group* consists of a service organization (which we will call the first organization) and one or more of the following: (1) any service organization that is a shareholder or partner in the first organization, and that regularly performs services for the first organization, or that is regularly associated with the first organization in performing services for third persons; or (2) any other organization if a significant portion of its business is the performance of services (for the first organization, for organizations described in subparagraph [A] "management organizations," or for both) of a type usually performed in that field by employees, *and* 10 percent or more of the interests in the organization is held by persons who are highly compensated employees (within the meaning of Section 414[q]) of the first organization or an organization described in subparagraph (A).

For our purposes, the term "affiliated service group" also includes a group consisting of an organization the principal business of which is performing, on a regular and continuing basis, management functions for an organization (and for any related organizations), as well as the organization(s) receiving the service.

Employee Leasing

A *leased employee* is any person who is not an employee of the medical practice, and who: (1) provides services to the medical practice through an agreement between the medical practice and the leasing organization; (2) has performed these services for the medical practice (and any related persons) on a substantially full-time basis for at least one year; and (3) performs these services under the primary direction or control of the medical practice. The leased employee must be treated as an employee of the medical practice, and contributions or benefits that are provided by the leasing organization for services performed for the medical practice must be treated as if the medical practice provided them.

This is not to say that a medical practice cannot use leased employees; rather, the decision to use leased employees should not be based on retirement-plan considerations. The rules are complex and the perceived savings sometimes illusionary. In any case, the company must consult an employee benefits specialist to evaluate its own particular situation.

TAX IMPOSED ON CERTAIN BUILT-IN GAINS UNDER SECTION 1374

The major tax difference between a C- (regular) corporation and an S- (small business) corporation is who pays the tax. The tax on the taxable income of a C-corp is paid by the corporation. The S-corp rarely pays tax on its taxable income; rather, the taxable income is passed through to the shareholders and taxed on the shareholders' individual tax returns. Circumstances may have dictated the medical practice to operate as a C-corp in the past, but, given the harsh tax effects of the personal service company rules, the practitioner may be considering a change to S-corp status. The rules of Section 1374 will give the medical practitioner cause to pause, and certainly require a great deal of planning before proceeding.

The general rule states that if, for any taxable year beginning in the recognition period, an S-corp has a net recognized built-in gain, the income of that corporation is taxed for that year. The amount of this tax, imposed by subsection (b), is computed by applying the highest rate of tax specified in Section 11(b) to the net recognized built-in gain of the S-corp for the taxable year. The tax does not apply to a corporation that has always been an S Corporation. A *net unrealized built-in gain* is the amount (if any) by which the fair market value of the assets of the S-corp, as of the beginning of its first taxable year for which an election under Section 1362(a) is in effect, exceeds the aggregate adjusted bases of the assets at that time.

The *recognition period* is the 10-year period beginning with the first day of the first taxable year for which the corporation was an S-corporation. (For any amount that may be included as income under Section 593(e), the recognition period follows the same definition, except with no reference to the length of the period.)

With respect to any taxable year in the recognition period, the net recognized built-in gain is the lesser of (1) the amount that would be the taxable income of the S-corp for that taxable year if *only* recognized built-in gains and recognized built-in losses were taken into account, or (2) the corporation's taxable income for that taxable year (determined as provided in Section 1375[b][1][B]).

A *recognized built-in gain* is any gain realized during the recognition period on the disposition of any asset, except to the extent that (1) the S-corp did not hold that asset as of the beginning of the first taxable year for which it was an S-corp, or (2) the gain exceeds the excess (if any) of the asset's fair market value as of the beginning of that first taxable year, over the adjusted basis of the asset as of that time.

A *recognized built-in loss* is any loss realized during the recognition period on the disposition of any asset, to the extent that (1) the S-corp did not hold the asset as of the beginning of its first taxable year as an S-corp, and (2) the loss does not exceed the excess of its adjusted basis as of the beginning of that taxable year, over the asset's fair market value as of that time.

Any item of income that is properly taken into account during the recognition period but is attributable to periods before the first taxable year for which the corporation was an S-corp shall be treated as a recognized built-in gain for the taxable year in which it is properly taken into account.

Any amount that is allowable as a deduction during the recognition period (determined without regard to any carryover) but that is attributable to periods before that first taxable year shall be treated as a recognized built-in loss for the taxable year in which it is allowable as a deduction.

The amount of the net unrealized built-in gain must be properly adjusted for amounts that would be treated as recognized built-in gains or losses under this paragraph, if those amounts were properly taken into account (or allowable as a deduction) during the recognition period.

Treatment of Transfer of Assets from C-Corporation to S-Corporation

In general, except to the extent provided in regulations, if an S-corporation acquires any asset and its basis in that asset is determined wholly or partly by reference to the basis of the asset (or any other property) in the hands of a C-corporation, then a tax is imposed on any net recognized built-in gain attributable to any such assets for any taxable year beginning in the recognition period. The amount of tax shall be determined under the rules of this section.

Computation of Tax

The tax imposed on the income of an S-corporation by Section 1374(a) for any taxable year during the recognition period is computed as follows:

1. The net recognized built-in gain of the corporation must be determined for the taxable year under Section 1374(d)(2) and Section 1.1374-2.

2. The net recognized built-in gain must be reduced (but not below zero) by any net operating loss and capital loss carryforward allowed under Section 1374(b)(2) and Section 1.1374-5.

3. A tentative tax is computed by applying the rate of tax determined under Section 1374(b)(1) for the taxable year to the amount determined under paragraph (a)(2) of this section.

4. The final tax is computed by reducing the tentative tax (but not below zero) by any credit allowed under Section 1374(b)(3) and Section 1.1374-6.

Anti-Trafficking Rules 1.1374-1(b)

If Section 382 (ownership changes), 383 (certain capital losses and excess credits), or 384 (use of preacquisition losses) would have applied to limit the use of a corporation's recognized built-in loss or Section

1374 attributes at the beginning of the first day of the recognition period if the corporation had remained a C-corporation, these sections apply to limit their use in determining the S-corporation's pre-limitation amount, taxable income limitation, net unrealized built-in gain limitation, deductions against net recognized built-in gain, and credits against the Section 1374 tax.

Section 1374 attributes are the loss carryforwards allowed under Section 1374(b)(2) as a deduction against net recognized built-in gain and the credit and credit carryforwards allowed under Section 1374(b)(3) as a credit against the Section 1374 tax.

The recognition period is the 10-year (120-month) period beginning on the first day the corporation is an S-corp or the day an S-corp acquires assets in a Section 1374(d)(8) transaction. For example, if the first day of the recognition period is July 14, 1996, the last day of the recognition period is July 13, 2006. If the recognition period for certain assets ends during an S-corp's taxable year (for example, because the corporation was on a fiscal year as a C-corp and changed to a calendar year as an S-corp, or because an S-corp acquired assets in a Section 1374(d)(8) transaction during a taxable year), the S-corp must determine its pre-limitation amount (as defined in Section 1.1374-2[a][1]) for the year as if the corporation's books were closed at the end of the recognition period.

For purposes of Section 1374(c)(1), if the basis of an asset of the S-corp is determined (in whole or in part) by reference to the basis of the asset (or any other property) in the hands of another corporation, the other corporation is a predecessor corporation of the S-corporation.

An S-corporation's net unrealized built-in gain is the total of the following: (1) the amount that would be the amount realized if, at the beginning of the first day of the recognition period, the corporation had remained a C-corp and had sold all its assets at fair market value to an unrelated party that assumed all its liabilities; decreased by (2) any liability of the corporation that would be included in the amount realized on the sale referred to in paragraph (a)(1) of this section, but only if the corporation would be allowed a deduction on payment of the liability; decreased by (3) the aggregate adjusted bases of the corporation's assets at the time of the sale referred to in paragraph (a)(1) of this section; increased or decreased by (4) the corporation's Section 481 adjustments that would be taken into account on the sale referred to in paragraph (a)(1) of this section; and increased by (5) any recog-

Exhibit 8.3
Net unrealized built-in gain

Assets	FMV	Basis
Building	500,000	900,000
Accounts Receivable	300,000	0
Goodwill	250,000	0
Total	1,050,000	900,000

Liabilities	Amount
Mortgage	200,000
Accounts Payable	100,000
Total	300,000

nized built-in loss that would not be allowed as a deduction under Section 382, 383, or 384 on the sale referred to in paragraph (a)(1) of this section.

The rules of this section are illustrated by the following example: Medical Corp, a calendar year C-corp using the cash method, elects to become an S-corp on January 1, 1996. On December 31, 1995, Medical Corp has assets and liabilities as shown in Exhibit 8.3. Further, Medical Corp must include a total of $60,000 in taxable income in 1996, 1997, and 1998 under Section 481(a).

If, on December 31, 1995, Medical Corp sold all its assets to a third party that assumed all its liabilities, Medical Corp's amount realized would be $1,050,000 ($750,000 cash received + $300,000 liabilities assumed = $1,050,000). Thus, Medical Corp's net unrealized built-in gain is determined as follows:

Amount realized	$1,050,000)
Deduction allowed	(100,000)
Basic of X's assets	(900,000)
Section 481 adjustments	60,000)
Net unrealized built-in gain	$110,000)

SPECIAL ALLOCATION RULES FOR CERTAIN ASSET ACQUISITIONS UNDER SECTION 1060

In the case of any applicable asset acquisition, for purposes of determining both the transferee's basis in such assets and the gain or loss of the transferor with respect to the acquisition, the consideration received for the assets shall be allocated among them in the same manner as amounts are allocated to assets under Section 338(b)(5). If, in connection with an applicable asset acquisition, the transferee and transferor agree in writing as to the allocation of any consideration, or as to the fair market value of any of the assets, their agreement shall be binding on both the transferee and transferor unless the Secretary determines that such allocation (or fair market value) is not appropriate.

Under regulations, the transferor and transferee in an applicable asset acquisition shall, at such times and in such manner as may be provided in such regulations, furnish to the Secretary the following information:

- The amount of the consideration received for the assets which is allocated to Section 197 intangibles

- Any modification of the amount described in paragraph (1)

- Any other information with respect to other assets transferred in such acquisition as the Secretary deems necessary to carry out the provisions of this section

For purposes of this section, the term *applicable asset acquisition* means any transfer (whether directly or indirectly) of assets that constitute a trade or business, and with respect to which the transferee's basis in such assets is determined wholly by reference to the consideration paid for such assets. A transfer shall not be treated as failing to be an applicable asset acquisition merely because Section 1031 applies to a portion of the assets transferred.

Patient Information and Communication

Patient Financial Policy

It is the goal of _____ to provide the best care on your behalf. It is also our desire to assist you in the financial arrangements related to this care. Therefore, it is important for you to fully understand our insurance, credit, and collections policies. Please read the following information carefully and feel free to ask any questions you may have in any area. We ask that you sign this statement when you have read and understand each point covered.

Upon registration each patient is asked to complete our Patient Information Form, a Medical Information Sheet, and a Financial Responsibility Waiver. A copy of your primary and secondary insurance cards will be requested for verification of insurance coverage and benefits.

If you have been referred to this office by your primary care physician and belong to an insurance plan that requires precertification or referral for this office visit, we request that you have this information available before you visit a physician. Failure to supply this information may postpone your visit to the physician or make you responsible for the full balance of your account.

Your signature will be requested for the following: Release of Medical Information for insurance purposes and assignment, Release of Medical Information to the primary care physician. Assignment of Benefits, Insurance Waiver, and Financial Responsibility Waiver.

Payment for the patient portion is due at the date of service. If unusual circumstances should make it impossible for you to meet these terms, we invite you to discuss with our office options available to you. We will work with you to arrive at a mutually agreeable payment plan. We accept American Express, MasterCard, and Visa.

If you have health insurance, it should be understood that this is an agreement between you and your insurance carrier to pay for medical care. Our office is able to file your insurance claims for you. We hope that this will alleviate part of the burden of necessary paperwork. Your doctor's bill is an agreement between you and this office. You are ultimately responsible for the payment of your bill regardless of the status of your insurance claim. The only exception to the above policy apply to those patients who are covered by insurance companies that our office has contracted to provide services within their fee schedule. These companies are:

_____

_____

_____

These contracts are subject to change with or without notice. All co-pays are due at the time of service.

You will receive regular statements (every 25 days) from our office informing you of the status of your balance. Feel free to call our office should you have any questions. If we have not received any payments after 120 days from the date of service, we reserve the right to refer your account balance to an outside collection agency where you will be responsible for all collection and legal fees. I also understand that there will be an $18.00 fee for all checks presented for payment with non-sufficient funds (bad checks). You will also be billed separately by the hospital or other source, if it applies, for certain lab fees, radiology fees, and/or out-patient or in-patient procedures.

I have read and understand the above financial policy.

Signed _____   Date _____

Patient Information

(please print)

Date _____

Patient Name _____ Age ___ Birthdate _____

Address _____ City _____ State ___ Zip_____

Home Phone _____ Work Phone _____ Other Phone _____

Social Security # _____ Sex: (M)/(F) Marital Status: (S)(M)(D)(Sep)

Employer _____ Occupation _____

Emergency Contact _____ Phone _____

Spouse/Guarantor Name _____ SS# _____

Spouse/Guarantor Birthdate _____ Occupation _____

Spouse/Guarantor Employer _____ Phone _____

How did you hear about us? _____

Referring Physician _____ Phone _____

Insurance Information

Primary

Company Name _____ ID# _____ Grp# _____

Policy # _____ Insurance Address _____

Policy Holder's Name _____   Policy Holder's SS# _____

Secondary

Company Name _____   ID# _____   Grp# _____

Policy # _____   Insurance Address _____

MasterCard/Visa # _____   Driver's License # _____

Permission For Treatment: I hereby authorize the physician and/or assistants for the care of the patient named on this record to administer any treatment as may be deemed necessary including examinations or treatment that may be ordered to be performed by clinical personnel. I am aware that the practice of medicine is not an exact science and I acknowledge that no guarantees have been made to me as the result of examinations or treatments to be performed.

Permission for Release of Medical Information: I understand and agree that any of the above information may be used, if necessary, for purposes of communication for appointment changes, accounts receivable, emergencies, etc. Information from my medical records may be released, if necessary, for insurance purposes.

Assignment of Benefits: I hereby authorized my insurance company(s) to make payment(s) as stipulated in my policy(s) for any services furnished and that such payment(s) be paid directly to the provider of the services. I also understand that I am financially responsible for all services provided and agree to pay upon demand or as agreed for the related charges or remaining charges following my insurance payment(s).

Signature: _____   Date: _____

Financial Responsibility Waiver

I understand that if my insurance benefits and/or positive verification of my eligibility/coverage are not approved by my health plan at the time of service or in the future, then I am **financially responsible** and agree to pay for all charges related to services provided by:

Subscriber's Name _____

Patient's Name _____

Address _____

City, State, Zip _____

Telephone Number _____

Insurance Carrier _____

Employer Group _____

Group Policy Number _____

I have read the above and understand my financial responsibility to
_____ and hereby affix my
signature as an acknowledgement of this understanding.

Patient's Signature _____

Date _____

Receptionist _____

No Response from Insurance

Patient: _____

Account No.: _____

Service Date: _____

Balance: _____

Your insurance carrier was billed over thirty (30) days ago, but has not paid as of today. They have had ample time to pay this claim. We are now required to look to you for the payment of this claim.

Please mail the balance in full today or contact your insurance carrier to arrange for payment.

We appreciate your cooperation and support in assisting us to clear your account balance.

If you have any questions regarding this situation, please call our office at the number listed above. Thank you in advance for your cooperation.

Medicare Waiver

Name of Patient _____ Medicare # _____

PHYSICIAN NOTICE TO PATIENT ABOUT MEDICARE

Medicare will pay only for services that it determines to be "reasonable and necessary" under Section 1862 (a)(1) of the Medicare law. If Medicare determines that a particular service, although it would otherwise be covered, is "not reasonable and necessary" under Medicare program standards, Medicare will deny payment for that service. I believe that, in your case, Medicare is likely to deny payment for the following reasons:

❑ Medicare does not usually pay for this many many visits or treatments.

❑ Medicare usually does not pay for this shot.

❑ Medicare usually does not pay for this service.

❑ Medicare usually does not pay for this many shots.

❑ Medicare usually pays for only one nursing home visit per month.

❑ Medicare does not pay for this because it is a treatment that has yet to be proven effective.

❑ Medicare does not pay for this office visit unless it was needed because of an emergency.

❑ Medicare usually does not pay for like services by more than one doctor during the same time period.

❑ Medicare usually does not pay for this many services within this period of time.

❑ Medicare usually does not pay for more than one visit a day.

❑ Medicare usually does not pay for such an extensive procedure.

❑ Medicare usually does not pay for like services by more than one doctor of the same specialty.

❑ Medicare usually does not pay for this equipment.

❑ Medicare usually does not pay for this lab test.

❑ Routine screenings are a non-covered Medicare expense.

❑ Other: _____

_____

Service Date:	Procedure:	Description:	Change:
_____	_____	_____	_____
_____	_____	_____	_____

Medicare Beneficiary Agreement

I have been notified by my physician that he/she believes that, in my case, Medicare is likely to deny payment for the services identified, for the reasons checked. If Medicare denies payment, I agree to be personally and fully responsible for payment.

_____

Beneficiary Signature   Date

Financial Agreement

Date: _____

Patient: _____

Account Number: _____

Account Balance as of Date: _____

Beginning on _____ , I agree to _____ payments of _____ ,
due on the _____ day of each month.

I understand my account will be considered delinquent if my scheduled
payment is more than five (5) days late. I further understand that I may
be legally responsible for any/all collection costs incurred as a result of
the delinquency of my account balance if I default on this agreement.

I have read the above description of this agreement, and I agree to the
terms.

_____

Responsible Party Name

_____   _____

Responsible Party Signature   Date

_____   _____

Authorized Signature From Name of Practice   Date

Rescheduled Appointment

Date: _____

Dear: _____

Our records indicate that you did not return for your follow-up visit, which was scheduled on _____. Dr. _____ would like to see you again to make sure that there are no complications. Please call our office at your earliest convenience to schedule an appointment.

Thank you.

Sincerely,

Receptionist

Policies and Procedures

Financial Policy Guidelines and Considerations

1. Formalize the practice's existing collection procedure and commit it to writing.

2. Review the collection requirements of each insurance plan with which the practice participates.

3. Review the collection policy with physician and staff. Update this each time a new contract is signed.

4. Evaluate how the computer can assist in this process.

5. Include a set of complete instructions to comply with a "fair warning" policy.

6. Develop a protocol of strict adherence to fees as dictated by each plan. Educate patients and staff.

7. Develop a protocol in which only the manager will have the authority to negotiate fees.

8. Develop a schedule for sending final notices and turning patients over to collections. These should include procedures on refunds, no-shows, statements, and repayment agreements.

9. Develop a schedule for sending final notices and turning patients over to collections. These should be explained to the staff and patients.

10. Develop a procedure for formal dismissal of patients for noncompliance with instructions or payment, and for notifying the plan.

11. Obtain a fee schedule from every managed care or insurance plan in which the practice participates.

12. Obtain a list of appropriate copays per plan.

13. Obtain a list of service centers per plan.

14. Ensure a fee schedule that includes adjunct codes, supply codes, drug codes, and so on.

15. Ensure that the information provided includes surgical package definitions and time frames.

16. Develop and implement a financial policy brochure or form and have patients sign off on it.

17. Gather, incorporate, and educate staff on information relative to modifier use/recognition (both CPT and ICD9 codes).

Internal Financial Policy

1. Patients are responsible for all applicable charges at the time of service. This includes all deductibles, co-pays, co-insurance, and past due balances. Patients without insurance are required to pay the entire balance. Patients with insurance are required to pay the amount required by their insurance policies. Patients with primary and secondary insurance are not required to pay until insurance has paid. Medicare patients are required to pay 20% of the allowed amount if there is no secondary insurance. Patients with workers' compensation insurance do not have to pay any amount at the time of service.

2. The practice will file all insurance, both primary and secondary, for all patients.

3. Insurance claims will be filed daily. Statements will be sent out to patients the day after the date of service and on a 25-day cycle thereafter.

4. No patient will receive services without the proper referral number or form prior to the time of service. This information will be required at the time of appointment scheduling and no later than the time of service.

5. All patient insurance and workers' compensation insurance will be verified at the time of service. Front office staff will make a copy of all insurance cards that the patient has and will attempt to verify as time allows. Insurance will be verified thereafter.

6. All requests for medical records must be in writing and signed by the patient. A fee of $25.00 will be charged for review and copying of medical records and attending physician statements. This fee will be waived for referring physicians.

7. All patients are required to complete and sign the following forms: Medical Records Release, Financial Responsibility Waiver, Assignment of Benefits, and Patient Information Sheet.

8. There will be an $18.00 fee for returned checks, due immediately. Payment in full will be due immediately in cash, cashier's check, or credit card.

9. The practice will accept the following methods of payment: cash, check, or charge (American Express, Visa, MasterCard).

10. There will be a $25.00 charge for all broken appointments.

11. Patients who are insured with companies with which the practice is contracted are responsible for the contracted amount or fee.

12. The physician is the final source of determination on whether a patient is seen regardless of patient financial status.

13. Indigent care accounts will be written off with approval of the attending physician.

14. All balances that are less than $5.00 will be written off or adjusted on a monthly basis.

15. All write-offs and collection turn-overs will be at the determination of the administrator and/or physician.

16. All debit and credit adjustment must be documented daily.

17. The attending physician will determine whether a patient whose account has been turned over to a collection agency continue to be seen.

18. All private-pay patients will be turned over to collections if payment in full has not been received at 120 days after the time of service. The account will be turned over after 10 days from receipt of certified mail.

19. Private-pay patients with outstanding balances at 30, 60, 90, and 120 days will receive past due and/or collection letters.

20. It is at the physician's discretion whether to refill prescriptions for patients with past due balances of 60 days or more.

21. Patients will be released or fired as a patient at the determination of the attending physician. This will be done by certified mail and in a personal letter from the physician.

22. Insurance-only patients will be accepted at the determination of the attending physician. Insurance will be filed and the amount received by the insurance company will be considered payment in full.

23. Professional courtesies are permitted for referred physicians and their spouses only. Prior approval by the attending physician is necessary. If the patient has insurance, insurance will be filed and payment from the insurance company accepted as payment in full. The remaining amount will be adjusted from the account. If the patient does not have insurance, all charges will be adjusted off for services rendered.

24. When a patient is due a refund, the office will complete a check request form and send the completed check request form and supporting documentation to the accounts payable department. All refund requests must be approved by the administrator.

25. Discounts for the rendering of services will be determined by the attending physician. Prior approval is necessary.

26. Patients who have filed bankruptcy will be seen at the determination of the attending physician and may be on a cash basis if they have no insurance.

27. All probate accounts and accounts of deceased patients will be filed with the deceased patient's insurance company and money received applied to their accounts. All patient-responsible amounts will be due only after approval of the attending physician. Filing of charges with the probate will only be made at the prior approval of the attending physician.

28. It is at the determination of the attending physician when to render services to patients who are in collections.

29. When the decision has been made that a patient cannot pay the remaining balance of his or her account, the account may be resolved through a payment agreement in the form of a promissory note. The

terms shall consist of 20% down and four (4) monthly payments of 20% of the initial amount owed. This agreement shall be approved by both the physician and the administrator. No monthly contract or payment agreement shall be established for amounts less than $25.00.

30. All patients are encouraged to resolve payments on account and for services rendered by credit card, when available.

Accounts Receivable Action Plan

1. Review the financial classes and the aging of accounts that have an outstanding balance. This information can be obtained from the aged trial balance report. Review each account class by payer type and number of days old. An aged trial balance should be done weekly and worked daily for at least one to two hours. A majority of the time spent working the A/R should be concentrated on insurance accounts, which are usually easier and quicker to obtain.

2. Determine which accounts are:
   • Pending primary or secondary insurance payments.
   • Private pay after insurance has paid.
   • Initial private pay.

3. Initial private pay and private pay after insurance should receive a monthly letter, starting at 30+ days past due. This letter should be followed up with a personal telephone call at monthly or bi-monthly intervals. Payment arrangements and agreements can be made at this time. This will flush out any problem accounts as well as generate payments.

4. Accounts pending primary or secondary insurance payment will be researched, followed-up on, and resubmitted if necessary. Concentrate on the oldest accounts with the largest balance by payer type. Work each payer using this "largest, oldest, first" strategy.

5. After insurance claims within the filing limit have been billed, contact the insurance company for claim status.
Determine if:

- The claim has been received.
- The claim needs additional information before processing is complete.
- Payment has been made on the claim.

6. If the claim is not received following billing procedures, resubmit the claim after verifying all insurance data (address, policy number, etc.).

7. If the claim is received and not paid, press for payment. If additional information is needed, find out specifically what is necessary to release payment. Then take steps to acquire and send the needed information.

8. If payment has been made to the provider/practice:

- Verify address that the check and EOB were mailed.
- Obtain the amount of the check and the check number.
- Obtain the date the claim was processed and the check was mailed.

9. Involve patient in obtaining payment from an insurance carrier when any problems or delays are encountered. It should be part of the practice's financial policy that the patient is ultimately responsible for the charges incurred. All patients should receive statements monthly regardless of whether the patient has insurance.

Job Descriptions

Switchboard/Patient Services Representative

REPORTS TO: Office Coordinator

RESPONSIBILITIES:

Responsible for answering and directing phone calls as well as for taking messages. Assists patient in the completion of patient information forms. Assists in the filing of charts and copying of medical records.

DUTIES:

- Responsible for answering, directing, and taking messages of all phone calls.
- Assists patients in the completion of patient information forms.
- Assists in filing of charts, records, and reports.
- Assists in the copying of medical records.
- Labels patient charts.
- Completes patient appointment cards.
- Responsible for pulling charts for the next day.

JOB REQUIREMENTS:

Education and Background:

High school education or GED equivalent. Completion of a two-year Medical Assistant course preferable. Previous experience in medical practice is desirable.

Temperament:

Possesses a preference for dealing with people who are ill and need help. Possesses the skill to deal effectively with patients, physicians, and other employees.

Physical Requirements:

Ability to communicate clearly with patients over the phone and in person. Visual and manual dexterity for data entry. Ability to remain seated for extended periods of time.

JOB RELATIONSHIP:

Does not supervise any other employee. Reports to and receives supervision from the office coordinator.

Front Office Clerk

REPORTS TO: Office Coordinator

RESPONSIBILITIES:

Responsible for greeting patients/visitors and determining their needs, then directing accordingly. Ensures complete and correct capture of all needed patient information. Responsible for performing all check-in duties in accordance with practice policies.

DUTIES:

- Schedules patients following established office procedures.
- Answers telephone by the third ring, when needed.
- Obtains patient information such as name, address, referring physician, reason for visit, and authorization number.
- Updates established patient information.
- Makes reminder calls to patients prior to the day of the appointment.
- Updates and corrects returned mail.

- Obtains and distributes schedule for the next day of service.

- Greets patients and visitors. Determines their needs and directs them accordingly.

- Answers non-medical questions and gives non-medical information to patients within practice guidelines.

- Gives routine non-medical instructions in preparation for the patient's visit to the practice.

- Reviews all information sheets and forms after new patient completion. Ensures that all necessary information is completed. Assists new patients in completing the patient information sheet, if necessary.

- Prepares encounter form and attaches it to the medical record for use during the patient visit.

- Researches computer records to determine whether patient has visited the practice before.

- Checks with the patient for any changes in the patient's address, phone number, name, and insurance information. If there are any changes, updates the patient's medical records and the computer files. Also obtains all referral authorization when needed.

- Obtains copy of insurance card for patient file and verifies when needed.

- Enters all demographic data into computer.

- Places all medical records in clinical hold area, ready for back-office use.

- Responsible for overseeing and monitoring the waiting area. Maintains a neat and orderly waiting area.

- Enters patient charges into the computer and requests appropriate payment at the time of service. At the end of day confirms that charges for all patients who have been seen that day have been entered into the computer. Responsible for all encounter forms as well as for reviewing them for accuracy and completeness.

- Makes all follow-up appointments and other appointments as needed.

- Balances cash drawer to computer totals and encounter forms.

- Makes copies of all checks and completes deposit slip and batch form.

- Completes all end-of-day activities within established practice guidelines.

- Handles patient phone calls as needed.

- Performs other duties as assigned by the office coordinator to ensure operations.

JOB REQUIREMENTS:

Education and Background:

High school education or GED equivalent. Completion of a two-year Medical Assistant course would be an advantage. Previous experience in medical practice is desirable.

Temperament:

Possesses a preference for dealing with people who are ill and need help. Possesses the skill to deal effectively with patients, physicians, and other employees.

Physical Requirements:

Ability to communicate clearly with patients both over the phone and in person. Visual and manual dexterity for data entry. Ability to remain seated for extended periods of time.

JOB RELATIONSHIP:

Does not supervise any other employee. Reports to and receives supervision from the Office Coordinator in all matters.

Check-in/Receptionist

REPORTS TO: Office Coordinator

RESPONSIBILITIES:

Responsible for greeting patients/visitors, determining their needs and directing them accordingly. Ensures complete documentation of necessary patient information on all forms. Responsible for performing all check-in duties in accordance with practice guidelines.

DUTIES:

- Greets patients and visitors. Determines their needs and directs them accordingly.

- Answers non-medical questions and gives non-medical information to patients within practice guidelines.

- Gives routine non-medical instructions for the patient's visit.

- Reviews all information sheets and forms after new patient completion. Ensures that all necessary information is filled in. Assists new patients in completing the patient information sheet, if needed.

- Prepares encounter form and attaches it to the medical records for use with patient visit.

- Determines whether patient has visited the practice before.

- Checks with the patient for any changes in the patient's address, phone number, name, and insurance information, and updates changes in the computer and in patients medical records. Also obtains referral authorization when needed.

- Obtains copy and verification of insurance card for patient file when needed.

- Enters all demographic data into computer.

- Places medical record in clinical hold area, ready for back office use.

- Responsible for overseeing and monitoring the waiting area.

JOB REQUIREMENTS:

Education and Background:

High school education or GED equivalent. Completion of a two-year Medical Assistant course preferable. Previous experience in medical practice is desirable.

Temperament:

Possesses tolerance for people who are ill and need help. Possesses the skill to deal effectively with patients, physicians, and other employees.

Physical Requirements:

Ability to communicate clearly with patients over the phone and in person. Visual and manual dexterity for data entry. Ability to remain seated for extended periods of time.

JOB RELATIONSHIP:

Does not supervise any other employee. Reports to and receives supervision from the Office Coordinator in all matters.

Check-out / Cashier

REPORTS TO: Office Coordinator

RESPONSIBILITY:

Responsible for collection of patient payments at the time of service. Ensures complete and correct capture of all charges. Responsible for performing all checkout duties in accordance with practice policies. Monitors and reviews encounter forms for accuracy and completeness.

DUTIES:

- Greets patients and visitors at the checkout area. Determines their needs and directs them accordingly.

- Answers non-medical questions and gives non-medical information to patients as set by practice guidelines.

- Gives routine non-medical instructions for future visits or outside tests.

- Enters all patient charges into the computer and requests appropriate payment at the time of service. At the end of day confirms that charges for all patients who have been seen that day have been entered into the computer. Responsible for all encounter forms as well as for reviewing them for accuracy and completeness.

- Makes all follow-up appointments and other appointments as needed.

- Balances cash drawer to computer totals and encounter forms.

- Makes copies of all checks and completes deposit slip and batch form.

- Completes all end-of-day activities within practice guidelines.

- Handles patient phone calls as needed.

- Performs other duties as assigned by the office coordinator to ensure operations.

JOB REQUIREMENTS:

Education and Background:

High school education or GED equivalent. Completion of a two year Medical Assistant course preferable. Previous experience in a medical practice is desirable.

Temperament:

Possesses a tolerance for people who are ill and need help. Possesses the skill to deal effectively with patients, physicians, and other employees.

Physical Requirements:

Ability to communicate clearly with patients over the phone and in person. Visual and manual dexterity for data entry. Ability to remain seated for extended periods of time.

JOB RELATIONSHIP:

Does not supervise any other employee. Reports to and receives supervision from the Office Coordinator in all matters.

Medical Records/File Clerk

REPORTS TO: Office Coordinator

RESPONSIBILITIES:

Responsible for filing and pulling patient charts. Ensures proper place-
ment of reports and correspondence into chart. Primarily responsible
for copying medical records. Maintains a neat and clean chart area.

DUTIES:

- Pulls all charts for the next day of service.
- Files charts throughout the course of the day.
- Distributes faxes.
- Pulls and attaches lab and correspondence.
- Relieves at front desk when needed.
- Assists in patient calls as needed.

JOB REQUIREMENTS:

Education and Background:

High school education or GED equivalent. Completion of a two-year Medical Assistant course preferable. Previous experience in a medical practice is desirable.

Temperament:

Possesses a preference for dealing with people who are ill and need help. Possesses the skill to deal effectively with patients, physicians, and other employees.

Physical Requirements:

Ability to communicate clearly with patients over the phone and in person. Visual and manual dexterity for data entry. Ability to remain seated for extended periods of time and to carry several charts at one time.

JOB RELATIONSHIP:

Does not supervise any other employee. Reports to and receives supervision from the office coordinator in all matters.

Appointment Scheduler

REPORTS TO: Office Coordinator

RESPONSIBILITIES:

Schedules appointments according to the established guidelines. Obtains patient information from new patients and updates established patient information. Makes patient reminder calls prior to the visit. Updates return mail. Obtains a printed schedule for office for the next day of service.

DUTIES:

- Schedules patients according to established office procedures.

- Answers telephone by the third ring, as needed.

- Obtains patient information such as name, address, referring physician, reason for visit, and authorization number, and updates patient records.

- Makes reminder calls prior to the day of service.

- Updates and corrects return mail.

- Obtains and distributes schedule for the next day of service.

JOB REQUIREMENTS:

Education and Background:

High school education or GED equivalent. Completion of a two-year Medical Assistant course preferable. Previous experience in a medical practice is desirable.

Temperament:

Possesses a preference for dealing with people who are ill and need help. Possesses the skill to deal effectively with patients, physicians, and other employees.

Physical Requirements:

Ability to communicate clearly with patients over the phone and in person. Visual and manual dexterity for data entry. Ability to remain seated for extended periods of time.

JOB RELATIONSHIP:

Does not supervise any other employee. Reports to and receives supervision from the office coordinator in all matters.

Accounts Payable Clerk

REPORTS TO: Administrator

RESPONSIBILITIES:

Performs all accounts payable activities on a day-to-day basis. Handles all refunds and refund questions. Coordinates and maintains daily batch control and deposit summary information for all staff. Closes out at the end of day.

DUTIES:

- Performs all A/P functions. Supplies information to administrator for approval of all checks.

- Writes and researches all refund requests and checks to insurance companies, patients, and other A/P sources.

- Prepares information for monthly bank reconciliation.

- Handles all problem calls related to bills or refunds.

- Assists in the posting of Medicare, Blue Cross, and other payments as needed.

- Assists in collection activities as needed.

- Receives daily deposit information from all offices and operators.

- End-of-day batch control balancing.

- Closes at end of day.

JOB REQUIREMENTS:

Education and Background:

High school education or GED equivalent. Minimum two years' experience in accounts payable. Experience in capture of patient charges and payments in a physician or hospital setting. Insurance and collection experience is also desired.

Temperament:

Possesses a preference for dealing with people who are ill and need help. Possesses the skill to deal effectively with patients, doctors, other employees, and insurance companies.

Physical Requirements:

Ability to communicate clearly with patients and insurance companies over the phone and in person. Visual and manual dexterity for data entry. Ability to remain seated for extended periods of time.

JOB RELATIONSHIP:

Does not supervise any other employee. Reports to and receives supervision from the administrator.

Back-Office Coordinator

REPORTS TO: Administrator

RESPONSIBILITIES:

Responsible for supervising and coordinating all back-office/clinical activities and staff. Responsible for rendering professional clinical assistance to patients within the medical practice as directed by the physician. Is the liaison between the patient and the physician for establishing and maintaining quality patient care. Responsible for performing all duties in accordance with practice policies and procedures.

DUTIES:

- Assists in developing and recommending back-office staffing levels.

- Assists in hiring, training, and evaluating medical back-office employees.

- Monitors and/or supervises preventive maintenance schedules and/or quality control of medical office equipment.

- Assists in developing, implementing, and maintaining medical back-office operating procedures, including maintaining medical back-office procedure manual.

- Assists and supervises good patient/doctor workflow.

- Monitors/supervises dispensing of all patient prescriptions.

- Monitors/supervises inventory of all medical office supplies.

- Monitors/supervises OSHA, DEA, CLIA, and government guideline compliance.

- Monitors/supervises the copying of medical records.

- Monitors/supervises and maintains accurate filing methods.

- Assists management in special projects as needed.

- Reviews charts for waiting patients.

- Escorts patients into the exam area.

- Takes and records routine elements of systemic review, patient's history, present illness.

- Places patient in exam room and prepares patients for appropriate examination.

- Assists the physician with the treatment and procedures provided to the patient in the exam room.

- Assists the physician in patient contact in providing instruction, education, and advice on routine and minor medical questions. Does patient education in the office and on the telephone.

- Is proficient in performing all routine procedures needed and required by physician and type of practice.

- Schedules appointments for specific testing after conferring with the physician and the patient.

- Orders refills of prescriptions within established physician guidelines and supervision and posts to patient's chart.

- Determines disposition of physician telephone messages daily, in conjunction with the front office.

- Ensures accurate coding for E&M visits and procedures performed.

- Documents in the patient's chart the outcome and information of all telephone calls.

- Inventories and originates requisition orders for medical and drug supplies.

- Maintains sterile instruments, equipment, and tidy exam rooms.

- Maintains and adheres to all OSHA, DEA, CLIA, and government regulations.

- Organizes, stores, and refills medical supplies and medications in exam/treatment rooms.

- Performs lab and x-rays as needed.

- Directs patient flow in clinical areas.

- Reminds physician periodically to update medical records.

- Enhances and promotes a team atmosphere favorable to growth of the practice.

- Responsible for processing and charging outside laboratory tests and ensuring the appropriate paperwork is completed.

- Monitors compliance with requests for release of medical information.

- Identifies problems in the clinical and medical records functions, reports them, and offers suggestions for improvement.

- Maintains strictest confidentiality.

- Performs other duties as required or requested to assure a smooth operation of the practice.

- Promotes and practices the policies and procedures of the practice.

JOB REQUIREMENTS:

Education and Background:

Graduate from an accredited school of Medical Assistance or Nursing. Preferably five years of previous experience in physician office environment. At least two years' supervisory experience required. Experienced in all aspects of clinical office care.

Temperament:

Possesses a preference for dealing with people who are ill and need help and for performing services that will benefit and help people. Possesses a preference for scientific activities and for understanding and working with medical concepts while performing clinical duties. Possesses the same sense of discipline to work in accordance with accepted nursing and medical standards. Possesses the ability to deal tactfully and effectively with patients, parents, other employees, hospital staff, and physicians.

Physical Requirements:

Ability to communicate clearly with patients over the phone or in person. Ability to stand for extended periods of time. Ability to lift/stretch/bend in providing patient care. Auditory and visual acuity for monitoring patient status. Manual dexterity for operating patient testing equipment. Verbal ability to understand patients' medical records, physicians' orders, and to be compassionately communicative with patient, patient's family, and hospital staff.

JOB RELATIONSHIP:

Supervises all back-office/clinical employees. Reports to and receives supervision from the administrator and/or physician in all matters.

Office Coordinator

REPORTS TO: Administrator

RESPONSIBILITIES:

Responsible for the management and coordination of all administrative and financial concerns of the physician practice in accordance with the policies and procedures of the office. Responsible for all business affairs within the practice, including, but not limited to, receiving and greeting all patients and visitors, scheduling patients, patient record preparation and maintenance, preparation of patient charges for processing, processing incoming and outgoing mail, ordering supplies, end-of-day reports and balancing, preparation of monthly reports, filing insurance claims, and posting payments.

DUTIES:

- Works with management to develop long range plans and organizational policies.

- Develops budgets for practice and monitors approved budget to insure compliance. Makes appropriate corrections when practice is out of compliance with budget.

- Serves as physician liaison by establishing regular weekly visits.

- Implements, monitors, and insures compliance with practice policies and procedures.

- Insures that cross-training occurs.

- Initiates risk assessment by actively participating in assessing and resolving patient complaints.

- Assists in developing and recommending office staffing levels.

- Assists in hiring, training, and evaluating employees.

- Monitors and/or supervises preventive maintenance schedules and/or quality control of front-office equipment.

- Assists in developing, implementing, and maintaining medical front-office operating procedures, including maintaining medical front-office procedures manual.

- Assists and supervises front-office procedures and develops good patient/doctor work flow.

- Monitors/supervises inventory and ordering of all medical office supplies.

- Monitors/supervises OSHA, DEA, CLIA, and government guidelines compliance.

- Assists in developing, implementing, and maintaining medical records operating procedures, including maintaining medical records procedures manual.

- Monitors/supervises the copying of medical records.

- Monitors/supervises and maintains accurate filing methods.

- Assists management in special projects as needed.

- Monitors/supervises doctors' appointment schedules and handling of messages and patient phone calls.

- Monitors/supervises patient check-in/check-out procedures.

- Monitors/supervises all end-of-day procedures.

- Monitors/prepares all end-of-day, weekly, and/or monthly reports.

- Maintains current fee schedule and charge codes.

- Monitors/supervises money transactions and balancing of daysheets and computer.

- Monitors/supervises accurate charging and batching procedures.

- Manages time sheets/time cards.

- Follows up on scheduling of procedures.

- Insures all referrals are scheduled.

- Monitors/supervises accurate demographic and insurance information.

- Monitors proper disposition of mail.

- Maintains daily communication with administrator.

JOB REQUIREMENTS:

Education and Background:

Graduation from a Medical Office Assistant program or possession of at least an Associate Degree from an area college with a major relating to business administration/health care administration. Preferably five years of previous experience in a physician office environment. At least two years' supervisory experience required. Experienced in all aspects of medical office administration.

Temperament:

Possesses a preference for dealing with people who are ill and need help and for performing services that will benefit and help people. Possesses a preference for the use of financial activities to understand and work with management and financial concepts in a medical office setting. Possesses the sense of discipline to work in accordance with accepted business standards and the ability to deal tactfully and effectively with patients, parents, other employees, hospital staff, and physicians.

Physical Requirements:

Good speaking skills to communicate clearly with patients over the phone and in person. Ability to stand or sit for extended periods of time. Ability to lift/stretch/bend in providing patient care. Auditory and visual acuity. Manual dexterity for operating office equipment. The verbal ability to understand patients' medical records, physicians' orders, and to be compassionately communicative with patient, patient's family, and hospital staff.

JOB RELATIONSHIP:

Additional Forms

Insurance Filing Worksheet

Type of Service: _____ Inpatient _____ Office_____ Surgical _____

Other _____

Practice Name: _____

Worksheet Preparation Date:

Patient Last Name	Type of Insurance	Date Claim Prepared	Date of Last Service	Number of Days

Total number of days _____

Total number of claims _____

Average time to file a claim form _____

Front Desk Collection Analysis Worksheet

Practice Name: _____

Worksheet Preparation Date: _____

Date	Patient Name	Type of Insurance	Office Charge	Amount Collected

Total visits per worksheet _____

Total visits where collection occurred _____

Percent of visits collected _____ %

Financial Analysis Formulas

LIQUIDITY RATIOS

$$\text{Current Ratio} = \frac{\text{Current Assets}}{\text{Current Liabilities}}$$

Quick Ratio (also called Acid - Test Ratio) =

$$\frac{\text{Cash} + \text{Marketable Securities \& A/R}}{\text{Current Liabilities}}$$

ACTIVITY RATIOS

$$\text{Accounts Receivable Turnover} = \frac{\text{Net Revenue}}{\text{Average Accounts Receivable}}$$

$$\text{Inventory Turnover} = \frac{\text{Cost of Goods Sold}}{\text{Average Inventory}}$$

$$\text{Asset Turnover} = \frac{\text{Net Revenue}}{\text{Average Total Assets}}$$

PROFITABILITY RATIOS

$$\text{Return on Assets} = \frac{\text{Net Income}}{\text{Average Total Assets}}$$

$$\text{Profit Margin on Assets} = \frac{\text{Net Income}}{\text{Net Revenue (or Collections)}}$$

$$\text{Physician Compensation Profitability} =$$

$$\frac{\text{Physician Compensation \& Benefits}}{\text{Net Revenue (or Collections)}}$$

COVERAGE RATIOS

$$\text{Debt to Assets Ratio} = \frac{\text{Total Debt}}{\text{Total Assets}}$$

Index